wHispers

wHispers

when He is so precious even rocks sing

"Be still, and know..."
Psalm 46:10

Shirley Pieters Vogel

Shirley Pieters Vogel

PRINCIPIA
MEDIA

"Be still, and know that I am God!"

—Psalm 46:10

"The voice of the Spirit of God is as gentle as a summer breeze—
so gentle that unless you are living in complete fellowship
and oneness with God, you will never hear it."

—Oswald Chambers[1]

They tell me, Lord, that when I seem
To be in speech with you,
Since but one voice is heard, it's all a dream
One talker aping two.
Sometimes it is, yet not as they
Conceive it. Rather, I
Seek in myself the things I hoped to say,
But lo! My wells are dry.
Then seeing me empty, you forsake
The listener's role and through
My dumb lips breathe and into utterance wake
The thoughts I never knew.

—C. S. Lewis[2]

To my parents whom I love deeply…

…my mother, Jennie DeSeyn Pieters.

Thank you for your unwavering example of loving and trusting God even in the toughest of times.

…my father, Milton Adrian Pieters.

You were called Home early, but my memories of your faith – especially your kneeling in prayer at your bedside – remain imbedded in my heart.

Contents

Foreword

DO YOU ACTUALLY believe in prayer? Shirley Vogel does. For her, prayer involves not much talking, but a lot of listening. Like the Christians of old, Shirley has learned that God speaks to us in the silence of prayer and, further, that she can sometimes hear His whisper in the midst of the day's activities. A reader skeptical about prayer may suppose that Shirley must have had an easy life. In fact, she didn't.

After twenty five years of marriage, Con and Shirley Vogler were the Christian couple who had it all: children, grandchildren, financial security, and, of course, their church. Faith in God was the focal point of their lives. They served as elders, sang in the choir, and worshipped regularly with their children. Then one day Con announced "I'm just not happy," and that's where Shirley's wonderful story begins, her Pilgrim's Progress. Only this time it's not an allegory, its real life.

Shirley tells of the painful experience of her divorce, of the letter from a man she scarcely knew, and of a friendship blossoming into love and marriage. Through it all, she never gave up on God.

End of story? Far from it! Only four years after her remarriage, Shirley was diagnosed with a severe cardiac condition requiring immediate open heart surgery. Resting post-op in the ICU, Shirley was moved by deep gratitude she felt toward God. She gave herself entirely to God, to do whatever he might ask of her. Up to that point her role had been more as a helper than as a leader. She thought of herself as the simple "little gal from East Pal." Her religion was that of "a good girl who did what was expected." Now, however, she had really opened up the door to God. A change was at hand.

At her church in Brewster, Massachusetts, she became a deacon—then the deacon representative on the Pastoral Search Committee. Quite to her surprise, she was invited to chair the committee. She was being asked to change from helper to leader. She didn't want to do it, especially as it would require public speaking. God, however, made her realize that the chairmanship with the public speaking was exactly the "whatever" to which He was calling her. Under Shirley's leadership, the committee ran a successful campaign—not by a professionally orchestrated fund drive, but by church suppers and prayer. Following several more leadership positions, Shirley felt God calling her to establish a women's ministry with an ecumenical outreach—a ministry that ultimately drew participants from sixteen Cape Cod churches. Not bad for the "East Pal gal," but not the end of the story.

Though at home with God the Father, Shirley felt that Jesus and the Holy Spirit were known to her only intellectually. She wanted a personal relationship with Jesus and the Holy Spirit, and she let God know it. How this prayer was answered is the topic of Part Three of *wHispers*.

What makes this part really interesting is that it shows us a life that's serious about the apostle's admonition to "be constant in prayer." It's not a treatise on prayer, an instruction on prayer, or a collection of prayers. What we have—almost in journal format—is prayer not as an add-on or something hard for a practical person to find time for, or as reserved for dire moments, but as an integral part of daily life.

Shirley daily sets aside time for prayer in solitude. She often experiences what she believes is a direct communication from God: sometimes as words, sometimes as a picture she must interpret. She sees the hand of God pervasive in her surroundings. She finds much that is "God-sent" addressed especially to her. Thus, for instance, when anxious about a torn tendon and angry with herself for her own self-pity, she happens into a book sale with "only a few minutes to look." She's drawn immediately to "Not Me God," which turns out to be exactly what she needed to regain perspective.

For Shirley, the relationship of prayer and daily life is reciprocal. Prayer informs daily life; daily life informs prayer. Each supports the other; together they form a whole.

The inner circle of support, importantly social, consists of her husband, Stefan, a few intimate friends, and inspirational books from the Christian press. Stefan is her stay and support. Her women friends function as spiritual advisors. They guide, admonish, encourage, validate,

Foreword

and share intercessory prayer. As to reading, Shirley is a voracious book hound. For her, inspirational and devotional texts are like conversation with others on the same track. Her Christian reading often guides her to apropos passages of Holy Scripture.

Her life of prayer is affected, too, by the world beyond her intimate circle: the morning walk, outdoor nature, a daily journal, classes, small groups, ministries, corporate worship, and especially the sacrament of communion. The sometimes severe challenges can be very serious, yet, for Shirley, they are a path to a closer walk with God.

A common misconception about prayer is that it separates one from life. It leads to the ivory tower, the cloistered virtue, avoidance of the rough and tumble of real life. We can see, on the contrary that seeking to be constant in prayer, daily to discern God's will, calls forth a more intense engagement. It calls forth a complex pattern of movement in prayer among people, books, events, and surroundings. It's like a dance, choreographed by the Lord of the Dance.

As you read *wHispers*, I hope you will be strengthened in spirit by the quotes and inspiration you will find in each chapter, and as Shirley guides you through the account of her experiences, you may hear God's whispers within your heart.

David Light, RN, PhD

Acknowledgments

I AM THANKFUL to…

…Almighty God for the intimacy I enjoy with You as my Abba Father, my Jesus Savior, and my Holy Spirit. As you continually guide, teach and empower me, I feel very humbled and privileged to be used in Your service. There are no words big enough to describe my appreciation for physical healing so that I can share with others what You've taught me. May You be glorified through it all.

…Stefan, my husband and greatest fan. My ministry would be less effective without your help. What a wonderful and loving God-gift you are to me and all of our children. I love you very much.

…my children, Julie, Jenny and Jim, whom I love dearly. Thank you for loving me no-matter-what, and trusting me even when you don't fully understand the unusual ways in which God sometimes leads. Thanks for telling me you're proud of me!

…my wonderful stepdaughters, Heather, Lisa and Stefanie, for your loving encouragement that is so important to me.

…my family and friends who faithfully encourage and pray for me through many ministries and crises. You know who you are; your support and spiritual direction have made a difference. I cling especially to your written words that I've tucked into my Bible and my heart.

…Dwight Ritter for designing the beautiful wHispers logo, and Peter Spier for so freely sharing your expertise in graphic design publication.

…devout men and women of God; some who lived a long time ago, but still minister to me and many others through their devotional writings.

And many who currently serve the Lord. You demonstrate your passion for God in remarkable ways—your example inspires me.

...many whom I have served. In turn, you affirm and encourage me more than you'll ever know. Your promises to pray for me every day strengthened me when I couldn't pray for myself.

...the many caring people whom God uses to meet my medical needs and heal me. Most especially, I thank you, Dr. Lawrence McAuliffe, for supervising my care. Your expertise and sensitivity make a difference.

...you, the reader. As you learn more about God's love, power and faithfulness, may you develop a passion to hear His whispers to you, and to absorb the hope and truths that God wants you to share with others whom He puts in your life.

A Must-Read Introduction!
God's Gift of wHispers

"Call to me and I will answer you and tell you great and unsearchable things you do not know."

—Jeremiah 33:3(NIV)

MONDAY, APRIL 7, 2003 WAS no ordinary day! God's startling answer to my prayer that morning was so specific I had no doubt I was in His presence. Sitting at my dining room table early that morning, the warmth and wonder of God's love penetrated every part of me.

Three and a half months earlier I had suffered a stroke, after which concerned family and friends insisted I reduce my full time volunteer church work. As founder and coordinator of Caring Ministries at my church, that was easier said than done and I resumed ministry after only a few days. Rather than working less, demands on my time increased as women began coming to me wanting to talk about personal challenges and faith issues. It wasn't long when I recognized my new passion to minister to women. Still in fragile health, I wondered, *can this really be God's will?* I began praying about it and two months later I received a very surprising answer.

After reading Bill Hybels' book, *You're Too Busy Not to Pray*[3], writing my prayers had become an integral part of my time alone with God every morning. Early on that April day, I ended my prayer time by asking God to help me stay so close that I could hear even His most quiet whispers. My exact words were, "I rest in You, Abba—alert for Your voice and directions. Hold me so close, Holy Spirit, that I recognize and understand even Your most quiet whispers."

When I wrote "whispers," I knew immediately that I had just written the name for a new women's ministry. Even more startling was that in my mind's eye, I saw the word as "wHispers" —lower case letters except for a capital H! I knew instinctively that the H stood for He, Him, or His. Often looking at words as acronyms, I came up with words for the first five letters easily, "when He is so precious," but what to do with "e-r-s?" Searching my Bible concordance for "e" words, the one that stood out was "even", and for "r" it was "rock or rocks", and then I had it— "when He is so precious even rocks sing!"

I was thrilled with God's affirmation of a ministry to which I felt He was now leading me. When I had considered the possibility that this ministry could become a reality, I had unbelievers in mind. Now I wondered, *will women who don't have a personal relationship with the Lord understand the acronym; will they be inspired to want more, or will they be turned off?*

Then my husband, Stefan, came downstairs and knowing it was my "quiet time," didn't interrupt me. I called to him and explained what had happened, but only the first part of the acronym and I added, "I'm just not sure about 'e-r-s.'"

Stefan, only half awake, didn't respond and I wondered if he had even heard me. He went outside to get the newspaper and on his return, called out, "How about 'even rocks sing'?" I could hardly believe what I heard, but then delight took over. God had chosen to reaffirm this new ministry through Stefan!

For me, the acronym means if we love and trust God enough, we believe He can do anything! God can bring water from a rock as He did for the Israelites (Numbers 20:11), He can make rocks sing, and in a more practical sense, if we love and trust God enough He can make a real difference in our lives—no matter what the circumstances or how hopeless they may seem!

I believed that and I knew from experience that God doesn't assign us something and then desert us. But unequipped for this new task and not having a clue where to start, I felt like Mother Teresa who said, "I know God won't give me anything I can't handle. I just wish He didn't trust me so much!"

Remembering how many times God had already guided and empowered me to obey Him in situations foreign to me, I decided to go forward in faith again. *wHispers*, a successful ministry, is only one of many unique challenges God has used and continues to use to stretch me into a person He can use for His purposes.

A Must-Read Introduction!

Sometimes God asks what, in my limited understanding, seems impossible. Other times He tests my endurance to the point that I wonder if He has forgotten me. Through it all, I've learned the magic words are "center on God," and as long as I do that instead of focusing on myself, I can hear God's most quiet whispers. God's presence makes my heart sing, and more and more—even in times of deep distress—I know His peace and joy.

I'm learning my lessons well—not easily, and sometimes kicking and screaming, but well. We are told in Deuteronomy 6:5,

> You shall love the Lord your God with all your heart, and with all your soul, and with all your might.

I've found that loving God intimately means celebrating His blessings, but also trusting God when we don't understand why He permits things that upset and even devastate our lives and the lives of our loved ones.

My challenges have been many; intense, painful and so varied that listeners can always identify with some part of my story. When they share how God has used my testimony to give them hope and courage to go on, it makes every tear worthwhile.

Dear reader, as I write this book it's my prayer that both the trials and God's blessings on my life will be instrumental in drawing you into a new or deeper relationship with Jesus Christ. May you also know the richness of God's faithfulness and power; His love, grace and mercy.

It's my privilege to share with you how I came to understand in very real ways, the words of Nehemiah 8:10: "Do not be grieved, for the joy of the Lord is your strength."

Part One

Prayers By A Picket Fence

*"Trust in the Lord with all your heart, and lean not on your own
understanding; in all your ways acknowledge Him,
and He shall direct your paths."*

—Proverbs 3:5-6 (NKJV)

*"What shall you do in your present straits?
Constantly, incessantly offer your pains to the Lord.
Ask Him for strength to endure the pain. But above all
else, get into the habit of entertaining yourself with
God. Forget Him the very least you can. During
your pain, just adore Him."*

—Brother Lawrence[4]

Chapter 1

Storm Clouds on the Horizon

"…in quietness and trust is your strength…"

—Isaiah 30:15 (NIV)

MY HUSBAND, CON, and I were enjoying the last day of a late summer, sun-filled reunion week on a New Jersey beach with our children and grandchildren. Relaxing in lounge chairs, the adults read or visited while keeping watchful eyes as the children took turns burying each other in the sand and splashing in the rolling waves.

"Mom, Dad seems so quiet. Is something wrong?" Julie asked. I turned. Just beyond her sat Con, his hat pulled down over his face, exposing only his gray beard. A novel, open and face down, was about to slide from his lap. His quiet gentleness had attracted me when I first met him. After twenty-five years of marriage, he still possessed the same qualities.

"I don't think so, Julie, but I'll ask."

That evening, as I sat in front of a crackling campfire hugging my knees tucked under my chin, I counted my blessings—most especially our children. There they were. Jim with Jody, the girl who would one day be his wife, and Julie and Jenny with their families all nearby, tanned and happily tired, toasting marshmallows and wishing aloud that the end of our vacation could be delayed. Grateful for the love we shared, I dreaded the "good-byes" that had to be said in the morning when we would head in different directions.

The Announcement

I didn't remember my promise to our eldest daughter until later when I was packing. Con was in bed reading.

"Con, Julie's concerned because she thinks you've been unusually quiet. Will you tell her you're okay so she won't worry?"

He didn't answer, so I persisted, "You are, aren't you?"

He put the book down, but looked away. *Was something wrong? Was he ill?* Then he gave me a quick darting glance and an answer that would change all our lives forever, "I hadn't planned to tell you this right now, but I'm just not happy! I haven't been for a long time!"

To say I was surprised and confused is an understatement. After more than a quarter century together we knew each other well. I even thought that most of the time, we knew what the other was thinking. This time I was dead wrong!

"This isn't an ideal time to change jobs," I offered, "but if you're not happy, you should consider it."

"It's not my job. I love my job," he said quietly, his eyes avoiding mine.

When I realized he was talking about our marriage, I was stunned. *This can't be happening,* I thought. *Not us! Unhappy for a long time? He's always been a loving, caring husband and devoted father. What does he mean?*

I wanted to know more, but was too confused to ask. His uneasiness was clear as he continued to look anywhere but at me. He suggested we talk again in the morning and one of us, I don't remember who, turned off the lights. Awkwardly we said, "Good night," the first time ever without a kiss.

We lay in unfamiliar and painful silence, being careful not to touch each other. Rigid with fear, I stared into darkness, my thoughts racing. *How could things have changed so drastically and so quickly without my knowing? We've been comfortable with each other from the start and, for the most part, accepting of each other's faults. I must have missed something, but if there was a clue, I didn't catch it.*

Only last year we celebrated our silver anniversary, and now we're lying here next to each other, afraid to talk or touch!

The more I thought, the more confused I became. I loved being with him and I thought he felt the same about me. We were together whenever possible and we still walked hand in hand. With our children grown, we were beginning to enjoy more money and time for ourselves.

As a registered nurse, I had worked part time while our children were in school and Con, a college professor, completed his doctoral studies. Later, with his encouragement, I earned a B.S. degree, and he said he was proud of me.

As Christians, we spent a large part of our lives in church activities; serving as elders, singing in the choir, and worshipping regularly with our children. Faith in God was the focal point of our lives.

But now, everything was different! I could hardly lie still. I knew this had to be hard for him too, but I wanted to shake him and insist, "Our marriage is fine!" I didn't because I was afraid of what else he might say.

Tears slid down my cheeks and my chest ached as I tried not to make a sound. I pleaded silently, *God, with Your help, we can fix this. Surely Con's just tired, and after a good night's sleep he'll say, Forget it—nothing to worry about.*

The next morning I wasn't so sure. Looking at him still asleep, I wanted so much to erase our dialogue of the evening before, but when he awakened there was awkwardness—a sad new dimension in our marriage. He said he was sorry and I wanted to believe him, but at the same time he seemed pleased, self-assured, and even relieved. That worried me. Maybe Con didn't want to mend our marriage.

Dressing, I thanked God for being with me, and that assurance was my only comfort. For the first time, I had a problem I could no longer share with my best friend—he was the problem! And sadly, I thought, I guess I'm his. Wanting so much to believe that with God's help we would find a solution, I claimed the promise in Matthew 19:26, "With God all things are possible."

Keeping busy with breakfast and last-minute packing helped mask my worry, but I couldn't help wondering what the future would hold and if we would ever all be together again. Saying goodbye to our children and grandchildren was much harder than usual, but after hugs all around, Con and I began the ten-hour ride to Buffalo. It seemed endless and although there was a lot to say, we couldn't find the words. When we did speak, it wasn't about the bewildering state of our marriage, but of ordinary things like when to stop and where to eat. He looked straight ahead and rarely at me, as if he couldn't or didn't want to. His seeming indifference confused and frightened me further.

I became angry because I didn't know or understand the person he had become. How could he not care about my pain? And did he even think about what a possible separation or divorce would mean to our children if we didn't find an answer? When tears threatened, I turned and pretended I was sleeping or watching the countryside, but my throat ached as I held in the sobs. I didn't want him to know how much I hurt and I vowed never to cry in front of him.

Feeling helpless, I wondered why God would allow anything to harm our marriage. Yet, at the same time, I sensed His presence and wanted to trust Him. I tried to concentrate on a favorite Bible passage:

> Do not be anxious about anything, but in everything, by prayer and petition, with thanksgiving, present your requests to God. And the peace of God, which transcends all understanding, will guard your hearts and your minds in Christ Jesus.
>
> —Philippians 4:6-7 NIV

Finding it impossible not to worry, I did my best to trust God for the peace He promised.

It seemed that professional guidance would be the first step, so I asked, "Will you go to a marriage counselor with me?" At first, Con didn't answer, he just drove. Finally, he agreed, but insisted, "Not a Christian counselor." I asked why. He had no particular reason, but was definite about it. I still didn't understand.

I didn't understand much just then.

Sad Homecoming

We arrived home, clearly two separate people and it hurt. The ease and spontaneity of our relationship were gone and I hated feeling self-conscious. I felt he was constantly evaluating me and I worried about whether I was pleasing or annoying him. I was afraid that something I said might tip the scales and he'd leave, so I chose my words carefully.

I was still committed to the vows we had made twenty-six years earlier and I had trouble believing Con wasn't. My fears often resulted in tears, but I kept the promise I had made to myself—Con would not see me cry. I wept only when I was alone or running tap water or taking a shower—anything to conceal my sobs.

I continued to find comfort in Scripture, but I had trouble with Ephesians 5:19-20 (NIV):

> Sing and make music in your heart to the Lord, always giving thanks to God the Father for everything.

4

I didn't feel like making music and I argued instead, "But, God, how can I be thankful for this?" Eventually I began to understand. God didn't expect me to be thankful our marriage was in trouble, but He did want me to be grateful for His presence, my family, my health, and the many other people and good things in my life. Convinced that God would never leave me, I knew I wouldn't have to deal with my pain alone. We're assured of this in Hebrews 13:5–6,

> [God] has said, "I will never leave you or forsake you. So we can say with confidence "The Lord is my helper; I will not be afraid."

I was eager to find a marriage counselor and get started. Con agreed, but stuck to his word. "We both know what a Christian counselor will say. I want a more objective viewpoint."

I thought of a friend, an ordained minister who worked in the court system as a counselor. I knew Con liked him, but because Con had been emphatic about not having a Christian counselor, I was surprised when he agreed. I phoned for an appointment, but when I explained why I was calling, our friend's usual joviality gave way to stiff professionalism. "I can't be objective," he said, referring us to a colleague, twenty-five minutes from our home. Though disappointed, we knew he was right.

On a beautiful warm fall evening, we drove to our first meeting through hills brilliant with color. Normally, I would have relished the breathtaking beauty of it all, but now anxiety took over. It was all like a bad dream and the soft radio music Con selected depressed me further. *Had we really once danced to those same romantic ballads?* We didn't talk and my fear-filled questions went unasked. *What if counseling doesn't work? What if we can't find an answer?*

The farther we drove, the larger the lump in my throat seemed to grow, but Con seemed relaxed. I worried that he was just going through the motions of doing the respectable thing. Was he just biding his time or did he really want help for our troubled marriage? I didn't know, but, then I thought, *the same God who every year paints these hills in such an awesome way, leaf by leaf, is also in charge of my life, moment by moment. God cares and nothing is insignificant, including my pain.* That was comforting, but when we arrived at the office, I was feeling anything but confident.

Counseling

It was a lovely Victorian house in a picturesque village nestled in the hills. It was my favorite time of year, but the beauty around us and the aroma of the fallen leaves we shuffled through in the parking lot seemed only to heighten my pain. Before, often in good times, but especially in difficult, we would have held hands and I missed that. Now I wondered, *Do you even think about it? You're unhappy with me, why would you?* On the verge of tears, I led the way upstairs to a second-floor waiting room.

The office interior was strikingly dismal compared with the beauty outside. The drab avocado green plastic furniture, brown indoor-outdoor carpet and outdated magazines did little to lift my sagging spirit. I wondered what Con was thinking. Although he was flipping pages in a magazine, he seemed to be staring blankly ahead. I wanted to say, "Let's leave—we can fix this by ourselves! God will help us!" But I said nothing and we waited for the counselor who soon greeted us, and then he and Con left the waiting room together.

As I followed them down a hallway, feeling weak and jittery, I silently asked God to help us. I still couldn't accept that our marriage was in trouble.

However, when I heard Con start talking about his unhappiness, I was jarred back to reality. Con's ease in answering questions surprised me. He seemed to enjoy explaining his discontent, and this was so unlike his normally quiet self. Even when we were with good friends, he never seemed at ease with small talk. And now it seemed as if he wasn't talking about us, but some other couple. Sadly I thought, *that's pretty close to the truth. I'm not sure, either, who we are anymore.*

The therapist's questions were challenging, demanding honesty about all aspects of our married life, including sexual intimacy. Still, my determination to put our marriage back together enabled me to answer. I wanted our marriage to be stronger than ever before—because we were going to save it together.

I was shocked when the counselor confronted me. "Your behavior is unusual. Did you want this to happen?" he demanded.

"I don't understand."

"Generally," he explained, "a wife in your situation would be crying uncontrollably, perhaps hysterically. Why aren't you?"

I was shaken and tears threatened due to the counselor's blatant attack. I had no answer, but then God's indescribable peace washed over me. My tension and fear eased as God seemed to breathe an answer through me. "I don't want to cry here, and I can't promise I won't, but I know God is with me and will get me through this—hopefully, with Con, but if not, without him. The Lord will help me."

I looked at Con, expecting some sort of reassurance, comfort, or compassion, but there was none. He didn't even look at me. Where was the loving support and tender nurturing that Con was always ready to give? Instead, he seemed oblivious to what had just happened.

The counselor insisted, "Shirley, you're in denial!" I didn't argue, and I didn't tell the counselor I couldn't remember ever crying in front of anyone. Even when my father died, I held back my tears until I was alone. Until then, I had never seen my mother cry except when Dad or one of us kids gave her a special gift. Perhaps that was why, as the oldest of three children, I always thought I must be strong for those around me. Now, again, I couldn't or wouldn't share my tears.

The counselor had unnerved me and I doubted I would ever trust him, but that disappointment paled in the light of God's reassurance and grace. Whatever lay ahead, I knew I could trust God, who saw the whole picture. I had experienced God's peace before, but never like this. I knew at a deeper and profound level the reality of Paul's words in Philippians 4:7 (NKJV),

> And the peace of God, which surpasses all understanding, will guard your hearts and minds through Christ Jesus.

This was the first of many times the Holy Spirit would make His presence known to me. At that time, I didn't know the Third Person of the Trinity well, but the blessings of getting to know God more intimately would make each challenge worth the accompanying pain, doubt, and frustration.

Even as the session ended, Con couldn't explain what he wanted different in our marriage. He just repeated that he was unhappy.

Our Secret

Con and I decided not to worry our family or friends because we wanted to work out our problems without well-meaning interference. Having had honesty drummed into me from childhood, I felt as if we were living a life of deceit. It seemed wrong to pretend everything was all right, but because our marriage appeared so solid it wasn't difficult. After twenty-six years, who would suspect?

Later, I would realize that I was afraid to tell others about it. If I admitted we had a problem, I would be taking ownership and I didn't want to. Continuing to socialize and worship with the same people, only

God and we knew what was really happening in our marriage. When we talked with family and friends we pretended all was well. I continued to hope Con was just going through a phase; we would save our marriage and not have to worry our children and the rest of our family.

Keeping a secret also meant that in my worst crisis ever, I couldn't ask family and friends to pray for us. Con went to church services and activities with me, but showed little enthusiasm. I wondered what had happened to his faith and I couldn't be sure he was praying for us. And so it was God and me. My prayers became more frequent and intense. Still, I worried about our marriage and I couldn't bear the thought of hurting our children.

Con told me he had confided in a couple of colleagues. Also needing a friend's support, I suggested we tell close friends. We agreed on a couple from church whom we knew would keep our confidence and pray for us. I called and asked if we could stop by. We were greeted warmly in their home where we had enjoyed many meals and wonderful evenings. There was no easy way to tell them except to just say it. They were shocked and for a moment speechless, but then they hugged us and I was glad they knew. In my darkest moments, their love, encouragement, and prayers for us kept me going, and I knew our sad secret was safe.

Soon after our counseling sessions started, Con asked if I wanted to resume intimacy. "I'll understand if you say no," he added, but it wasn't a difficult decision for me. "I love you," I told him, "and I don't think it's possible to put our marriage back together with one of the most important parts missing."

Continuing Doubts

It wasn't long, however, before I began to wonder if he was appraising me and sometimes doubt and anger crept in. *Do you have someone else in mind? Do you wish I were her? How do I compare? Are you using me?*

I never verbalized my fears because I was afraid of his answers. Instead I tried to bury them and think positively.

Con had always been a man of few words. Sometimes I wished he would talk more, but then we would spend an evening with someone who was boorish and overbearing and I would appreciate Con just the way he was. Almost always thoughtful, kind, and gentle, our children adored him. It wasn't often that he became angry and then it usually was with good reason—when I was cranky or demanding.

There were no big revelations during the following months of counseling except for occasional petty things. When I told Con about a dinner invitation I had accepted for both of us, he became angry. "Don't make plans for me anymore without my okay!" So I agreed to check with him first. It seemed strange after having been the one to make all of our social arrangements for almost three decades, but it was a small request and easily met. Other than that, he expressed few complaints except to insist continually, "I'm just not happy."

*Whispers from **Your** Heart*

When I'm afraid, where do I look for courage, strength, and peace? Have I found it there? If not, why not?

When I feel helpless, do I ask for God's help, or try to solve the problem on my own? Explain.

I have known God's indescribable peace and it made me feel:

Chapter 2

Another Storm

*"For I, the Lord your God, hold your right hand;
it is I who say to you, 'Do not fear, I will help you.'"*

—Isaiah 41:13

SADLY IN THE middle of our struggle, we suddenly had more to think about than ourselves. Jenny and Jim's marriage was ending in divorce.

I received a phone call at work from three-year-old Jimmy who was crying. "Grandma, my Daddy went away," he sobbed, the last words barely understandable through his tears. Jim had spent the morning playing with the children and explaining that he would be living somewhere else. It was a situation they couldn't begin to comprehend and in their innocence and ignorance of what this would mean, they drew pictures for their Daddy to hang in his new home. After he left, however, Jimmy had cried, "I wanna talk to Grandma."

Later, Con and I went over to console Jenny and the children. Two-year-old Julie was too young to realize the significance of what had happened, but this was clearly not so with Jimmy who adored his Daddy and knew something was dreadfully wrong.

We played with his toys and read books and later I tucked a somber little boy into his bed and helped with his prayers. We began as usual, asking God to bless each family member by name, but we only got as far as "Mommy and Daddy" when I felt his little body shudder in my arms. His beautiful little face became contorted as he cried, "Oh Grandma, this isn't what I want." Weeping too, I held him close and prayed for God to comfort him, but that indelible image of Jimmy's grief would always bring tears.

We were devastated for Jenny and did what we could to support her, but looking back I wonder if we could have—should have done more. Emotionally Con and I were both stretched, and Jenny's pain was unbearable for all of us. We helped her help her two small hurting children who understood even less than we did.

Continuing to see our counselor, the only solid direction we received was to be open with each other. "Talk about what you're feeling." Our counseling sessions were expensive and we were relieved when the therapist said we could stop, but he re-emphasized the importance of expressing our feelings. We tried hard to do this and sometimes our efforts were gratifying and brought hope that we could save our marriage. We would make it!

On other occasions, communication was poor or lacking. Picnics in beautiful parks and walks along the river were awkward and depressing. Even a special weekend in Toronto, which I had hoped would be a romantic getaway and an opportunity to renew our marriage, fell flat. Nothing seemed to penetrate our discord. I had resorted to planning topics for discussion, but we never got beyond a couple of brief comments.

Con had never been dynamic or forceful; he would make his point quietly. And there was never any question of his loyalties. He was always ready to demonstrate that his family came first. A compassionate man, I now felt sorry for him as he struggled for answers. He was obviously torn between what he knew was right for us and our children, and what he thought he wanted for himself—freedom—a fresh start. He seemed to feel life was passing him by, and as time went on, I didn't know if he still had no answers or if he knew what he wanted, but lacked courage to say so.

Our twenty-seventh anniversary came and I can't remember where we went for dinner. There wasn't much to celebrate except that we were still together, uncomfortable as it was.

By this time I could "read" Con and whenever he was unusually quiet and wouldn't look at me, I'd ask, "Are you okay?" His answer was always, "I'm all right." I learned, however, that he really meant, *I'm not all right, but I don't want to talk about it.* Sometimes he'd say, "I didn't want to come home today," and I ached. Often he went alone to the river to "sit and think," and I'd feel inadequate and deserted, crying and worrying that he was trying to get up his nerve to leave. At the same time, trying to understand, I prayed for more patience.

12

Another Storm

A New Counselor

A few months later, we weren't making any headway and resumed counseling—this time with a woman who was described as very good and less expensive. Con liked her and I found comfort in her warm, open, and caring nature. When she encouraged us to share without reservation, I wasn't ready for Con's bold and painful confession. This time he looked directly at me and said, "I don't love you and I'm not sure if I ever loved you." The words hit hard. I had been trying to deal with what I thought was a temporary hiatus in our marriage, but this was different! He never loved me?

Since the first time he told me about his unhappiness, I had tried to understand his confusion and at the same time cope with my mounting disappointment and pain. It was like standing in the rolling surf, braced against a threatening undertow, one wave after another pounding against me. Con's new revelation was the big one that almost pulled me under. I was so devastated that for the first time, I doubted we could save our marriage. *If he never loved me, maybe there's nothing to build on?* At the same time, I wouldn't accept that. I couldn't!

My mind flashed back and in a moment captured so many loving memories—the first time he kissed me, his marriage proposal, and when just prior to the birth of our first baby, he wept out of helplessness because he couldn't do anything to relieve my pain. And what about his deep concern and then obvious relief, when my uterine tumors proved benign and only surgery was required? He was always there for me—I thought because he loved me and I had never doubted it.

The counselor was looking at me and waiting for my response, but I couldn't speak. My confusion and frustration turned to anger and I wanted to cry, but instead I demanded, "If that's true, why did you marry me?" It sounded more like an accusation than a question. He didn't answer me, but just looked down.

I recalled our first date. It was a fun evening and at the end Con said, "You're the kind of girl my Mom would have wanted me to marry."

Did Con marry me to please his mother who died when he was in high school? They had been very close and I knew he still missed her. *Could it be?*

I shared those thoughts and asked, "Is that why you married me—because of your mother?"

Expecting him to deny it and say, "Of course not," I was stunned when, without looking at me, Con answered softly, "I don't know." I

13

would never know either and I was beginning to wish I had never met him, but then I wouldn't have my precious children and grandchildren. In sessions that followed, the counselor tried over and over to help Con pinpoint the reasons for his discontent.

"What do you want Shirley to do differently?"

"How can you improve your marriage together?"

"Can you state the problem?"

But Con's now tiresome response persisted. "I'm just not happy." I thought if I heard it again, I'd scream! How could I help if he couldn't or wouldn't say what was wrong? Perhaps the counselor felt the same. She suggested we again stop counseling and work on our own. "Call me any time you need to," she said.

A New Challenge

It wasn't long afterward that Con started to find fault with me. He complained that I took too much time fussing with my hair and then he asked why I didn't use coarser language. I found that really bizarre. We had never used rough language or profanity in our home and neither did our children.

He began to compare me to Nancy, a colleague, in her early thirties and I was appalled when he said he had told her about some of our marital intimacies. I was angry and shouted, "That's inappropriate and an invasion of my privacy. Don't ever do it again!" When I asked why, he said, "I needed to talk to someone." Despite my rage, the next day he said that he had now told Nancy about my anger of the day before.

Hurt and frustrated by his behavior, I began crying and screamed, "You have no right to tell her these things! Don't you understand how humiliating it is?" This time he evidently understood my anger, but his promise not to confide in her again was soon broken.

The following day, Con announced, "Nancy wants to meet you for lunch," and I could hardly believe what he was suggesting. Wanting to forget that she even existed, I refused, but that wasn't the end of it!

A couple of days later, Nancy called and asked me to have lunch with her—to "clear the air," she said. I accepted because she sounded sincere and also because I was curious. Maybe I would get some answers. We decided on a small Greek restaurant for the following day.

First to arrive, I nervously looked around for a woman matching Con's description. Not finding her, I chose a table near the door and waited.

Another Storm

As I sat there I could hardly believe what I was doing. *How awkward this could be! Ridiculous! A wife isn't supposed to meet the "other woman" for lunch! Is that what she is?*

When Nancy arrived she was pleasant and not unattractive, but her language was coarse, her clothes appeared to have been taken from the ironing basket, her hair disheveled, and she wore no make-up. This was the role model Con had chosen for me; the woman to whom he was attracted.

"I need a haircut, badly," Nancy said, and when she apologized further for her appearance, I was uncomfortable. Had she read my mind? "I'm sorry and embarrassed," she continued, "to be in the middle of this dispute you and Con are having." She was candid and I found her believable.

"I'm aware of Con's infatuation with me, but I want you to know it's definitely one-sided. I'm fond of him, but he's more of a father figure for me. There's someone else in my life." Instinctively I knew she was trying to relieve my fears, but at the same time she had validated my suspicions and I felt sick and only picked at my souvlaki.

"Nancy, I didn't want to meet with you because I was worried about what you might say. Now I know this hasn't been easy for either of us." I thanked her for her kindness in helping me to understand. Her openness helped me relax and our time together was as pleasant as it could be under the circumstances.

During the thirty-minute drive home I tried to sort my feelings; grateful that Nancy wasn't interested in Con and disappointed that he cared for her. I understood why Con was drawn to Nancy's relaxed, down-to-earth, and caring personality. I liked her too!

When I arrived home, Con was eager to hear what had happened and asked, "How'd it go?"

"I like Nancy and I'm glad I went because now I know that she doesn't have a romantic interest in you. In fact, she's quite interested in someone else."

If Con was disappointed, he didn't show it and I didn't go into details because I didn't think he deserved to know. I purposefully didn't tell Con that Nancy had described him as a father figure. I'm not sure why, but perhaps because I knew he was sensitive about his receding hairline and I didn't want to embarrass him. It made me wonder *why do I still care?* Maybe I didn't tell him because I was just plain tired of talking about the whole mess.

A "New" Husband

Several weeks later, Nancy became engaged to be married. Con seemed to accept the news easily and made it clear that he wanted for us to attend a garden reception in their honor. I gave in to please him, but I resented going.

There I saw the "new" Con in action! Overnight, it seemed, he had become adept at social skills! He appeared relaxed and happy, exuding confidence! I felt awkward and sad. With Con following me in the receiving line, I tried to appear calm and sincere as I offered my best wishes to Nancy. She accepted graciously and introduced me to her fiancé. Walking away, I felt like crying; not because of anything they did or said, but just because I was there and they were happy and I was so miserable. *If only we could leave now*, I thought, but Con had already moved on and was having a great time talking and laughing with some of his colleagues.

Standing alone, I felt conspicuous as I looked around and wondered who else knew about Con's unhappiness with me and his interest in Nancy. Did they pity me? Humiliation took over and with my heart pounding and feeling dizzy, I headed inside to a powder room where I stayed until I calmed down.

After that party, I knew Con was bored with our life together. His interests lay outside our marriage; he wanted someone new. I didn't know how to change that and my feelings of inadequacy escalated. At the same time, his newfound self-assurance was not consistent and so I didn't know what to expect. Withdrawing, he would isolate himself and then bounce back and act happy again. He seemed to ride a seesaw on which my emotions bounced. Up and down, up and down…

A week later, I ran into a friend whose marriage had recently ended. She talked about her pain, but also of the deep conflict, hurt, and anger that had been inflicted on their children. Was that where we were headed?

When I saw couples our age laughing together or families enjoying picnics in a park, dinner on their patios, or worshiping together, I ached in envy. I wanted to tell them, *Don't take your marriage for granted—enjoy every moment!*

Through the years we had delighted in the happy times, but also had endured and grown together through hurts, disappointments, losses, and the inevitable adjustments. I remember how pleased Con was when I agreed to move our family to England for a year so that he could exchange his job and our home with a college professor there. Nine years earlier we had made a difficult decision when he was offered a job at SUNY College in Buffalo. Con knew that leaving family for the first time had proved difficult for me and I guess he thought a second move to England would be asking too much.

Five months into our stay in Lancashire, my father became critically ill. I flew back to New York state with Con's blessing and the reassurance of our wonderful British neighbors to assist us in any way. A year later when my father died, it was Con who held me and calmed me. I found my strength in his quiet composure and my faith in God. I relied on both.

Our joy, tears, and faith reinforced our oneness, but now the foundation of our marriage had serious cracks in it. We were arguing more and more.

A New Problem

I yearned for intimacy again—that natural bond of love and understanding which only matures after many years together. We had it once. Where did it go?

Not only was our relationship in jeopardy, but Con no longer seemed to have time for God. At least, he wouldn't talk about it and I believed God was the source of any hope for our marriage to survive.

When Con appeared unhappy, I slipped into the guilt trap of so many women. *What have I done wrong? What can I do to make it right?*

I was aware of my mistakes and our different personalities. Being more laid back, it must have been difficult for Con to put up with my insistence that things had to be just so. And I often got so involved with church activities that sometimes he seemed to resent it; maybe he felt neglected. Even though I prayed for guidance and tried to be a good wife and mother, I had failed miserably at times, but I wasn't ready to give up.

For almost a year we successfully lived our "lie." Sometimes I felt guilty about not being real with our family and friends, but we were sure it was the right decision and not difficult to carry out. I don't believe I ever lied intentionally about it to anyone, but I chose very carefully what I would or would not say. If that was a sin, it was a sin of omission.

Our oldest daughter Julie and her husband lived in Virginia, and our other daughter Jenny and her family lived nearby. Neither of them or our son, Jim, a college student who lived with us, ever suspected. When Con and I argued, it rarely happened in front of others and that didn't change despite the strain in our relationship. From all outward appearances, our marriage was solid.

Fall arrived and Con said he was going away for a weekend to sort out his feelings. He planned to rent a cabin in a state park. After he left, I prayed for God to replace Con's confusion with a deep desire to heal our marriage and to draw close to God again.

Sunday evening, on his return, he found me reading in the living room. "There's something I have to tell you," he said and the serious look on his face frightened me. *Is this it? Has he decided to leave me for good?*

"I didn't go alone," he admitted, "I took a friend with me; a woman." My stomach ached and I was so shocked that I couldn't speak. "Nothing happened," he explained, "we didn't sleep together." Then he hesitated and added, "Well, we slept in the same bed, but we never undressed."

I found his story incredible! At the same time I was relieved and wanted so much to believe him that I rationalized. *He didn't have to tell me any of this.*

"I want to believe you," I told him and neither of us ever brought it up again. I also didn't tell anyone else, which is probably just as well. I doubt anyone else would have swallowed his story and I would have felt foolish all over again if I admitted that I had.

A New Hope

After his weekend away, there was a wonderful change in Con. He seemed happier and actually eager to spend time with me. I couldn't be certain of what had happened on that weekend, but his time away seemed to have renewed his interest in me. Or perhaps it was relief that I hadn't insisted on pursing the subject further.

Gradually, I felt more relaxed and relieved that we were finally working our way out of a sad dilemma. In early November, when Con suggested that we attend a marriage enrichment weekend, I was thrilled. He did want our marriage to work and when I packed, I tucked in a lovely new negligee.

The program, designed to encourage communication in marriage, was explained at the first session. There would be group discussions, but the couples would do most of the "work" privately.

Each participant received a blank notebook, the kind with black and white marbled cardboard covers. In these we would write letters to our spouses, but only after spending time apart to think carefully about the assigned topics. This proved difficult as we strived for integrity while digging deeply into feelings that we had tried to suppress. Then each couple reunited to read and discuss their letters. It was painful, physically

18

exhausting and emotionally draining to hear truths about ourselves, many of which hurt to acknowledge. It was equally difficult to openly criticize each other, but we were told that success demanded honesty. At times we laughed and sometimes there were excruciating tears. Surprisingly, we were able to talk and love freely for the first time in many months, unhampered by worry or embarrassment.

During the group meetings, ballads from *Man of LaMancha* were played and the words from "The Impossible Dream" filled me with sadness and anxiety. For many years that song would continue to tear me apart to the point that I had to turn off the radio or television.

Still, I felt we were on the right track. I dreamed of success and was convinced that with God's help, we would attain that "unreachable star."

At the orientation, we had been told that on the last evening there would be a ceremony for all couples wanting to renew their marriage vows. I didn't dare think it would happen for us, but just before that service began, Con tenderly asked if I wanted to. I was delighted and after the brief ceremony, he held me close and I thanked God. Our marriage was all right again! With His help we had done it! The unreachable star was ours!

On Thanksgiving Day I awoke early. Although a turkey waited to be stuffed, I treated myself to a few extra minutes in bed and thanked God for the many blessings of the past year. First on my list was Con, who was still sleeping as I slipped out of bed and into my robe.

The incomparable aroma of a roasting turkey surrounded me as I prepared all the other traditional favorites. I set a place for us and each of our children and grandchildren, feeling more appreciative than ever for the love we shared. We had come too close to not being a complete family on this wonderful holiday, and I wondered *how will they react when we tell them about the past fifteen months?* Con and I had decided they had a right to know and we wanted to share our re-found happiness.

With everyone gathered around the dining room table, Con asked the blessing and my heart sang in grateful response. As usual we ate too much, but still managed to stuff in pumpkin and pecan pie, topped with whipped cream, of course. While the adults leisurely finished coffee and dessert, our grandchildren were excused and Con explained his earlier unhappiness, our ensuing counseling, and the marriage enrichment weekend. I felt compassion as they listened with obvious concern; their faces solemn. When their eyes met mine, they seemed to be asking *why didn't you tell us; are you all right?*

Con assured them, "Everything's fine. We're both happy. You don't have to worry, but we thought you should know." They glanced from him to me, appearing to not quite believe what they had heard. Even after I reassured them, it was clear from their serious expressions that it would take a while for everything to sink in. There was sadness in their eyes which I hadn't anticipated and I second-guessed our decision to tell them. Clearly, despite the happy ending, we had taken something precious and irreplaceable from our children and that void was filled with uncertainty.

Whispers from *Your* Heart

In a disagreement, how do I express my feelings? Am I honest and open to discussion?

What is my "impossible dream"? How can I trust God with it?

In what ways do I acknowledge God's answers and blessings?

Chapter 3

A Different Life

"Do not fear or be dismayed...the Lord will be with you."
—2 Chronicles 20:17

DURING THE WEEKS that followed, Con and I cherished each other and our time together. Eagerly sharing thoughts, both positive and negative, we wouldn't again forget how important it was to be open about our feelings.

Our marriage seemed better than ever, and the intervening days until Christmas were filled with joy and anticipation. It was a happy and busy time, and perhaps that's why I didn't notice the subtle changes as Con reverted to his quiet more introspective self of only six weeks before.

It was a fun time of buying gifts and hiding them throughout the house and baking many tins of everyone's favorite homemade cookies. I hung fragrant boughs of Douglas fir, pine, and red-berried holly on lamp posts, the fence gate, mirrors, chandelier, and the back door with our old sleigh bells—any place I could attach the boughs with red velvet ribbons.

Many of the angels in my collection, which were displayed behind the glass door of our old desk, were moved to their special places throughout the house. As I picked up my favorite, made by Jimmy in first grade, the head fell off. It had been reattached earlier with a toothpick and cellophane tape, now yellow and dried out. About eight inches tall, its light blue construction paper dress had faded and the wings were tattered. I carefully mended it again, amused by the cockeyed little face with its red crayoned mouth and blue dotted eyes. Then, I set it aside until it could be placed at the top of our tree.

Our old crèche, candles, poinsettias, and as perfect a tree as possible would all play a part in my dream for our best-ever Christmas. The most important part of Christmas was family—just being together to worship on Christmas Eve, to sing carols and exchange gifts. It was a time to notice the wonder on our grandchildren's faces and to feel joy in our hearts, not only for the Christ child, but for another family Christmas for us—which almost didn't happen!

Julie and her husband, Bob, came home, and Jenny and her children also joined us for family dinners and times of sharing and celebration. The laughter and tender moments that make family gatherings so special passed much too quickly.

On a couple of occasions I noticed Con sitting deep in thought. He seemed preoccupied and unaware of the laughter and activity going on around him. It happened again at our New Year's Eve party, so when we were alone in the kitchen I asked, "Are you all right?" His familiar quick glance tugged at my heart. Even though he said, "I'm okay," I knew he wasn't. We needed to talk, but that would have to wait until our guests had left. That was 3 A.M. and we fell exhausted into our bed.

Later that day we took Julie and Bob to the airport. Hugging me good-bye, Julie whispered, "Mom, I'm worried, please talk with Dad. It's important." I didn't understand Julie's concern and I wondered what she knew, but with no opportunity to ask, I was still puzzled as they walked away to board the plane. Riding home, I didn't mention Julie's comment because I hoped Con would take the initiative. It seemed I was the only one monitoring our relationship and this time I wanted Con to tell me what was bothering him. He didn't and I decided to wait.

Lightning Strikes

The next morning, on January 2, Con and I were having breakfast in the still decorated dining room where we had enjoyed so many celebrations over the years. After lively holiday fun, our house seemed too quiet. Jim was there, but he was still sleeping.

As I refilled our coffee mugs, I thought, *He's not going to say anything; I'll have to bring it up.* "Con, I'm concerned. Sometimes you seem quiet and unhappy again. Can we talk about it?"

He listened and nodded silently in agreement. I thought he looked pale and tired, but suddenly he stood up, almost tipping his chair over. "You're right," he said. "I'm not happy and I'm out of here!"

24

I couldn't believe it! We just needed to talk—like the counselors had said, "Be open with each other!" I was speechless as he abruptly left the dining room, grabbed his jacket from the closet, and opened the back door.

Even then, for the tiniest moment, I expected him to change his mind and say, *No, let's try again,* but he didn't. He left, and the Christmas bells on our door jingled just as merrily as they had for twenty-seven years, but this time they signaled the end of our marriage.

I froze. I couldn't move and I wanted to scream, *what do you mean, you're not happy? For eighteen months you said that again and again, but you never said why! Do you know why? I wanted to please you and I really tried. And, now you're gone,* I thought bitterly, *only two months after we renewed our wedding vows and that was your idea!*

My head ached and I was gripping the coffee mug so tightly that my fingernails cut into my flesh. Trembling, I released it and stood up, but I didn't know what to do. *Should I go after him? I don't know where he's going.* Defeated, I sat on the couch in front of our beautiful Christmas tree and did nothing. *He's gone. Our marriage is over. What now, God?*

I felt strange—senseless—like a block of wood. I couldn't think clearly and I felt powerless. I just sat there until I heard Jim walking around upstairs and then I panicked. How could I tell my son his father had left and wasn't coming back? No one should have to do that.

I waited a while to compose myself and asked God to help me find the right words. Then I climbed the stairs to his room—the same stairs from which I had often awakened my children by calling, "Happy faces in the morning!" or "Wake up little rosebuds, wake uh-up!" Emotions rushed back and with my heart pounding and eyes burning, I whispered a prayer for God to calm and help me.

Jim was back in his bed, propped up and reading, his thick black hair disheveled against the pillow. With dark eyes sparkling, he gave me his familiar, affectionate greeting, "What's up, Shirl?" I didn't want to answer, but I had no choice. Moving his legs over, he made room for me to sit, and I did my best to tell him.

"Jim, I hate to tell you this, but your father has again decided he's not happy, and he's left."

"Where is he?"

"I don't know," I replied, and then I told him what I could. "I'm so sorry, Jim." He said it wasn't my fault, but not much else. He just looked sad and confused. I knew he was trying to be brave for me, and my heart broke for him. This was so different from comforting him as a child, when I could just cuddle him in his blue-footed jammies until he wiggled off my lap, his troubles forgotten. Now, twenty-two years old, all I could do was hug him and leave him alone to deal with it.

Ripple Effects

I went downstairs as I had so many times after hearing my children's prayers and tucking them in for the night. *Oh God, there must be something else I could have said to help Jim, but I don't know what. I'm not very good at this. Please help us.*

I was glad I hadn't cried in front of Jim. My tears would only make it harder for him and I was determined to be strong for my children.

Julie, Jenny, and others also had to be told. *Eventually,* I thought, *I can't face it now.*

Jim came down a short time later. "Is it okay if I go out for a while? Will you be all right?"

"I'll be okay. You go ahead." I guessed he needed to talk to one of his friends or maybe look for his Dad. I didn't ask.

Later the phone rang, startling me. I wasn't ready to talk to anyone, but I made myself pick it up. I trembled when I heard Con's familiar, "It's me," but it was so strange. He sounded nervous and hesitant, as if he didn't know what to say. My husband of twenty-seven years suddenly seemed a stranger. "I'll be house-sitting for Ken who's going to California for a few weeks. Okay, if I stop by to get some clothes?"

Hanging up the phone, my life seemed surreal. When Con arrived, we were pathetic as we searched for what to say. Then, his quietness gave way to arrogance and he actually seemed pleased with himself. I just wanted him to collect his things and go, but first I said, "Jim knows. Will you call Julie and Jenny? I just can't." *Besides,* I thought bitterly, *You left, you tell them!*

Thinking about their inevitable sadness made me tearful and I didn't want Con to see me cry. I only wanted him to go, but I worried about how he would tell our daughters. Seeming so self-focused and excited about his freedom, would he be sensitive to their pain? Still, I knew he loved them.

When Julie called and I heard her struggle with what to say, my heart broke again. "Are you all right, Mom?"

"I will be, honey. Try not to worry. I know this is hard for you too." The miles between her home in Virginia and mine in western New York seemed greater than ever. "Julie, I have to ask. Why did you tell me at the airport that it was important for your father and me to talk?"

"When I was packing," she explained, "Dad came to our room and said, 'No matter what happens, remember I love you.'"

Jenny also called me, searching for words to reassure me, but like Julie and Jim, her pain and confusion were great. I wanted to protect them, but only God could help us. Many years later I would learn that Con had told Jenny on New Year's Eve that he again wasn't happy and didn't think he could stay with me.

Now that he had left, I couldn't get away from the questions that had haunted me for too long and for which I had no answers: Why does Con no longer want me? Why can't I still make him happy? What does he want so desperately that it outweighs our children's happiness and mine?

Devastation

At bedtime I was physically exhausted, but so restless and wide awake that I doubted I could sleep. Walking into our bedroom and seeing Con's partially emptied closet, I closed the door as if I could hide the truth that he was gone. In the large wedding portrait over the bed, we both looked young and happy as we shared the dreams of every young couple in love. His wavy, brown hair was now gray and mostly gone, but I didn't love him any less. I thought we'd grow old together. He was the devoted and tender husband I had hoped for and a loving and gentle father to our children. *What happened?*

I lifted the beautiful cherry-framed photograph from its hanger and carried it to a storage closet, but my emotions were a jumbled mess that couldn't be tucked away as easily as the portrait.

Ready for bed, I knelt to pray, but for a long time I just rested there, my head heavy against the mattress until finally, words came. "Lord, I don't understand. I really believed with Your help we could save our marriage. I asked You to heal us and I really thought You would—I thought I just needed to be patient and trust You. Can I trust You?" Even as I asked the question, I remembered the many times I had known God's strength and peace. "I'm so grateful Father, but Con's gone!" Then I realized that all three of us had to want our marriage to survive and now it was clear that Con didn't care enough.

I pleaded with God to stay close, but lying alone in our bed, I was overwhelmed with self-pity and fears. My brain worked overtime, playing out every possibility I might ever have to face. Eventually, I cried myself to sleep and when I awakened in the middle of the night and remembered that Con was gone, I reached out in the dark to an empty pillow. It wasn't just a bad dream. Our marriage was over and I was alone.

The next morning I wondered if Con missed me or if he was happy because he had finally made his big move. And were our children sadly remembering what had happened? Did they think their father would change his mind? I didn't. He now had his freedom; what he wanted all along.

I didn't know what my future held, but God's presence was real and I knew I could trust Him. I wondered where Con would find strength. Right now he was happy and looking forward to a new life, but what if things weren't as wonderful as he anticipated? He hadn't shown any interest in God for a long time.

Suddenly I realized I hadn't eaten since Con left. I sat at the dining room table for my first meal alone and it was dreadful. As I paused to give thanks, I prayed, "Father, we thank You…," and then realizing there was no "we," I cried instead.

I couldn't eat and I began to understand why so many lonely people eat their meal from the cooking pan in front of a TV. Surely I wasn't the first to wonder, *why bother to set the table or create a lovely presentation when there's no one else to enjoy it?*

Clearing the table, I vowed not to give in to self-pity. Always optimistic, I would continue to look to the future with hope and take one day at a time. Meanwhile, I needed to keep busy.

Our Christmas tree no longer was "magical." Instead, just seeing it saddened me and I decided to get rid of it. As I removed the ornaments and sat on the floor, wistfully wrapping each one in tissue, I realized I had to separate Con's ornaments from the rest. I wondered, *where will he be next Christmas…and me…and our children?* Surely we wouldn't be together. There would never be another family Christmas for us, and that realization put me over the edge. Overpowered by grief amidst strings of lights, cartons of ornaments, and crumpled tissue paper, I collapsed on the floor and sobbed as never before.

Whispers from *Your* Heart

**When it seems my life is falling apart, can I thank God for what I
have left? Why or why not?*

*Have I ever felt too despondent to pray? What happened?

*Can I feel God's presence in painful times? How do I know its God?

Chapter 4

Repercussions

"Be still before the Lord, and wait patiently for him."

—Psalm 37:7

I FOUND STRENGTH in worship services and often sermons seemed to have been written just for me. Sometimes, songs about God's love and faithfulness made me cry—perhaps because there seems to be such a fine line between intense joy and deep despair. Praising God reinforced my faith in Him and as with any relationship, the more I centered on God and talked with Him, the closer I felt to Him. Needing to believe that God understood and cared, I clung to God's words for Hezekiah in Isaiah 38:5: "I have heard your prayer, I have seen your tears."

As time went on, my concern was more for my children than myself. I talked frequently with them, but didn't really know how they were coping. And although they were supportive, I worried, *Do they feel I'm to blame? Do they feel closer to their father?* Because Con was more laid back and I was home more than he, I had been the disciplinarian most of the time.

Still, I didn't delve too deeply into my children's feelings or express mine in detail, and they limited their comments as well. They were in a difficult place—between two people they loved and I was determined never to put their father down. That would only make their already unbearable situation more difficult.

Friends

Talking with my closest friends, I asked them to let others know what had happened. Their reactions were almost word for word the same. "I can't believe it. You're the last couple I would ever have thought this would happen to."

As our counselor had predicted at one of our first sessions, many of our married friends evaluated their own relationships and wondered if the same thing could happen to them. Some reacted positively, determined to appreciate each other and strengthen their marriage. Others, to my surprise, actually seemed jealous of my new "freedom" and one gal even said so!

Friends tried to understand my situation, but that's impossible unless you've been there. I became frustrated with some who nagged at their spouses about insignificant things. Although I had probably done more than my share of "nit-picking," I had learned a lesson. Now I wanted to shake them and say, "Just focus on the important issues and love each other!" Perhaps my reaction reflected the guilt I was feeling. If I had been more tolerant and not insisted on my own way so often…I would never know and it was too late now.

I was surprised when Melanie, a young widow and one of my closest friends, said that divorce was worse than losing a spouse by death. "Death is final. The person is gone forever and those who are left know what they have to deal with. On the other hand," she explained, "in divorce the former spouse often remains in the picture to various degrees. This can mean more pain, confusion, and frustration—intentional and otherwise—for the spouse and the children as their separate lives occasionally connect." I would grasp this truth more clearly later on.

I listened carefully out of a deep respect for my good friend, whose faith in God never wavered. Melanie had trusted God for strength to put aside her own fears and sadness in order to sustain her husband, Al, through endless diabetic and related crises. When Al died, Melanie trusted God for strength to go on without her husband, and she continued to believe in a God who has promised to see us through life's circumstances. Her unwavering confidence in God shined through her tears of loneliness and His presence helped fill the unbearable void of widowhood.

Many years later, Melanie shared her reflections of those days,

At this time I was trying to help my brother through a difficult time after finding out his wife had a relationship with someone else for the previous five years. And I was still dealing with my grief of losing my husband at age thirty-seven just six years before and leaving me with three young boys to raise alone with no family around. I cried, then, asking myself why life had to be so cruel, but at the same time reassuring myself that we have a God who really cares and has promised to see us through life's circumstances.

I remember driving down Shirley's street and slowing down when I saw her sitting on the ground scraping her large picket fence, and my heart went out to her as she did this menial task. I remember thinking how much it hurts to lose whether by death or divorce. After a few minutes I pulled myself together, drove back to Shirley's home and shared some precious moments with my friend.

When I stopped to talk with Shirley, I found her to be more of a comfort to me than I'm sure I was to her. She had a wonderful positive outlook and was trusting God for His answers to her heartaches. Although our circumstances were different, our loss was deep, hurtful, and shared.

I believe God puts us in circumstances so that we may at a later time be a help to those in like circumstances. Because of my loss I could be there for Shirley, not necessarily to give answers but to put a hand on her shoulder thus saying, "I've been there, I know, I feel your pain and you will come through this."

I will always remember Al's memorial service when we all sang Melanie's chosen hymn, "It Is Well with My Soul." These reassuring words were written by Horatio G. Spafford after two major traumas in his life; first, the great Chicago Fire of October 1871, which ruined him financially. And a short time later while crossing the Atlantic, all four of his daughters died in a collision with another ship. Gratefully, his wife survived and Spafford took a ship to meet her, passing near the spot where his daughters drowned. There, he said, the Holy Spirit inspired him to write the following words of eternal hope for all believers, regardless of the immensity of our pain here on earth.

It Is Well With My Soul

When peace like a river attendeth my way,
When sorrow like sea billows roll;
Whatever my lot,
Thou hast taught me to say,
"It is well; it is well with my soul."[5]

Despite Melanie's great loss, she could sing these words with integrity; confident that God knew her pain and would provide. He was already blessing her with strength and the deep joy of His presence, and in years to come He would give her another loving husband.

I don't know that Melanie ever questioned God about Al's illness and death; most likely she did. That is surely understandable, but Melanie's faith in God's love for her never wavered.

Melanie is a marvelous example of a woman who trusted God through the toughest of times, and she continues to inspire and encourage me today. Her example gave me a benchmark for which to strive.

Other friends were also generous with hugs, encouragement, and offers such as, "Is there anything I can do?" and "Call any time you need me—day or night." Several treated me to lunch or dinner during the first couple of weeks, but then except for a few, I didn't hear from them and that was okay. They were busy and I was tired of trying to explain a painful situation I still didn't understand. I felt their love and found comfort in knowing they were praying for me, and that they were close by if I needed them— "even in the middle of the night."

Other Responses

Con's decision to live with Jenny and her children until his apartment was available troubled me. I had hoped we could be stabilizing factors in the lives of our grandchildren, but instead, Grandpa left Grandma and I didn't begin to know how to help them understand. Sadly, I didn't have to. They said nothing and I wondered if they thought that Daddy left, so why not Grandpa? I would talk to them later, when they were ready.

Some of our friends were angry with Con, but tried to love and forgive him even though they felt he was wrong. Others wanted nothing to do with him and this upset Jenny, who said Christians should not be so quick to criticize and pass judgment, but instead to love and forgive. Con seemed to have lost interest in church and made little effort to contact even church friends of more than twenty years. With the exception of a few friendships that he chose to keep, he focused on starting new ones, mostly with thirty and forty-year old coeds at the college. At least, those were the ones he told me about.

One of our friends, while trying to comfort me, said, "It'll all blow over. He'll be back in six weeks." I was surprised by my reaction. I didn't want him back. I was defeated. I was fed up. It was over! I realized then that the eighteen months of counseling and "working through" so many difficult issues had prepared me for my new situation. Although I had been optimistic, I couldn't help considering what I would do if Con did leave, and indirectly that had softened the blow when it happened. In anger, I said that I would not give him a chance to leave me again.

Before, I would have trusted him with my life, but now he was gone and I would go on.

Con's Reaction

Although Con had made it clear he wanted to leave, he obviously had to dig deep for the nerve to do so and at first he acted uncertain about his new freedom. His reticence, however, was short-lived.

Each time he came to collect a few more things or talk about the legal aspects of our separation, he seemed more arrogant. Clearly delighted with his freedom, Con made no effort to conceal his feelings.

He reminded me of a little kid with a new toy, and although I resented his flippant comments, I said nothing. I wouldn't give him the satisfaction of knowing that I was hurting and lonely. He seemed nonchalant and carefree, while I could only deal with life one day at a time. Looking too far ahead overwhelmed me.

At times, he didn't seem to have a clue about what I was feeling or going through. Once when we talked about his having left, I said "I'm grateful you didn't have an affair. That would have made me feel worse—even more rejected."

His response seemed callous. "You shouldn't feel rejected."

I didn't answer. There was no point. Obviously our perceptions of rejection weren't even close!

Still, when I needed a different car, he offered to help me find one and a few days later he phoned.

"I've found a car. Do you want to see it?"

While driving to the showroom, he explained in a too light-hearted manner, "I told the salesman all about us." Again, my privacy had been invaded, but he seemed pleased with himself as he related their conversation in detail. When I met the salesman, my self-esteem was at rock bottom. I felt ashamed, like something tossed aside and I couldn't wait to get out of there. We agreed on the car, but at that point I would have settled for anything!

A couple of days later, a phone call from Con left me smiling and feeling smug.

"May I stop by and get my extra wallet? I was doing my laundry," he explained, "and I forgot to empty my pants pockets."

Then his unfortunate decision to dry his sodden wallet in the microwave had resulted in something closely resembling a piece of beef jerky.

I wanted to shout *Hooray! Double hooray!*, but I didn't. I wasn't ready to laugh with him; to resume any kind of normal relationship. I wasn't proud of my feelings and I didn't care! I was glad he ruined his wallet! Was that because I didn't want him to manage easily without me?

When he arrived, my delight in his mishap fizzled as he talked openly and excitedly about his new romances. He said more than I wanted to hear, but I didn't stop him and my curiosity annoyed me.

Unlike Con, I didn't care if I ever dated again. When I wasn't working I kept busy with church activities, chores, embroidery projects—anything to pass the time. Occasionally I went to a movie or enjoyed dinner with Melanie. Those were the bright spots in my life because she always reassured me of God's love and lifted my spirits.

Telling Mom

A month had passed and I still hadn't told my mother or my brothers, Don and Larry, that Con had left. They didn't even know about his earlier unhappiness or our counseling. A hundred miles separated us and although we talked weekly, it wasn't difficult to keep my secret, but I couldn't put the trip off forever. I dreaded telling my mom in particular, because I knew it would break her heart.

Jenny made time in her hectic schedule to go with me, and we were greeted with the usual big hugs from my tiny five-foot mother. "It's so nice you both could come."

I had told her Con wouldn't be coming and she seemed to like the idea of our first "girl" visit. After talking for a little while, I suggested we go to Don's home to say good-bye to my nephew who was returning to college. It would be easier to tell them all together.

I wondered how I would do that, but right away, Don asked, "Where's Con?"

"He's busy," I answered, trying to sound normal, but then glancing at Jenny, I knew I had to just say it. So, with my heart pounding, I added in a shaky voice, "I have something to tell you. Con's left me."

There was total silence.

My sister-in-law, Ann, appeared shocked and my stunned brother asked, "What happened?"

Repercussions

Before I could answer, Mom got up and left. I could hear her crying in the next room and I wanted to comfort her, but couldn't move. When she came back I hugged her trembling body, feeling guilty to cause her such pain. She asked, "When did it happen?"

"A month ago."

"You should have told me right away," she scolded.

"Mom, I couldn't tell you over the phone."

I answered her questions as briefly as possible and promised we would talk more later. My head was pounding and I was on the verge of tears, but not wanting to upset them even more, I said I was okay. They knew I wasn't, but no one said so.

Ann shook her head and said what I had come to expect, "You're the last couple I would ever have believed this could happen to.

It was good that Jenny and I could spend the rest of the day with Mom. With a shaky voice, she asked God's blessing on our lunch, but her confidence in God to carry all of us through this new crisis was solid. Her unwavering faith through many painful times now also strengthened and encouraged us.

When Larry, my younger brother, came over, he, too, wrapped his big arms around each one of us, but after hearing my news, he lost his composure and left the room.

It was Mom who followed and tried to console him—my little mom, who had to quit school after sixth grade to work and help support her. family. Life wasn't any easier after she married my father and they settled down in the tiny town of East Palmyra, NY. Their great love, however, overcame their financial hardship and they delighted in each other and in their three children all of whom were born in July. When I turned three, Don turned two and Larry was born! More than once she and Dad were teased about chilly October nights.

My father worked hard and Mom always took great pride in her responsibilities as wife and mother, especially in her clean home and sparkling laundry. As a child, I didn't have many clothes, but those I had were starched, ironed, and carefully hung or folded. I still feel sad when I think back to how shabby some of her clothes were. She sacrificed personal things in order to buy clothes for the rest of us.

The relationship she and my father enjoyed until his death at fifty-nine, was exactly what God intended a marriage to be—one of loving trust and total commitment. Mom had been so happy that ours had seemed the same. Sometimes Con had made the two hour trip alone to get Mom for a visit. With plenty of time to talk, they had grown close and that made our separation even harder for Mom to accept.

When she and Larry returned to the kitchen, she said, "I just can't believe it's true," but despite her anguish, Mom assured me, "God will take care of you. I believe in you and your faith will see you through. You'll be okay."

However, as she waved good-bye from her doorway, I knew she was again on the verge of tears. She appeared even smaller than usual and I drove away with a heavy heart.

Support Group

Mom was right. I continued to trust God, but sometimes I had to make myself pray and read Scripture, and then I was glad I did because I always found reassurance of God's care. A favorite was Proverbs 3:5-6 (NASB):

> Trust in the Lord with all your heart and do not lean on your own understanding. In all your ways acknowledge Him, and He will make your paths straight.

I claimed that promise and I found comfort in believing that God would show me what to do each step of the way. I didn't know where my path would lead, but God did.

I phoned to update our marriage counselor, but Con had already told her our news. She said she was sorry, expressed her concern for me, and encouraged me to attend a support group for women in transition that was beginning a few days later.

Driving to the first meeting, I was again suddenly overwhelmed by all that had happened. *How did I arrive at this place? Never in my wildest dreams did I think I would need a support group. How could a marriage like ours...?"* There were no answers—at least not good answers. I had to let it all go.

Proverbs 3:5-6 came to mind and this time I was blessed anew. I was amazed that for so many years I had skipped over the phrase, "...lean not on your own understanding." What this now said to me was that there are some things we can never understand in this life, such as the death of a child, intense suffering, or the end of a marriage. God alone knows the answers to some questions, but one day we'll understand. For now, He just wants us to trust Him—no matter what!

I was one of eight women in the support group and although we greeted each other warmly, I sensed that the others were as uneasy as I. A coffee pot gurgled as we settled into molded plastic chairs around a large stained and chipped Formica-topped table. We were asked to introduce ourselves and briefly explain our situations. This was clearly upsetting for everyone—some cried as they described their crises. The counselors, however, skillfully encouraged and helped us to share our pain, anger, disappointment, and feeble attempts to cope.

Six of the women were past fifty (one of them, seventy), and two in their twenties. They all were in various stages of divorce proceedings following their husbands leaving them for other women. My personal pain paled in comparison to what I felt for those who had suffered humiliation much worse than mine and in some cases, abuse. I was most concerned for those who seemed to have no hope; their faces reflecting absolute despair.

Weekly for the next ten weeks, we would climb the stairs to meet in this sparsely furnished room over a pharmacy. The battered furniture seemed to mirror the shabbiness we tried to mask, but we bonded through our tears, laughter, and the intimacy of sharing our pain with others who could understand. Driving home from those sessions, I felt emotionally bankrupt and I never slept well those nights.

God's Strength

As time went on, we talked about how we got through each day. Open about my faith and my confidence that God is always with me, I shared a favorite Bible verse hoping it would encourage the others, Isaiah 43:1-3:

> Do not fear, for I have redeemed you; I have called you by name, you are mine. When you pass through the waters, I will be with you; and through the rivers, they shall not overwhelm you; when you walk through fire you shall not be burned, and the flame shall not consume you. For I am the Lord your God.

God definitely was with me in the waters of grief that threatened to overflow me. Many of my friends and co-workers marveled at my ability to cope. The only explanation I had was, "You're seeing God's strength in me." I remembered a radio comment by Chuck Swindoll that I had jotted down several years before:

"Faith is like a lens...it doesn't change the situation, just your perspective."

More and more, I found that to be true. As I trusted God, my faith grew and I believed God could make something beautiful even out of my miserable situation. I purchased a refrigerator magnet that paraphrases Psalm 138:8, "God is perfecting that thing that concerneth me." Twenty years later it's on my refrigerator and it's still true! I am a work in progress, have been since birth, and will be until I go to be with the Lord.

I began worshipping at a different church that I had visited occasionally, and I joined a Sunday school class for adult singles. We learned from a Christian perspective about coping with relational stress, disappointment, and discouragement. Although I missed my other church friends, God was meeting my needs through this group and through the pastor's sermons.

One Sunday, I was more lonely than usual. Perhaps it was because it was a beautiful, warm, early spring day that should be shared with someone. I wrote in my diary, "...feeling this void so urgently even though I know God will provide for all my needs and that He alone knows what they are and when they must be satisfied."

Driving to the evening worship service, I stopped for a red light, and there facing me in his convertible, was Con and one of his new younger friends. They didn't seem to be having a great time. She was filing her nails and they weren't even talking. Even so, it was the first time I saw him with someone else. It was upsetting and I couldn't wait to get away before he saw me alone in my car.

Entering the sanctuary with a heavy heart, I seated myself next to a tiny gray-haired lady. "I'm Grandma Rose," she said, a smile lighting up her face. We talked for a while, but when the service began, I still felt miserable. Later when we sang a song about God's love, Grandma Rose unexpectedly reached over and gently took my hand—just when I desperately needed someone to cherish me. It was as if her hands were the loving hands of Jesus and her face radiated Christ's love. Grandma Rose sitting next to me right then was no coincidence, but God's beautiful and direct way to ease my loneliness.

When the service ended I turned to Grandma Rose. "I must tell you what happened this evening. I came here sad and lonely, but when we sang about God's love I prayed that I could feel it and that's when you reached over and touched me! I felt God's love through you." Grandma Rose beamed with joy and I had a splendid new friend whom I believe was one of God's angels. Driving home I was more certain than ever—God loved me! I didn't have a clue about my future, but I was at peace. God would unfold His plan for my life when He knew I was ready.

Medical Alert

Several days later, I was about to drive from a parking lot onto a major highway, when suddenly, I felt faint. Able to pull over and park, I lowered my head until the lightheadedness passed, but my heart was pounding and erratic. Eventually, when it resumed a more normal beat, I drove home and called my doctor.

The first time something like that happened had been several years earlier when I was working in a doctor's office. My chest suddenly felt like an unbalanced washing machine in the spin cycle, one side fighting the other. A couple of minutes seemed forever, and when the jerking stopped, my heart skipped and raced so forcefully I thought it might burst.

Medical tests led to the diagnosis of a prolapsed mitral valve in which the valve closes improperly. Medication regulated my pulse and I was assured that my life wouldn't be affected otherwise. That proved to be true until this parking lot episode.

After examining me and a new EKG, my doctor said he didn't know what was wrong, and added rather lightly, "Could be stress. You may have to learn to live with it." That wasn't easy—it was scary! I missed talking to Con and, also, his concern and support, and I didn't want to worry my children. Gratefully, the symptoms were infrequent and became less severe.

My Son, My Valentine

On Valentine's Day, my co-workers at the elementary school where I was school nurse happily chatted about cards and gifts from their husbands and boyfriends. I tried to share their enthusiasm, but it was difficult because I knew I wouldn't receive any. I was wrong. When I arrived home I found lovely flowers and a card, which was signed, "Love, Jim (your son)."

I laughed because he had been signing his correspondence that way since his first postcard from camp when he was five—as if we would forget who he was! Now his love and sensitivity brought tears, but they were happy tears.

Shift in Perspective

Jim's days were full with school, friends, and his job and although we lived in the same house, I didn't see much of him. As the weeks passed, I became lonelier. I missed having someone special in my life; someone who needed me, too. At the same time, I wasn't ready for and didn't want a new relationship; my ambivalence bewildered me. Emotionally fragile, I needed to be God-focused and not self-centered.

In Psalm 150:6, we're told to praise God in all things, and in 1 Thessalonians 5:18 to give thanks in all circumstances. Instead I wanted to argue, *but God, this is different...don't You understand? This is my marriage!*

Those days were tough, but greater than my tears and fears was an underlying sense of God's peace for which I was grateful. I didn't know what my future held, but God did and I could trust Him. Sometimes, however, I felt abandoned. Intellectually I knew God was with me, but I couldn't feel Him. I had to choose to believe in His promises never to leave me, and sitting on the floor in front of the stereo I made myself sing songs glorifying God. With a squeaky, trembling voice I did my best to sing worship choruses such as *You are Lord*.

> You are Lord, You are Lord,
> You have risen from the dead and You are Lord.
> Every knee shall bow, every tongue proclaim,
> that Jesus Christ is Lord!

I believed that if I made myself praise God, eventually I would again want to. I also decided to stop complaining and, instead, to look for the good remaining in my life; to stop feeling sorry for myself. When I prayed, I began to listen for His answers rather than tell Him what I wanted. More and more I could sense God's power in my life. For example, during a particular sermon God's direction couldn't have been more specific. The pastor who was talking about our needs and relationships, compared turkeys who will eat anything, to eagles who are more particular. He said, "It's difficult to live like a turkey when you're an eagle." The lesson for me was that God would always meet my needs. In particular, the analogy demonstrated that I should never settle for just anyone, but to be patient and particular; an eagle who waited for God's direction and timing.

Awkward Moments and Humorous Incidents

There were incidents that demanded composure, and sometimes humor. One evening as I entered a church service, I was delighted when a friend I hadn't seen in at least fifteen years called to me. We hugged, and then immediately she asked, "Why aren't you wearing your wedding ring?" For a moment, I was stunned. I couldn't believe she had noticed so quickly and I was shocked at her insensitivity. Surely someone must have told her.

I explained as briefly as I could that Con and I were no longer together. I remember her reaction well—total silence! She and her friends just looked at me for what seemed to be forever, and it was then I recalled that she was a member of a very conservative church. Obviously, she didn't know what to say, but I didn't either. Feeling flustered and humiliated, I excused myself.

Another time, I attended theater with close friends with whom Con and I had enjoyed front-row season tickets for many years. He had exchanged his pass, which was then resold to the attractive gentleman I found sitting next to me and it appeared I had a very handsome date! The floor show involved interaction between the comedians and the audience, and this made for some awkward moments when romantic comments were directed to me and my "partner." He was a good sport and we did our best to go along with the fun, but I was relieved when it was over.

As time went on, I became more confident as a "single" and might have accepted an invitation to dinner or a show, but I wouldn't go looking. After a twenty-seven year commitment to one man, I was hesitant about dating and couldn't imagine becoming intimate with anyone else. If ever there was to be someone new in my life, he would have to find me. But as my story played out, I would see that I was only half right. The *someone new* would find me, but it was God who would send him.

Whispers from *Your* Heart

In difficult situations, how have I trusted God's promises in Proverbs 3:5-6? "Trust in the Lord with all your heart and do not lean on your own understanding. In all your ways acknowledge Him, and He will make your paths straight (NASB)."

Who are the friends I can count on for support? Can others rely on me?

Has God placed an angel in my life? How do I know he/she is a special gift?

Chapter 5

Choices

"Because you are precious in my sight, and honored, and I love you..."

—Isaiah 43:4

ABOUT TWO MONTHS after Con left, a letter arrived from Stefan Vogel, Con's best friend from Army days—thirty-four years earlier. After basic training, both were assigned to radio school where a similarity in last names brought them together. Vogler always followed Vogel at roll calls. With a joint assignment in Austria, they soon became travel mates and chess partners. After both had married, their friendship continued long distance with correspondence only at Christmas and on the births of our children. This time, however, Stefan wrote about the sudden death of his wife, Marie.

We had visited them for three days—seventeen years earlier—when we were on vacation; the only time we were ever together. While Stefan and Con reminisced, Marie and I bonded as we cared for our children and prepared meals. Now I recalled little about Stefan except that he played his guitar and sang for the children, but I remembered Marie well. Her generous and loving manner had impressed me, and I could still feel her big bear hug greeting on their back porch. Hoping my fond memories of Marie might help Stefan and his three daughters, I wrote them a letter, and at the end I added, "There's been a change here as well. Con wanted his freedom and has left our marriage. I'll forward your letter to him."

About a week later, I was surprised to receive a response from Stefan. He expressed his concern over Con's leaving, and asked how I was coping. Because we both had enjoyed wonderful marriages that had ended abruptly, we found we had a lot in common and our letters continued on a regular basis between my home in Kenmore, New York, and his in York, Maine. I became fascinated with Stefan and looked forward to his letters.

He told me about Beth, a longtime friend and colleague. "She's the one I call when I need to talk. I love her and some day I hope to marry her. It just feels like the right thing to do and at this stage in my life, one relationship is enough." Stefan seemed content with his life. Then he wrote, "Are you dating anyone?"

"No," I answered, "and it's all right. I'm not ready." But why did I wish he would call me when he needed to talk, instead of Beth?

Stefan became my confidante. His experience was different, but he understood my disappointment, heartache, and concern for my children's loss and confusion. We also shared a deep faith in God. I thought Beth was pretty fortunate to have Stefan's interest.

Stefan invited all of his friends, including me, to visit him on the Maine coast. I declined, but Con accepted and went there during spring break instead of our original plans to visit our friends, Joni and Ralph, in Phoenix.

I considered canceling my plans for Phoenix too, but Joni insisted it would be good for me to go and she was right. Another couple joined us and we all piled into an RV and headed for Mexico. Both couples had been married for about thirty years and were still very much in love. Yet, their sensitivity toward me resulted in my never feeling like a "fifth wheel."

For the next several days, we enjoyed a beautiful beach on the sunny Gulf of Mexico and ate mostly giant shrimp which Ralph grilled, barbecued or steamed—a good buy at $5 a pound!

Tear Drop or Petal?

Walking alone on the beach early one morning, I found a shell—only a piece, really, like others in my collection. The once jagged edges were now worn satin smooth from being tumbled repeatedly in the surf. The lesson for me was that as broken shells are transformed into new and unique objects, I also was in process. God was changing my brokenness into something beautiful; I just had to wait and see.

The shell I found that day was shaped like a teardrop, or was it a delicate petal? The choice was mine. I could choose a symbol of my pain and sadness, or something beautiful to represent my faith in God and

Choices

my hope for the future. I still have the "petal" which symbolizes for me the beautiful words in Song of Solomon 2:11:

> For now the winter is past, the rain is over and gone.

Whispers from *Your* Heart

*When and how do I leave room for God to act in my life?

*How has God touched my life in unique ways?

*Despite the hurt, why and how can I choose joy?

Chapter 6

God's Soap Opera

*"The flowers appear on the earth; the time of singing has come,
and the voice of the turtledove is heard in our land."*

—Song of Solomon 2:12

I ARRIVED HOME from my trip to Arizona and Mexico feeling totally refreshed. A few days later, Con stopped in, and after making it clear that he was enjoying his freedom, he described his visit with Stefan in York, Maine.

"After three days there, I told Stefan, 'You and Shirley would be just right for each other'."

Suddenly he had my full attention!

"And, of course," Con continued, "Stefan asked, 'Why would I want her if you don't?'"

Rather arrogantly, Con looked at me, and said, "I told him you're attractive and nice, but just not for me anymore."

The more he talked, the more I felt like a hand-me-down and I wanted to say, "You big jerk! First you dump me, and then you give me away!" but I didn't. I refused to feed his self-satisfaction.

In spite of my annoyance, my interest in Stefan was piqued, but still I declined his invitation to visit. He was planning to marry Beth and besides, as I wrote to him, "I'm just old-fashioned enough to believe that if we ever see each other again, you'll have to visit me first."

Several days later there was another letter. I laughed as I tried to decipher some badly jumbled words, which were always a part of Stefan's letters because he typed too fast and didn't take time for corrections. This time there was a reason for his haste.

He was preparing to drive his daughters Lisa and Heather to Louisville, KY, to see their younger sister, Stefanie, in a play. Then he would drive Stefanie, her two cats, and the rest of her belongings back to York and the other girls would fly home to return to work.

Stefan agreed with my decision not to visit him and I was disappointed. I mean, really disappointed! *Ridiculous,* I thought, *he's only a pen pal!*

But, the following morning I still felt "down," and that puzzled me. I had managed to think positively in really tough situations—why couldn't I let this go?

Scraping and Praying for a "Sign"

It was a beautiful, warm Saturday morning. While eating a leisurely breakfast on the porch, I noticed the blistered paint on our picket fence. It desperately needed a face-lift and I needed to keep busy.

For five hot hours I scraped and thought and wondered and prayed about Stefan and my unexpected disappointment. I tried to make sense of feelings I didn't want or understand and eventually I was able to be honest with God and myself. *I'm fond of him and jealous of his relationship with Beth. I really do want to see him and I'm miserable because he agreed with my decision not to visit him.* The whole thing was ridiculous and I was disgusted with myself!

There's so much I don't know about him. We may not even get along, and besides, he lives in New England and I doubt I'll ever see him again. It's just as well. But I couldn't shake my disappointment. I doubted I would ever marry again, but if I did, Stefan seemed to be the kind of man I would want.

I asked God to clarify my confusion. "Please, Father, I don't understand my feelings and I don't want them. I'm like a teenager with a crush, and I'm not ready for a new relationship. I'm trusting You to sort this out and I'll try to forget him."

Salty drops of perspiration were stinging my eyes. Tired of scraping and itchy paint flakes that were sticking to my damp skin, I quit. Collecting my tools and latching the gate, I added a p.s. to my prayer, "God, I know You're always with me, but today I could sure use a sign that You are."

I didn't know what I wanted God to do or say, and I certainly had no idea of how amazing His "sign" would be!

God's Answer

The coolness of the house welcomed me and after a refreshing shower, I felt renewed. After a few chores, I curled up in a favorite chair to answer Stefan's letter, but I had barely started when the phone rang.

I answered and a beautiful deep voice with what I call a "Kennedy" accent, asked, "May I speak with Shirley?" I identified myself and then heard, "This is Stefan," and I knew immediately that God was giving me the sign for which I had asked! I was certain! The call was remarkable because we had not talked since we visited the Vogels seventeen years earlier.

Sometimes it's difficult to "read" God—to know if something is really from the Lord. On occasion there seems to be no answer, or at least not the one we hoped for. But this time there was no question and it didn't matter what Stefan said. Just that he called was enough because God was showing me He loved me; He had heard my prayers, and He cared about my pain and confusion!

"I'm calling from a theater in Louisville," Stefan explained. I smiled when he added, "I hadn't planned to visit you, but the idea unexpectedly came to me." Later, we would determine this to be the time that I had said my p.s. prayer! "I decided I can just as well take a different route home and my daughters think it's a great idea. They'll all fly home with the cats. Is that all right?"

"It's a wonderful idea." He accepted my invitation to stay with Jim and me and promised to call again with his arrival time on Monday.

I hung up in a daze, hardly believing what had happened, and I couldn't stop smiling. God had answered my prayers before, but never so dramatically, and this time He chose to do so through Stefan! "Thank You, God," I whispered, "I still don't know what my future holds, but You're in control and whatever happens is all right."

When I called Mom, and then Melanie, I laughed and said, "You'll never believe what's happened!" They knew that Stefan and I had been corresponding, and they were as surprised as I was about God's direct response and happy for me. They gave no reprimands or warnings—just radiated joy and acceptance.

After dinner, I was still wound up so I cleaned the room Stefan would be using—a job I had been putting off. I dusted, vacuumed, washed windows, and laundered the curtains, bedspreads, and canopy covers. I wondered if Stefan would mind sleeping in a bed with a dotted Swiss canopy and bedspread.

I had no trouble falling asleep, but the next two mornings I awakened at 4:30 and could not go back to sleep. My appetite also was affected and I ate little. I didn't understand what was happening to me. Remembering that Beth was the focus of Stefan's life, I asked God to help me put Stefan's visit in perspective and not read more into it than I should.

I couldn't remember what Stefan looked like and so I searched for a slide of him that Con had from Army days. I finally found it after sorting through four Kodak carousels and I wondered why I was going to so much trouble.

It was a side view of Stefan sitting at a desk, lighting a pipe. *Slim, blond, good-looking*, I thought, *but, perhaps not anymore*. I would soon find out, but somehow it didn't seem to matter.

Stefan called again on Sunday. He would arrive late on Monday and leave early Wednesday, so I arranged to take Tuesday off from my job as school nurse. I wanted to take him to Niagara Falls, our main tourist attraction, but I wasn't sure I knew the way. When Con and I had gone together, he always drove and I never paid attention, so Melanie took me on a trial run so that Stefan and I wouldn't get lost.

Stefan's Visit

On Monday afternoon, Stefan called to say he was making better time than expected and would arrive at six. Not prepared to cook and with no time to shop, I said, "That's even better. We'll go out for dinner—my treat." Not a big deal for many, perhaps, but it was for me. I had never treated a guy to a meal before or, for that matter, used a credit card in a restaurant. Con always took care of that.

Stefan accepted my invitation for that evening and asked me to make a reservation at my favorite restaurant for Tuesday evening and we said good-bye. Our ease in talking made me certain we would enjoy our time together.

Trying to read while I waited for him, I couldn't concentrate and a few minutes before six, Stefan drove up in his dark blue station wagon. I watched him get out and as he walked up the porch steps I went out to greet him, feeling totally comfortable. Prepared to shake hands, I was surprised when instead, Stefan smiled and said, "I guess a hug is in order." He, too, was relaxed and I liked his looks and manner right away.

While Stefan showered and changed, I absent-mindedly flipped magazine pages. *There's something special about this whole situation. Or, is it just that my life has become so routine that anything new is exciting?*

Because Stefan's car seats were packed to the roof with Stefanie's things, I drove to the restaurant. Stefan was a gentleman who seated me first and made me feel special. I liked the way he studied the menu through his horn-rimmed half glasses, but he had barely started reading, when he closed it and said, "I'll have the lamb chops, they're one of my favorites." His easy decision impressed me, because I always have trouble deciding. That evening I just chose something—I don't remember what.

There was never a lull in our conversation. It seemed as if we were old friends and I was intrigued with him from the start.

Stefan had lost thirty pounds, but hadn't found time to have his trousers altered. I laughed when he showed me how he tried to make them look neat by smoothing the fabric in front, and then gathering the extra four inches of cloth on his belt in back. I hadn't noticed because of his jacket, but always a perfectionist, I was surprised at my light-hearted reaction. Before, that type of thing would have been unacceptable and now it seemed insignificant. I felt guilty as I realized it was just the kind of thing I would have picked at Con about.

I had no trouble figuring the tip on the tab and presented it and my card without difficulty. Whew! Then I took Stefan to see Niagara Falls from the Canadian side and we didn't get lost! Two boosts for my self-esteem and it felt good! This all followed on the heels of Jim teaching me how to fill my gas tank and operate a car wash which had been fun even though we both ended up soaked when he "accidentally" sprayed me and I had to get even.

As Stefan and I talked and walked near the magnificent misty falls, I became tired and unsteady on my high-heeled shoes. Lack of sleep was catching up with me and I wanted to hold his arm for support, but held back as I didn't want to appear forward.

Jim arrived home soon after we did, met Stefan, and then the two of us chatted happily until 2 A.M., continuing to fill in the gaps not covered by our letters.

Tuesday was perfect; a sunny, cool, sweater and jeans type day. Before breakfast we walked around my neighborhood, and later we visited the zoo where we enjoyed the antics of monkeys and bears, but mostly we enjoyed getting to know each other. For lunch we bought pita sandwiches at a health-food kiosk, and ate them on a nearby deserted bleacher—not the Ritz, but we couldn't have enjoyed it more.

We returned to Niagara Falls; this time on the American side where we took an elevator down to view the awesome falls from below. A stranger, seeing my camera, offered to photograph us and our happiness was captured on film.

We walked along the rapids and then sat on a bench to watch the swirling, powerful current of the Niagara River and the swooping, screaming gulls. We talked non-stop about our children, feelings, experiences, Marie's death, Con's leaving, Stefan's job as school principal and mine as school nurse. Stefan would later describe our ease in talking with each other "like stepping into an old shoe."

He told me more about Beth, a friend and colleague of eleven years, who lived about two hours from his home. "We've only dated once, but we write letters, talk frequently on the phone, and are comfortable with each other. We're close friends and it just seems to me it's right that we're together. When we went out for dinner I talked to Beth about marriage, but she was non-committal. Recently I wrote a letter, asking for an answer. She's wonderful," he added. "I'm eager to hear how she feels about a future with me."

Now I better understood, but my heart was not in sync with my brain. Instead, my emotions were spinning, not unlike the water in the whirlpools before us.

At least, I consoled myself, *we're having fun today and I know that I can carry on a sensible conversation with a man other than Con and not totally fall apart!*

Stefan went on to tell me about his adjustment to single life. "I've mastered laundry skills except for ironing, so I just take my shirts out before the dryer shuts off and hang them. Works great!" His solution for meals was simple, but sadly the same day after day. Juice and an English muffin for breakfast, tossed salad and roll for lunch, and every Sunday after church, he stopped and purchased seven frozen meals which he microwaved for dinner each evening. "They're nutritious and low calorie," he added.

Pathetic I thought. *Hopefully, Beth will take better care of him.*

Stefan seemed as reluctant as I was to leave that idyllic place. Did he, too, not want our time together to end? Clearly we both enjoyed this opportunity to support and encourage each other in person and although we didn't talk about it, I sensed a deeper bonding. When we returned home, Stefan asked about my shell and angel collections displayed behind the glass door of my antique desk. I told him about my favorites and where I had found them. I explained what the "petal" shell meant to me, and I thought he was listening, but when I paused and looked at

Stefan, he said quietly, "I'm going to kiss you." He gently lifted my chin, and it was sweet and wonderful. We looked at each other, embraced for a moment, and without saying another word, Stefan smiled and went to shower and dress for dinner.

I was in a daze. I went into my bedroom and sat on the end of the bed, smiling at the wonder of it all. I couldn't believe it! He kissed me! I thought kissing another man would be awkward, but I didn't have time to think about it. It wasn't awkward at all—it was wonderful—as if it were supposed to happen!

But then Beth came to mind.

"God, I don't know what's going on. Stefan is even nicer than I thought he'd be, but what about Beth? I don't want any of us to get hurt. Please sort this out." And at that moment quietness flowed through me—a beautiful peace. I would just enjoy this time with Stefan.

I slipped on a simple white dress. It was the only thing I had purchased since Con left and at the time I wondered when I would wear it, never suspecting it would be on a date. I anticipated a wonderful evening and then Stefan would go home and that would be the end of it. If nothing more came of our friendship, his interest had boosted my confidence, affirmed a new self-image, and with God's help, I would carry on.

Stefan loved my "knock-out" dress, as he called it, and his admiring look made me feel more special than I had in a long time. As we walked into the Asa Ransom House, filled with antiques and costumed waitresses, he looked around admiringly and I knew he was pleased with my choice of restaurant.

Our table was ready and Stefan winked at me when the hostess said, "Mr. and Mrs. Vogel, please follow me." Coincidence? Perhaps, and fun!

Stefan moved his chair closer so we could talk more easily and at one point, he said, "They won't mistake us for an old married couple—we never take our eyes off each other!"

Although he had a long travel day ahead, our intention of going to bed early did not happen. Instead, we sang hymns and took turns playing the piano, and then he entertained me by playing Con's guitar and singing folk songs.

I was impressed with Stefan's goodness, and sorry for the pain he had suffered after Marie's death. We talked about trusting God and relying on His faithfulness to us, and I gave Stefan a blue glass dove of peace to hang in a window of his home.

Suddenly, he kissed me again and said, much to my delight, "I don't understand why Con left. The grass can't be any greener than this!" He was new and different and I loved being with him.

One of the songs we sang, "What a Difference a Day Makes," I secretly claimed as "ours." It was a special, romantic evening and one I knew I would never forget. Just before Stefan went to bed, my son arrived home in time to say good-night. Jim told me he liked Stefan. "Nice guy," he said, and I agreed.

Goodbye

The next morning as I fixed breakfast, I doubted I would ever see Stefan again. Although I told myself it was all right and that God was in control, I wasn't hungry.

Because Stefan was trying to stop smoking, I gave him a bag of hard candies for his trip and said, "When you're tempted to have a cigarette, have a candy instead." He didn't seem convinced, but said he would try. He hugged and kissed me and then, still holding my face in his hands, he said tenderly, "There's a lot of love here. I'll have to trust God to close one of these doors."

I wanted to say "I love you too," but again I thought of Beth and I didn't. Stefan was also trusting God for direction and I couldn't ask for more than that. Still, as he drove away, part of me went with him.

I marveled at how someone I hadn't seen in seventeen years had impacted my life so deeply, but it would be best to forget Stefan. Beth was waiting for him.

God, why have You answered my prayer in this way? Perhaps it would have been better if I hadn't seen Stefan at all. I didn't tell him about my prayers by the picket fence. Maybe I should have—I probably won't get another opportunity.

An hour later, I was back at school, comforting and treating tearful children with assorted bumps and bruises. When I wasn't busy with thermometers and ice packs, Stefan came to mind. Twice I was surprised by highway phone calls from him, "…just to say hello," he said, but I was pleased he was thinking about me, too.

Indeed, What a Difference a Day Makes!!!

At 6 P.M. he called again, this time from his home in York. "Shirley, sit down. I want to read something to you." So, seated at my old oak kitchen table, I heard Beth's response to Stefan's proposal of marriage. She said he was a dear friend, but because of family matters she couldn't consider a deeper relationship.

I was surprised at her answer.

"What do you think about that?" Stefan asked.

I didn't have time to think and so I said my first thought, "I think God answers prayers."

"I do too. I thought about you all the way home," he added, "and I knew before I got here that our relationship was the right one. Shirley, I love you. Will you marry me?"

He took my breath away. I was delighted and amazed! Although Stefan had acted as if he loved me, I didn't dare believe it and I had never considered a proposal! But I knew I would marry him. No hesitation. No questions. No fears. No matter we had been together only two evenings and a day! My answer was, "I love you too, but I don't want to answer your proposal over the phone."

"I hoped you loved me," he said and I could hear his happiness. "Will you come here this weekend to see where I live?"

Would I? I couldn't wait to see him again! "Stefan, I'd love to."

"I'll be happy to buy your plane ticket," he offered, but I told him that wasn't necessary. Our joy couldn't be contained and our excitement mounted as we realized the extent of God's blessing on us. We didn't want to say goodbye, but eventually and reluctantly, we ended our extraordinary phone call.

I have no idea how long I sat there with a grin that felt permanently etched on my face. God had touched our lives in a very special way and I laughed aloud when I remembered the song I had chosen as "ours"—"What A Difference A Day Makes!" A day can make a wonderful difference—especially when we give it over to God!

I was deeply grateful to God for answering my prayers in such a specific and astonishing way. He had transformed my confusion into crystal clear direction for my life. I knew I could trust Him even in this surprising situation which seemed too good to be true. In less than three days God had turned my life around.

Only a week before, I thought just dating someone would be awkward, and here I was about to accept a proposal of marriage! *And when I do, I'll tell Stefan about my picket fence prayers. He'll love that!*

Although I was certain about God's hand in all that had happened, I doubted that my family and friends would easily accept my news. They knew how difficult it was for me to make decisions—even when choosing an ice cream flavor I was always the last person to order! I was also very sensible about matters that were much less serious than getting married, so why shouldn't they wonder?

God, how can I explain all of this? I decided to say as little as possible to anyone until after I visited Stefan.

What about Stefan's daughters? Will they welcome their father's news—only four months after their mother's death? In spite of my questions, I had no doubt that all of this was God's idea. He had brought us together and He would take care of the details and that included helping our six children accept another change in their lives. "Even more than that," I prayed, "help all of us to love each other."

The next two days were a happy blur of phone calls. I ordered a round trip ticket to Boston which Jim picked up, and when he handed it to me, I said, "Jim, this is so strange—I feel like a teenager."

"I know, Mom," he replied, "I feel like your dad!"

Damp Weather, Warm Hearts

Friday evening 7 P.M. arrived, but because of bad weather in New York, the airplane didn't. After two seemingly unending hours, the plane arrived and my usual apprehension about flying was displaced by euphoria. Totally at ease as I boarded, I wanted to reassure anyone who was afraid of flying, "There's nothing to worry about. This plane is safe!" I was certain that after blessing Stefan and me in such a marvelous way, God wouldn't allow anything to mar our happiness. Soon the twinkling lights of Boston greeted us and as the massive plane touched down, I asked God to bless our weekend together.

Across the waiting room full of people, we saw each other immediately and when Stefan wrapped his arms around me, I knew I was exactly where I wanted to be and where God had put me. During the ninety-minute ride to his home we held hands, and totally fascinated, I hardly stopped looking at him as we talked happily about all that had transpired. I thought he was very handsome and his blue eyes seemed to penetrate mine when he said he loved me. And I liked his bushy eyebrows that reminded me of Andy Rooney. I was in love and nothing mattered but us.

Reminding me of the bag of hard candy I had given him for his trip home, Stefan said he only smoked three cigarettes during the ten-hour trip and none since our remarkable phone call. "Cold turkey—never could do it before! After Marie died, I thought my life, too, was over, but now I have you and a new and wonderful reason to live." God was still taking care of details and Stefan would never smoke again.

It was almost midnight when we entered the driveway to his lovely log cabin home nestled beneath tall birches and hemlocks. With a post and beam addition, it was much larger than I had pictured and every room was aglow. When I commented, he smiled and said he had asked his youngest daughter, Steffie, to turn all the lights on because he wanted me to feel as welcome as possible. His thoughtfulness made him even more precious and I was convinced that I wanted to be wherever he was.

Molly, his Golden Retriever, barked her greeting from the kennel and Steffie came outside to welcome us. Smiling, she embraced me and I was reminded of her mother's hug so many years before. Marie had taught her children well. Inside, Stefanie offered me chocolate chip cookies which she had made just for me. It was her first visit home since her mother had died, and now I was there. It must have been difficult, but Stefanie didn't let it show, or were we too enthralled with each other to notice?

"Come, I'll show you my house," Stefan offered and we began a tour of his warm and inviting home. We started in the cozy kitchen/family room with its back stairs and wood-burning stove and then the large dining room with a huge stone fireplace. These rooms along with a bath and two upstairs bedrooms had made up the original log cabin.

It contrasted beautifully with the more contemporary post and beam addition which had a spacious living room with circular staircase leading to a loft and master bedroom. On the parlor grand were several photographs that provided another look at what would be my new family. There was also a small study, two more baths and two more bedrooms.

On the bedside table in the guest room, I was delighted to find three long-stemmed yellow roses and a card which read, "I Love You." I turned to thank him and his face reflected the extraordinary love I felt for him. We embraced and no words were necessary.

Later, lying in bed, the night was absolutely still except for the occasional clang of a bell buoy in the harbor. I was reminded of childhood nights when an eerie train whistle blasted the evening silence and made me feel lonely. That night in York was entirely different. Feeling loved and grateful, I prayed, "Thank You, God. Only You could have done this!"

I awakened to the soft whisper of rain against the window and for a few minutes I was still—just lying there, remembering, delighting in the roses and thanking God for my unexpected happiness.

Soon, good-morning hugs were shared and the three of us found our way to the quaint Golden Pineapple Restaurant. The heat from the wood stove, the smell of the burning logs, and the coziness of small rooms were inviting after the dampness outside. I loved the crooked, wide pine plank floors which creaked as we were led to our table.

As Steffie ordered, I realized how beautiful she was with naturally curly, dark red hair and blue eyes that sparkled when she smiled at the waitress. While enjoying stacks of delicious blueberry pancakes, dripping with butter and native maple syrup, we happily filled her in on all the details of the past week. I wondered what she was thinking. Was it difficult for her to hear her father's excitement over me? She seemed to like me, as I did her.

Later, Stefan took me on a driving tour of nearby towns and beaches. The persistent rainy, gray day was no match for our happiness; nothing could dampen our spirits!

Proposal

We celebrated our love by having dinner at Clay Hill Farm, an elegant old inn in nearby Cape Neddick. "Shirley, you look so beautiful, everyone here is watching you," Stefan bubbled. I doubted that, but his delight and obvious pride in being with me made me feel cherished. We talked about many things, and I shared with him God's miraculous answer to my picket fence prayers. He, too, was amazed as everyone else is when they hear it.

Later, with such tenderness that I could hardly answer, he asked for a second time, "I love you so very much, will you marry me?"

"I love you too, Stefan. Of course I'll marry you!" What a contrast to my bewilderment of only a week before.

Stefan was totally unselfish, even offering to sell his home if I didn't like it. "If you don't want to leave your family, I'll move to Buffalo." He said he liked the way I had decorated my home and was especially impressed with a wall hanging of a Danish proverb that I had embroidered, "What we are is God's gift to us; what we become is our gift to God."

"More than anything," Stefan said, "I want to make you happy and I find it impossible to tell you how much I love you."

"Stefan, I do understand, I feel the same love for you."

On Sunday we attended church together for the first time. We held hands and sang hymns of praise and gratitude that seemed to have been written just for us. We knew God was smiling at our happiness.

God's Soap Opera

Driving to Boston to have lunch with Stefan's three daughters, I wondered aloud, "I hope they like me." Stefan assured me, "They'll love you."

Introductions were made, and while I was being greeted warmly with hugs, I heard someone whisper, "She looks nice," and I was put at ease. His girls were just as pretty as Stefan had said and what a variety—Stefanie, the redhead, Heather, a brunette, and Lisa, blond!

We became acquainted over plates of shrimp stir-fry. At first, I felt a bit awkward—like a new kid on the block, but soon we were all talking easily. There was much laughter as the girls and Heather's husband, Steve, teased their Dad by telling me about his "bad traits." A fun time was too soon over and Stefan and Stefanie took me to catch my flight home.

On the drive to Logan, Stefan and I agonized over having to be apart. We had something very special and it was difficult to say goodbye.

Whispers from *Your* Heart

How have I been flexible or rigid with life issues? How can I improve?

When I asked God for a "sign," how did He answer me?

When I receive a special blessing, do I see God or coincidence?

Chapter 7

Telling Family and Friends

"This God—his way is perfect; the promise of the Lord proves true; he is a shield for all who take refuge in him."

—2 Samuel 22:31

DURING MY FLIGHT home, I relived details of our perfect weekend, marveling at the wonderful way I had been welcomed by Stefan's children. God had thought of everything!

Next, I had to tell the news to my family and friends—most of whom didn't even know there was a Stefan in my life. Less than a week before he was only a pen pal. Even I could hardly believe all that had happened so quickly! *How will I explain this extraordinary relationship that Stefan and I share, and how can I expect them to believe me? Everything seems unreal and marvelous at the same time.* When I arrived home, it was too late to call anyone.

At school the next day, memories of the most loving, romantic time of my life overshadowed everything else. Co-workers hugged me and said, "You look so happy," and then a dozen long-stemmed red roses arrived—my first ever! There was such excitement, you would have thought they were for everyone, but the attached envelope had my name on it! All that was printed on the card inside was "etc."—a secret message which made me laugh and which I shared with no one. The beautiful roses thrilled me, but at that point, dandelions would have done as well. The romantic charm of it all was exciting and the love we shared almost beyond belief.

I knew that if I could have custom-designed my future, it wouldn't have been so splendid. "God, only You could do this! Thank You," I whispered.

Role Reversal

My concern about the reactions of my children and family soon became realities. "On the rebound," some said. They thought my decision to remarry so quickly was foolish and irresponsible, and they worried that I'd be hurt again. I too had heard disappointing and painful stories of second marriages that didn't work, but I knew this was different.

"This is God's idea!" I insisted. "Trust me. You know I've always been sensible," but they persisted. Eventually the elation I felt over Stefan conflicted with my worry about hurting them. Jenny's life was by no means easy and trouble free, and what about my son? Where would he live if I moved? Should I stay nearby? Still, I found it impossible to believe that God's answer to my picket fence prayers could in any way harm me or my children. Lovingly, friends tried to change my mind. "Wait a while and think it over," they said.

One Saturday morning I was surprised when Jim got up earlier than usual and then Jenny appeared at the back door. "Mom, we need to talk." They were clearly joining forces. We sat around the redwood table on the back porch and for the first time, I was "mothered" by my children.

A few weeks later, Julie and Bob arrived from Virginia. I suspected their need to also caution me, but they had trouble getting started and at lunch we talked about everything else. When they presented me with a Mother's Day gift of wind chimes, I decided to help them out. "I love them. They're perfect for the back porch of my new home in York!" That was all they needed and again, there was role reversal, with my receiving firm, loving, and sincere advice.

"We know you think you're doing the right thing, but what if you're wrong? We don't want you to be hurt again."

But after my children said what they wanted to say and what they thought I needed to hear, they listened to me. In the end, respecting my faith and sincerity, they reluctantly accepted my plans.

I had a new appreciation of my children's devotion and compassion; they were adults whom I loved and admired. Con and I had done a good job of raising our family, and hopefully, Con's and my brokenness would not compromise their values, but make them stronger.

Sometimes, however, I wondered if Stefan and I were being too hasty. My children were still hurting and adjusting, and for Stefan's daughters, their mother's death was a wound that would take a long time to heal. Ecstatic over our own happiness, we didn't fully appreciate until later, our children's ambivalent feelings; how much their sense of personal loss conflicted with their love for us. A lot had happened in only five months!

Surprise Reactions

I had hesitated to tell Mom because even though she had been pleased about Stefan's visit, I didn't know how she would feel about my marrying him so quickly. I needn't have worried.

"Mom, you're not going to believe this! Stefan and I are going to be married!" But Mom not only believed me, she accepted our decision easily even though she had never met Stefan.

"I trust you and God," she said. "You deserve much happiness."

I invited Con to come over because I didn't want him to hear our news from someone else and his reaction also surprised me. Standing in the kitchen facing him and separated only by the almost palpable awkwardness so common those days, I wondered, *What will you think, Con, since you were the one who first planted the idea in Stefan's mind?*

"Stefan and I are very much in love and we're engaged to be married."

Con appeared stunned, but then he stepped forward, took my hands, and said in a voice shaky with emotion, "I'm happy for you." His eyes filled with tears as he added, "I never wanted to hurt you."

"I know that; I saw your struggle. I hope some day you'll find happiness too."

Con's tears were unexpected even though I knew him to be a kind and thoughtful man who would not intentionally hurt anyone. He had struggled unsuccessfully to fit back into his mold of a loving and devoted husband, and like so many others, Con learned it's impossible to leave a marriage without hurting those who love him most. He made his choice and each of us, including Con, suffered and dealt with it in our own ways.

Sometimes I felt foolish for having given him twenty-seven years of my life and I wished I'd never met him, but then I wouldn't have my children. I could no longer remember the special times we had shared;

perhaps that was a defense mechanism. If I thought about the good times, my loss was magnified and I wasn't sure I could cope with more pain.

Our marriage was over and now I wanted our relationship to be civil; especially for our children. I would not make their situation more painful by criticizing their father. I wondered if one day he would regret his decision. Would he find happiness?

Some of our friends and my co-workers were impatient with my concern for Con and made comments I would not repeat. Others said, "If you feel that way, you must be in shock! I wouldn't care what happened to him if he'd left me." And, "You should have left him first!"

Friends of more than twenty years worried about my hasty decision to remarry. One said, "Wait six months. If Stefan really loves you, he will still love you in six months," but I held fast. I was certain, but what I considered God's direct response to my prayer was too much for even my most devout Christian friends. They also believe God can do anything, but they were torn between wanting to believe me and the possibility that I was reading "God's will" into mere coincidence. They tried to be supportive, but it was easy to read between the lines of their transparent comments.

I responded enthusiastically, repeating our wonderful story which, for me, held no doubt—it was crystal clear! Although it was difficult for my friends to accept, eventually they gave me their blessing. Only later, when I could be more objective, would I understand that if the situation had been reversed, I would have been equally concerned for them.

Others reacted with no apparent attempt at tactfulness. One actually said she was jealous and wished her husband would leave so that she could find someone to make her as happy as I was! I could find no words to respond. Although I realized she was half-kidding, her bluntness shocked me. Some, with whom I had worshipped for twenty years, suddenly didn't know how to relate to me. They were polite, but distant when our paths crossed. This was confusing; I just wanted to be loved and know that our friendships remained solid. When one of them suggested to a mutual friend that Stefan and I had probably had an affair and that was why Con left, I wept in disappointment.

A wonderful note from Melanie lifted my spirits:

I have a wonderful peace that God is in control of your life by seeing a sincere Christian maturity in you. It is always hard to understand why things happen to us because we live so much in the present, but God sees a full picture of past, present, and FUTURE and this is where our faith comes in …If we're close to Him we'll always be sensitive to His leading—I know you are and therefore I can encourage and support you.

*Whispers from **Your** Heart*

Can I be happy for a friend who gets what I'm praying for? How do I react?

Do my friends consider me an encourager? Why or why not?

Do I believe God can do anything? If not, why not?

Chapter 8

Making New Memories

*"Now faith is the assurance of things hoped for,
the conviction of things not seen."*

—Hebrews 11:1

RETURNING TO NEW England for the July 4th holiday, I searched
the airport's crowded waiting area for Stefan and saw a new side of
him. Waving broadly, he was looking at me through huge, red-rimmed
sunglasses—the kind a circus clown might wear! We laughed, embraced,
and as comical as Stefan looked, I knew that I was at home in his arms.
Driving back to Maine, I was eager to meet the rest of his family.

Our first attempt to prepare and serve a lobster bake together was
fun—especially for Stefan. He donned an over-sized red chef's hat and
a navy blue bib apron imprinted with a white image of the schooner,
Stephen Taber, on which he had vacationed in Penobscot Bay. Placing
two large kettles over the fire, he tried to convince this novice that the
first order of business was to "gag" the lobsters with bits of white muslin.
"This," he said, "will prevent their crying out as they meet their deaths in
the boiling water." Although I thought the procedure cruel, I was eager
to fit in and ready to cooperate. Fortunately, behind her father's back,
Lisa raised her eyebrows to alert me to Stefan's nonsense.

The holiday was a huge success and I felt acceptance in the welcome
hugs from Stefan's aunt, his sisters, and their families. The warm weather
was perfect for our afternoon on the large side porch, shaded by towering
birch trees. Some of us relaxed on white, cast iron furniture with its
yellow flowered cushions, while others enjoyed the cedar hot tub nearby.
I listened carefully as many of Stefan's family took turns reminiscing and

sharing favorite family stories. They explained that this was to better acquaint me with their family and to give me an honest picture of Stefan. I especially enjoyed watching his six-foot, good natured, eighty-year-old Aunt Ruth standing tall and reciting with great animation and obvious enjoyment, a humorous poem. I felt love and approval that day; more than I could have hoped for.

Stefan's sisters spoke openly and with delight about similarities between Marie and me; even our handwriting. We were both raised in small towns and later enjoyed nursing careers, cooking, decorating our homes, and for both of us, faith and family were most important. Thinking back to my only visit with Marie, I better understood why we immediately seemed best friends.

Later, I wondered, *I'm about to become not only Stefan's wife, but stepmother to his children. Will the traits that Marie and I shared make it easier for my new family to accept me, or will I be a frequent reminder of what they miss in their beloved Marie? I have to make sure they know that I can't and don't want to take Marie's place in their lives. With God's help, Stefan and I will both be accepted by our new families.*

A genuine love for others had been nourished in Stefan's family. Their hearts proved large enough to hold special memories of Marie, and to make room for me. They understood the extraordinary way God had brought Stefan and me together, and their happiness for us proved genuine.

Marriage Plans

The next day Stefan and I selected a pattern for matching wedding rings. The goldsmith would make each ring of two circles of yellow gold, joined by a center rope of rose gold. Engraved on the inside would be *Proverbs 3:5-6*, referring to our wedding Scripture:

> Trust in the Lord with all your heart and do not lean on your own understanding. In all your ways acknowledge Him, and He will make your paths straight (NASB).

We had each tried to live by that advice for many years and now, together, we were trusting God for our future. It was an exciting and fun time of planning a simple, private wedding ceremony as we continued to marvel at how much God must love us!

Returning home, my children and friends tried to be supportive and say the right things, but enthusiasm was lacking. Except for Jim's brief meetings with Stefan, however, no one knew him. I was certain they would change their minds when they met Stefan and could see how happy we were together.

Jumbled Emotions

I put my house on the market and began sorting a twenty-seven year accumulation of household goods, and boxes of odds and ends. I was transported to the past and without a second thought, discarded faded scrapbooks bursting with mementos of my bridal showers.

I wept as I looked through happy photographs of our children's baby and school years; such joyful times, and now they were hurting. There were many boxes of labeled slides, identifying family celebrations and trips, the most memorable being our year in England. It was an exciting and challenging year, packed with unique experiences. One of my favorite slides is of a Scottish castle with me waving a scarf in feigned "distress" from an opening high in the huge stone fortress and Con struggling to get a foothold to climb the outer wall and rescue his "damsel." With a sigh, I put the box of memories aside without opening it.

So many changes! I could hardly believe the complete turnaround my life had taken since Con first announced his unhappiness less than two years earlier. My life as I had known it for twenty-seven years was over. And when he walked out on January 2, my focus went from saving my marriage to survival for me and damage control for my children.

Now, only seven months later, I was going to marry Stefan and there in front of me was the large wedding portrait of Con and me. We had been so proud of it and now, I couldn't imagine who would want such a painful reminder of a huge disappointment. Removing the picture from its beautiful cherry frame, I tore it into several pieces. My tangled feelings confused me; sadness, anger, confusion, and even relief to be rid of it. It was time to move on and I stuffed the portrait pieces into a brown paper bag with other discards.

Pain-filled Memories and Revelation

I found the journals from our marriage encounter weekend and not having looked at them since, I felt compelled to read them. Memories rushed back and my stomach knotted as I read Con's beautiful letters and promises, and again I didn't understand how a relationship of love and trust could just vanish.

However, those feelings of disbelief and confusion at that moment would pale in comparison to what I would feel a couple of years later when Con became engaged to remarry. It wasn't his engagement that upset me, but rather learning from Jenny that the Catholic Church had annulled our marriage of twenty-seven years. Con told her this was necessary before he could marry his fiancée who was a member of the Roman Catholic Church.

I was angry and when I said that I didn't understand, Jenny explained, "It's as if your marriage never took place."

"I know that, Jen, but it's absurd! I haven't even been contacted! Can they erase our marriage just like that? What about our marriage ceremony in front of God and a church full of witnesses? What about all of the wedding anniversaries we celebrated? What about our children? Is it all a lie?" I knew it wasn't, but I couldn't press Jenny any further. She looked as upset as I felt and she didn't have any answers either. Even if she did, it wouldn't have made any difference. For me the whole idea was preposterous and an incredible insult to me and our children.

Years later, I learned that the annulment of our marriage was also difficult for Con to accept. If our marriage wasn't recognized as "real," then were our children considered illegitimate?

But, back to our marriage encounter journals. As I continued to read I considered sending them to Con in hopes of making him feel foolish. Instead, I dropped them into the brown bag with other discards. We had both suffered enough. It was over. My "impossible dream" had turned into an agonizing nightmare, but my anger had resurfaced and it would be harder to get rid of that than the journals.

Next was a tattered box of favorite writings, cartoons, and mementos that I had collected since nursing school days. In it were two poems that Con had written on sheets of paper, torn from a small spiral bound notebook. They were undated, but I remembered reading them before—perhaps ten years earlier. Still, the words were familiar. The first was short and simple, but it made me wonder again why he had chosen to give it all up.

There is a sadness in so
much happiness for two.
Perhaps it's just that the

whole world should be
so lucky.

Passionate and beautiful, I thought. The other poem was also passionate, but shocking!

Constant as the stars I cannot
be. I am but flesh.
Her face before me no longer
seen. In yesterdays, she was
my being.

Time and tide Gibraltar
wear.
My inconstant heart does not
resist, the beckoning of
Adventure's Kiss.
My heart, once prostrate at her feet,
Now with wanderlust doth retreat.

I was stunned! *I must have read it before; how could I not have noticed? Why didn't I understand? Maybe then we could have saved our marriage. Did my sense of security in our marriage blind me?*

I sat on the closet floor, my thoughts and emotions a mess. I felt sad because our marriage hadn't been as special to him; foolish because unintentional as it may have been, he deceived me; and angry because I still didn't understand how he could do this!

My legs cramped from sitting so long on the floor and emotionally I was exhausted. I put the poems back in the box and went to the kitchen to brew a pot of coffee. It was a small room, but my favorite with its warm, pine paneling and blue-and-white-checked gingham curtains. I wondered why it didn't bother me more to leave my home which held so many good memories. The happiest ones were of my children and me, or them with their father. Those of Con and me—once sterling, were now tarnished and painful to think about. They made me feel foolish and that part of my life seemed like a book I had once read, and now wanted to leave on the shelf.

The ringing phone interrupted my wistful thoughts, and Stefan's "I love you" placed a smile on my face. Then he literally put a song in my heart as he sang lyrics to me that he had paraphrased from a song he had once heard, "Red is the Rose." The romantic lyrics tied my life in

Kenmore to the beautiful roses he had sent and I was thrilled anew with this special man whom God had sent to love me.

Kenmore Rose

Come over the hill, my bonny Kenmore lass,
Come over the hill to your darling…
You choose the road, love, and I'll make the vow,
And I'll be your true love, forever.

Chorus:

Red is the rose that in yonder garden grows
Fair is the lily of the valley
Clear is the water that flows from the falls
But my love is fairer than any.
'Twas down by Niagara Falls that we strayed,
The moon and the stars, they were shining,
The moon shone its rays on her locks of dark brown hair,
And she swore she'd be my love forever.

Chorus

'Twas not for the parting of my dear friend Beth,
'Twas not for the grief of Marie,
'Twas all for the love of my precious Kenmore lass
That my heart is joyous forever.

Chorus

I knew I would miss my family and friends and I worried about not being near to help my children. But convinced that it was God's will, I could go in peace knowing He would continue to meet all of our needs.

Stefan and I talked at least three times a day and our exorbitant monthly telephone bills of between two and three hundred dollars must have delighted the telephone company. Stefan, of course, insisted that was just one more excellent reason to get married quickly— "We can't afford to stay single!"

When Stefan came to stay with Jim and me, we spent a lot of time with my family and friends. I was delighted when Jenny, who had strong reservations, seemed to like him. After an especially relaxing and fun-filled afternoon with Jen and her fiancé, David, I knew they were willing to accept Stefan as part of my life and theirs.

Stefan's many years of experience with young children made him fun and appealing to my grandchildren. They loved him immediately—his folk singing and sleight of hand trick—and asked him repeatedly, "Please do it again! Take off your thumb!"

A few days later, however, Stefan's presence confused Julie, my five year old granddaughter. Stefan and I were in the back seat of Jenny's van and Julie was sitting in front of us. At one point, she turned and looked first at Stefan and then at me, and asked, "Grandma, do you still love Grandpa Con?" Her confusion was clearly reflected in her blue eyes, which had already seen too much sadness in her young years. Silently asking God for the right words, I told her, "I love your Grandpa Con, but he no longer wants to live with me."

"And now you love Stefan?"

"Yes, Julie, Stefan and I love each other very much." She looked thoughtfully again at both of us and I was very relieved when she asked no more questions. How do you explain divorce to a child? I looked at the back of her little blond head wondering what she was thinking and wishing I could give her better answers.

As I had hoped, our enthusiasm was infectious and seeing the love and goodness Stefan and I shared soon outweighed the concern of our family and friends. A few held fast to their doubts and tried to persuade us to wait, but at that stage in our lives, we didn't want to "take our time." In mid-life, we didn't know how long we would have together, but we agreed that if God only blessed us with a few years, it would be worth it.

Jim

I felt guilty about Jim's having to move out of our home, but he seemed to like the idea of having his own place. Although he was invited to live with his father, he chose privacy instead and found an apartment, which I helped decorate. We had fun cleaning, hanging wallpaper, and making the apartment "his." Drapes, furniture, and dishes from our house found a new home there and I hoped their familiarity would make his place more comfortable, rather than be disturbing reminders of what used to be.

Jim's obvious excitement about his first "bachelor pad" eased some of my regrets, but I knew I'd miss him and his delightful sense of humor. I would always remember his thoughtfulness with flowers on Valentine's

Day and later on my birthday, when he presented me with a framed Monet print to hang over my bed in the place vacated by the wedding portrait.

Concerns about not being around to help Jenny with her children were lightened when she and David married. We were impressed by his obvious love for Jenny and her children, and because this was David's first marriage, they had a formal wedding ceremony.

I was proud to be there with Stefan and happily introduced him to Julie, Bob, and extended family and friends. I was relieved to see their immediate fondness for him. The situation was awkward, however, because Con and his date also were there and I worried about our children; it had to be painful with both parents there, but apart.

Our grandchildren's excitement over being included in the marriage ceremony seemed to overshadow their confusion over our new family structure, but more changes were coming. A few weeks later Stefan and I would be married, and during the next two years both their daddy and grandfather would re-marry. Then they would have parents, step-parents, and five sets of grandparents! For the moment, however, they were laughing in the arms of their mother and stepfather as the foursome danced around the floor together.

Pure Joy!

With our wedding date fast arriving, we tried to be sensitive to the inevitable mixed emotions of our children. Only eight months since my marriage ended, and seven months after Marie's death, we knew they were all still in various stages of grieving. We decided not to have an elaborate affair which they would feel obligated to attend. We made it clear that although we would love to have them join us, we would understand if they didn't travel all the way to York for the ceremony.

Stefan and I were married on a beautiful August afternoon on the side lawn of Stefan's home. Stefanie, Heather, and a few friends who lived nearby, attended our ceremony. Sunlight filtered through a canopy of lofty birches, fragrant cedars, and hemlocks which, with the delicate Queen Anne's lace rimming the lawn, made an exquisite wedding chapel.

The traditional ceremony became uniquely ours as a minister, who was also Stefan's best friend from college, read some of our favorite Scriptures. Included were some verses from the Sermon on the Mount in Matthew 5, and Proverbs 3:5-6. The birds seemed to sing more merrily than usual and their music provided the perfect background for the reading of the love chapter, 1 Corinthians 13. Holly and Bruce, two of our closest friends, stood nearby as our honor attendants.

Holding hands and looking into each other's eyes, we pledged our love and I still could hardly believe the miracle that was ours. The warmth of God's presence and His blessing were on our marriage, and I was convinced that no one had ever been as much in love! Heart-wrenching losses had proved fertile ground for new-found contentment. Earlier pain proved to be a blessing in disguise because it made us more appreciative of our new happiness.

Several years later my brother, Larry, would quote an unnamed author, "There is no such thing as a coincidence—just God remaining anonymous." Immediately, I thought of God's answer to my picket fence prayers.

After receiving happy hugs and warm congratulations at a reception on the side porch, we registered at the York Harbor Inn—one of York's oldest and finest. It was filled with antique furniture, tiled fireplaces, wavy windows and creaking, crooked wide-boarded floors. In our room, the old brass bed had been rubbed to a glow. The quilted coverlet of many brightly-colored remnants had been pieced together in a lovely design. Above it, delicate white curtains billowed gently in puffs of fresh ocean air that came through the open windows. A perfect touch was a lovely pink, purple, and yellow flower arrangement sent, "With love from Holly and Bruce."

We walked along the winding York River leading to the village beach where Stefan had brought me on that rainy day in June. Climbing the rocks, we sat side by side on the rugged ledge, our arms around each other and our legs dangling above the sandy beach. As we watched the glistening swells of water break on boulders below, our hearts overflowed anew with love and gratitude for what God had done. His blessings, like the waves, just kept coming.

We rediscovered the joys of marital love, but some deeply entrenched habits and expectations formed during our first marriages were no longer suitable. We were a new couple and we needed to pay attention to what we were saying and expecting from each other.

This was true even with our names. Occasionally, Stefan would call me Marie or I would call him Con. We both did it and could laugh about it. For many years it would continue to be embarrassing for relatives and friends who still apologize all over the place if they slip up.

Fun!

For our first Christmas, we wrote a newsletter from our log cabin home. For my part, I explained that I had become adept at tending both the wood stove and coal furnace, which was true. Jokingly, I added that I had found it extremely difficult to catch our Thanksgiving Day turkey which I had to chase back and forth across our yard several times before tackling it!

As it turned out, I was too convincing for an elderly aunt who wrote to express her concern that I had moved to a tough life in a very backward community with no modern appliances!

We had included with our Christmas letter a photograph of us in colonial costume taking part in a historic celebration at the old town tavern. Evidently, the photo strengthened my aunt's fears! I wrote a long letter to assure her of my happiness and that I did have many conveniences!

As we combined furniture from our first marriages, Stefan's house and our lives became more entwined. I missed my family, but found it comforting to remember that the God who had so marvelously answered my prayers was also with my loved ones even though hundreds of miles separated us. God's "omnipresence," His being with all of us at the same time—regardless of where we are, took on greater significance for me.

Stefan introduced me to being a school principal's wife, sailing, lobster bakes, cross-country skiing, and all that makes living in New England so special. In return I introduced him to "Grandparent-hood" which is a joy-filled adventure in itself!

We were blessed not only with our own happiness, but also with no stepchildren problems. From the start all of them loved us enough to be patient with mid-life parents acting like the newlyweds we were—absolutely "gaga!"

From the beginning, Stefan and I have taken turns saying grace before meals and often, when it's his turn at breakfast, he begins, "Good morning, Father!" The first time I heard it, I'm embarrassed to admit that I was tempted to lower my voice and say, "Good morning, Stefan," but he continued. "I thank You first for dear Shirley, the light of my life, and for the love that we share. It's so wonderful that Shirley and I can slide down the back side of life together."

We were delightfully happy and after living in York for only a year, Stefan was invited to become principal of the elementary school in Wellfleet, MA on beautiful Cape Cod. He accepted and there we purchased the first home we checked out. Stefan enjoyed his new job and we found a church family with whom we enjoyed worshipping and serving God.

Trouble in Paradise

In the fourth year of our life together, as episodes of my racing, irregular heartbeats became more frequent and intense, my medication became less effective. Suddenly, our joy-filled ride down the backside of life was bumpy!

This "bump" grew into such substantial proportions that our journey together was threatened. Our road twisted and veered off the course we had anticipated, and this was only the first of many challenges ahead.

Whispers from Your Heart

In what ways have I grown closer to God?

Why do I believe God has a plan for my life?

What is the greatest blessing God has given me?

Part Two

Whatevers

*"I am the Lord, the God of all flesh; is anything too hard for me?
...Call to me and I will answer you, and will tell you great and
hidden things that you have not known."*

—Jeremiah 32:27, 33:3

*"It ought to be tremendously helpful to be able to acquire the habit of
reaching out strongly after God's thoughts, and to ask, 'God, what
have you to put into my mind now if only I can be large enough?'"*

—Frank Laubach[6]

Chapter 1

Blessings of a Fragile Heart

But this I call to mind, and therefore I have hope: The steadfast love of the Lord never ceases, his mercies never come to an end; they are new every morning; great is your faithfulness.

—Lamentations 3:21-23

THERE I SAT, once more like Raggedy Ann, bent at the waist with my head between my knees. But unlike the still, small heart painted on the doll's chest, mine was racing and skipping.

After five years of marriage, my joy-filled ride with Stefan "down the backside of life" had become rough and worrisome. My increasing episodes of light-headedness and a rapid, irregular heart beat stumped my new physician, Dr. Mathis, as they had my previous doctors. No one could figure out why this occurred only when I was quiet, never physically active. Sometimes I would be typing, or stirring something on the stove, but never at the gym or when doing something strenuous. To increase blood flow to my brain and relieve the faintness, I would slump in my chair like Raggedy Ann.

These frightening symptoms were embarrassing when we dined with friends. Most of them didn't know I had a problem and not wanting to alarm them or Stefan; I would drop my napkin and feign difficulty in picking it up. Sometimes lowering my head worked, but if not I had to take my medication and wait it out.

Despite more diagnostic tests Dr. Mathis remained bewildered, and when my symptoms intensified he acted as if I was imagining them. More than once he mumbled, "I don't know, everything looks normal," and

I would leave his office feeling confused and insecure. *Was he missing something?*

One night, my pounding heart startled me out of a sound sleep. As it jerked inside my lurching chest, I could hardly sit up to swallow the medication my terrified husband brought me. Gradually my heart quieted down and my pulse stabilized, but in the morning I called Dr. Mathis who said to come in for another EKG.

Reading the results, Dr. Mathis said, "If I only had this to go by, I'd ship you off to Boston, but you're fine." Opening the door to leave, he added, "Enjoy the holidays."

Enjoy the holidays? I needed answers and so I asked about my medication. "Should I change the dose?"

"If it makes you feel better, take it," he said abruptly, leaving me with still unanswered questions. *What did he mean, "If I had only this to go by…?"* Uncertain and feeling rejected, I wept as I dressed. Clearly, he was frustrated by my persistent and not easily understood symptoms, but so was I!

As one of three part-time nurses working in his office, I was scheduled to work two days later, and it was then I forced myself to ask for a second opinion. I didn't want Dr. Mathis to think my trust was gone, but the last episode had terrified me and his dubious response forced me to speak up.

"I know my symptoms aren't 'by the book,' but they scare me and I need to know more." My attempt at tactfulness was ignored or went unnoticed. Instead, Dr. Mathis snapped, "Shirley, you don't need a second opinion, but I'll arrange it if that's what you want!" His glaring eyes asked, *Why won't you believe me?* I was tempted to give in, but I didn't and walking away, Dr. Mathis said, "Call me tomorrow." Hurt, but relieved, I prayed he would find someone who could help me.

The next day Dr. Mathis said I should return to his office for reports and notes from my file for my appointment with Dr. James, a cardiologist at Brigham and Women's Hospital in Boston. However, when I went to get my medical records, Dr. Mathis had left without selecting them, and as I made copies of what I thought might be needed, I wondered why he hadn't done so and if I was being punished.

Alarming Test Results

The next morning Dr. James, a cardiologist, listened so carefully to my story that I felt I was the only person who mattered to him at that moment. This was such a contrast to Dr. Mathis, who often flipped rapidly through my file looking for something while asking me the same question three or four times. After an exam and EKG which showed no significant changes, he sent me for an echo-cardiogram.

Having had many of these tests several years earlier when my prolapsed mitral valve was diagnosed, I wasn't worried. It was a brief and painless procedure, but this time, the results were alarming!

My first clue was when the small room suddenly filled with medical students and interns, all straining to see the monitor. I knew from my nursing experience that this meant there was something extraordinary to see, and this time it was my heart they were craning their necks to view on the screen!

No one said much so I assumed the doctors had been filled in on what to expect before entering. After most had left the room, the remaining doctor drew a crude diagram of a heart with four chambers, not unlike the open back of a doll house with two rooms up and two down. She said, "You have a hole in your heart; an atrial septal defect," and pointing between the two upper chambers, she said, "It's there. Your cardiologist will explain the rest to you."

Feeling shaky, I went to find Stefan who was also alarmed at this unexpected news, and we returned to Dr. James for more answers.

"Why do I have this?" I asked.

"It's congenital."

"Can't be," I insisted. "I've had many echos—wouldn't they have found it then?"

"Earlier machines weren't sophisticated enough. The hole must be closed."

Stefan pleaded, "But she looks well and exercises regularly."

Looking at Stefan, Dr. James gently explained, "Without closure, Shirley's at risk of a stroke or heart failure."

I had two options. One was open-heart surgery—*with a forever ugly scar*, I thought! Unlike bypass surgery which is done on the outside of the heart, this meant cutting my heart open and working inside. Dr. James insisted that it was routine surgery. Our eyes met, and I said, "Routine—unless it's your heart!"

The other choice was a less invasive procedure of inserting and threading a catheter through a blood vessel in my groin into my heart. An "umbrella" or "clam-like device" would be threaded through the catheter and secured over both sides of the hole. I didn't want something mechanical in my heart, but it sounded better than cutting it open. Then I learned that the procedure was still so experimental I would be only the third person to ever have this device implanted! Deciding was difficult and so we prayed for guidance, trusting God for the right decision.

There were many trips to Boston for procedures to determine the exact size and location of the defect. Under light sedation, I even swallowed a tiny "camera" which found a second hole, making the "umbrella" a less likely choice.

I asked Dr. James my defining question whenever I have to make a tough medical decision. "If I were your wife or mother, what would you advise me to do?" He said that with two holes, he would not recommend the "umbrella". The dreaded scar would become a reality.

For the most part, God blessed me with a wonderful sense of peace, but Stefan couldn't stop worrying. His first wife had died unexpectedly and the possibility of also losing me was too much. There were times when neither of us could find words of strength or reassurance, and we just held each other.

Open Heart Surgery

On a sunny June day, Stefan drove me back to the Brigham and Women's Hospital, this time for surgery the next day. As we traveled the Mid-Cape highway, I wasn't feeling particularly morbid, but I wondered if I would ever see that splendid view of Bass River again. My thoughts were strangely objective. *If I don't survive, others will still enjoy that seascape and life will go on. There'll be tears from those who love me, but as time goes on they'll miss me less and less. That's life!*

I didn't understand my detachment. I was so unlike many patients in my nursing career whom I had comforted as they faced surgery. Gratefully, I was able to tuck those thoughts away and focus on God's promises of love, protection, and hope in Psalm 46:1-2:

> God is our refuge and strength, a very present help in trouble. Therefore we will not fear.

The next day, Stefan arrived early; the strain of our ordeal shadowing his smile. I thought, *O God, what You've given us is so precious! I know Stefan said at the beginning, "If we only have a few years together, it'll be worth it," but I don't think he meant it—neither of us is ready to let go. We* tried to be strong for each other, but when Stefan sat on the bed and held me, we both wept.

Like most people, I didn't want to give up control of my life to anyone. I didn't want to be put to sleep so that someone could saw my ribs apart and cut into my heart! I chose not to think about that, but to trust God and picture myself resting in His arms, and there I found peace.

Intravenous fluids were started, an aide helped me onto a gurney, and Stefan was permitted to accompany us as far as the preoperative area where he kissed me and whispered, "I'll be praying for you." I promised to pray for him, too, and I did, as they rolled me away. Then I concentrated on Psalm 4:8, which I had memorized to focus on when I went to sleep:

> I will both lie down and sleep in peace; for You alone, O Lord, make me lie down in safety.

The next thing I heard was a pulsating motor and, "Shirley, wake up. Your surgery is over." I was alive! I wanted to say, "Thank You, God," but I couldn't even whisper—a tube in my throat felt like a garden hose! Still, despite my unintelligible sounds, the nurse understood and promised to remove it as soon as I could breathe on my own. Her quiet, gentle voice was reassuring, and when I awakened again the tube was gone. Stefan was standing next to me with Dr. Gregory, the surgeon, who explained, "I found not two, but three holes." Smiling, he added, "Shirley, you made the right choice. You'll be fine. Everything went smoothly."

My ICU Prayer

The rest of the day was a sleepy blur, but that night lying in my ICU bed, I was wide awake and deeply grateful to God for successful surgery. I knew joy more profoundly than ever before; it seemed to be bubbling out of me and I couldn't stop smiling! When I asked the nurse to open the drapes so I could see the city lights, she teased, "Shirley, there must be something wrong with you—you're not supposed to act like this the night after heart surgery."

But, I couldn't thank God enough. I was alive! And so grateful that I rededicated my life to serving Him. "Father, I give You me for 'whatever'." That simple, heart-felt prayer would change my life in unimaginable ways!

After four days I was discharged, and in our dining room I found a "welcome home" surprise from Stefan—a word processor to encourage me in my writing and to keep me occupied in my recovery. Stefan had placed it on a table beneath the Danish proverb that he had liked so much the first time he visited me: "What we are is God's gift to us; what we become is our gift to God." Neither of us realized then how fitting those words would be to my future.

During my recovery I felt God's love, and the scar I had dreaded I now consider my "life line" - a small price to pay for feeling well again. A week after surgery, our pastor welcomed me back to worship, and announced with a laugh, "The indomitable iron woman has returned."

Whispers from *Your* Heart

*When I was afraid, how did God reassure and strengthen me?

*How did I show my gratitude?

*In what ways have I trusted God with my life?

*What was God's response?

Chapter 2

God's Love and Provision

"Trust in the Lord, and do good; so you will live in the land, and enjoy security. Take delight in the Lord, and he will give you the desires of your heart."

—Psalm 37:3-4

I CELEBRATED MY renewed strength by becoming more involved in church work. I hadn't forgotten my "whatever" prayer and I was about to find out God hadn't forgotten either. As a deacon and retired nurse with concerns about congregational needs, I started a visitation team and prayer chain. I didn't realize it then, but those two ministries were the beginning of "Caring Ministries," something much larger that the Lord would help me set in place.

I also agreed to be the Deacon Representative on the pastoral search committee which was being formed to find a replacement for our retiring minister. While Stefan and I enjoyed a week in Florida, I read Charles Stanley's book, *The Source of My Strength.*

Later, I would see how God used it to prepare my heart for what He wanted to do in my life. My shyness provided fertile soil for the seeds that God planted and nourished through Stanley, and his words proved prophetic for the ministries God would give me. Stanley wrote of God's great love, a powerful antidote for my feelings of inadequacy:

God couldn't possibly love you more than He loves you right now. God couldn't possibly approve of you more than He does today.

You are His child, and He loves you just the way you are—right now. He knows that you are in the process of becoming, but He also takes

91

responsibility for what you will become and how fast you will become it. He says to you…"Let Me do the work in you."[7]

I marvel at God's grace in reassuring me this way; using Stanley's words to guide and encourage me:

When you have…a restlessness in your soul—that can be one of the most exciting times of your life. God is at work in you; He is about to move into a deeper, more fulfilling experience in your walk with Him.

That's the time when you need to…make sure that everything is right between you and God…wait in eager anticipation for God to reveal your next move…start evaluating what you *don't* want in your life, *don't* want out of life, and *don't* want to do or be in life. Very often the Lord leads us into His will by giving us a great distaste for what isn't His will… look for the Lord to give you strong impressions—or checks in your spirit to guide you into His path… [8]

I thank God for leading me to Stanley's book just as God was answering my "whatever" prayer and beginning to unfold His plans for the rest of my life! My manuscript about my growing sense of God's direction, power, grace, and empowerment was always in the back of my mind, but I seldom found time to work on it. I would wait fifteen years before God would tell me, "It's time to finish your book."

God Whispers

Before I go further I want to explain what I've come to know about God's whispers. Psalm 46:10 says, "Be still and know that I am God."

As I spent more time with God, reading His Word and being still before Him, I came to the place where I could hear His whispers. Some have questioned my certainty about God speaking to me, but as I've heard others say, "I just know it in my knower!"

I know God's Spirit is whispering when suddenly my confusion is replaced with clarity, unrest is transformed into an indescribable peace; I feel compelled to do something I've never done before and feel incapable of doing, or when a new thought comes unexpectedly and uninvited—something I know is not mine! Often in quietness, words of instruction or direction are formed in my mind.

For example, while Stefan and I were on vacation in Florida, the rest of the search committee was elected. On my return I learned that the committee would meet to select a chairperson, and as I was driving to the first committee meeting, I wondered who it would be.

It might be you.

No, I've never even been on a pastoral search committee.

You wouldn't have to do it alone. Besides, you said "whatever."

I pulled into the parking lot, stopped my car, and just sat there for a while. God's voice wasn't audible, but He couldn't have spoken more clearly if it had been.

"Okay God," I whispered, "I'll accept if nominated, but I won't volunteer!"

Waiting for the meeting to start, I sat next to Helen, the wife of a retired minister. Indicating some documents in front of her, she explained that the first thing for the new chairman to do was contact the area minister who would guide us through the process. Clearly, God had selected Helen, and I was relieved.

The church clerk brought the meeting to order, and Helen nominated someone else who accepted. *Great,* I thought, *he's perfect,* but my relief was short-lived. I sat there a bit stunned as I was nominated, I accepted, and was elected by secret ballot! Then the clerk stood up and said, "Shirley, the meeting is yours," and she left!

I panicked until I recalled Helen's directions and realized that God had already begun helping me! After explaining that I would contact our Area Minister and invite him to meet with us, I closed our meeting in prayer.

God knew all along what would happen! He was beginning to show me the truth and power of Paul's words to the Philippians 4:13 (NKJV), "I can do all things through Christ who strengthens me."

Driving home and recalling my earlier "conversation" with God, I had a new understanding of what joy in the Lord is and a great anticipation that God had a very special plan that included me! Any apprehension was countered with wonder as to why God had chosen me. I felt confident and energized because I believed this new responsibility was God's response to my "whatever" prayer.

I didn't have a clue about what I would be doing, but I had wonderful peace because my ability to believe that God knew what He was doing was greater than my fear of the unknown, and by the time I arrived home my heart was singing.

It was only when I told Stefan what had happened that his rather incredulous look made me realize what a huge responsibility I had taken on. He asked, "Who did you vote for?"

"I voted for Jim. I thought that was the polite thing to do. Everything happened so fast that it never occurred to me to vote for myself! Jim's better qualified than I and it just seemed the right thing to do! It was, wasn't it?"

Smiling and in his gentle way, Stefan said, "Usually, if someone wants a particular job, they vote to get it."

That night I knelt by my bed and asked God for wisdom and understanding, and before falling asleep I felt assured that God had already chosen our new pastor. If I did my best with my "whatever," God would help us find "whomever," and in the bliss that came from being fully ignorant of the challenges that lay ahead, I slept well.

When our Area Minister, Hector Cortez, explained the pastoral search process to the committee, I learned that public speaking would be a big part of my job and I wondered if God had chosen the wrong person. I hated public speaking! I could never stand in front of a group and make sense. Even as an adult, I couldn't find the courage to teach a class of five-year-olds a Sunday school lesson, but public speaking was exactly what God had in mind!

What impacted me most was Hector's prayer for the Holy Spirit to anoint us as we trusted Him for direction. The prayer was so beautifully simplistic and sincere, yet confident, that it made me want to know the Holy Spirit as Hector did, and that resolve would later be strengthened by my friend Carol's comment, "I just love the Holy Spirit so much!" I wanted to love the Holy Sprit as Hector and Carol did.

The Transformation of "Chubbette"

I had been a shy and self-conscious child, sometimes brought to tears by classmates taunting, "Fatty, Fatty, two by four…" I wasn't grossly overweight, but I was chubby; a fact confirmed by the "Chubbette" label in some of my dresses.

In seventh grade as I compared myself to slimmer friends, my self-image was further distorted. I can still feel the heat of my red face one day, when reading aloud I pronounced depot phonetically: "Deepot!" The laughter from my classmates was so painful I wished I could sink through the floor, and one day, a few months later, I thought I might!

God's Love and Provision

The entire class was excited about our new desks and as we all sat down for the first time, the screw on my seat had not been tightened and I dropped to the floor with a loud crash.

It didn't get easier in high school when I had to stand before my class and present oral reports; I wanted to be sick those days. Although I knew my material, when the dreaded moment arrived I failed miserably. Only someone who shares this deep fear can understand the pain and humiliation of a blushing face, rubbery legs, and eyes so watery one cannot read his or her notes.

Years later, an invitation to help with my daughter's pre-school Bible class again set me in a panic. After confiding my fears to Laura, the head teacher, she affirmed the abilities she was sure God had given me and said she would pray for me. I never did teach that class, but God nourished and grew the seeds Laura had planted, and later I agreed to present devotions at women's fellowship meetings, and to lead a panel discussion. I was comfortable with these women who were like sisters to me.

But addressing our church was a different story. I wished so much that I had qualified my "whatever." If only I had added, "Anything but public speaking!"

Shirley, just do your best and trust Me. I sighed…a big sigh…

Before my first presentation to the church, and those that followed, I prepared carefully, read my notes repeatedly, and asked my husband and a friend, Helen, to pray for me. Still, even before I was introduced, my heart raced and I worried about becoming lightheaded, or even fainting in front of the entire congregation! Despite heart medication, stress would sometimes initiate symptoms, and so it was one more thing for which to trust God. Gradually I became more comfortable with speaking, but never at ease.

Sometimes God affirmed me through people in fun ways. One Sunday after I spoke, a gentleman walked up, shook my hand and said, "Shirley, that was wonderful. You're just as good as Maggie Thatcher!" I knew I wasn't any prime minister—especially Britain's Maggie Thatcher, but God used this man's enthusiasm to encourage me and reward my determination to obey Him.

A few minutes later, a visitor asked if I would teach her how to be a public speaker! I told her briefly how I had become one, and how much I was relying on God's help. Later, as I reflected on that conversation, I laughed aloud. In my late fifties God was helping me overcome my greatest fear!

Pats on the back from my church family were wonderful, but nothing compared to God's loving embrace through that experience. When I sought the Lord's will, He gave me direction, strength, confidence, empowerment, and joy.

Over a year later, I introduced our pastor-elect to the congregation. We had trusted God, and with wholehearted confidence I could say, "Doug, we know that God *has chosen you*." (1 Thessalonians 1:4)

The church's agreement was made clear in a unanimous vote and our new pastor found love, acceptance, and joy, and our church experienced a fresh sense of optimism and excitement.

Whispers from Your Heart

*When God asked me to do something that scared me, how did I respond?

*When I trusted God for what seemed impossible, what happened?

*How do I know God is in control of my life?

*How do I know that God has or has not whispered to me?

Chapter 3

A Greater Stretch

"What is impossible for mortals is possible for God."

—Luke 18:27

WITH GOD'S HELP my "whatever" became a success and because I had repeatedly gone to my knees, I had a maturing faith and growing love for the Lord.

It wasn't long before our church grew and a group was formed to study space needs, a building committee followed, and then a fundraising team. Right from the start, the fundraising process was unusual, and for me it began in an almost incredible way when Pastor Doug asked me to meet with him, but didn't say why.

We had met frequently, but for the first time Doug asked the secretary to hold his calls, and when he also closed the door to his cramped office I said, "This must be serious." Doug just smiled and began talking about the Capital Fund Campaign. Then, pointing to a large organizational chart in front of him, he identified all of the sub-committee chairpersons and explained their duties.

I was perplexed. *Why is he telling me this?*

Then he laughed and said, "You can see I went through all of them."

I wondered why he was laughing, but naïve and unsuspecting, I said, "Good! You want me to do something at the bottom." He just laughed some more and said, "No, it's the job at the top we want you to take." I couldn't believe it!

"What? Why me? Of all the people in this church, why choose me?"

Doug explained that the Campaign Fund Raising Committee consisted of the members of the Building Fund Committee that had been meeting for six months. No one, however, felt they were the person to chair a campaign so they agreed to pray about it for a week. When they met again, my name was the only one that came up!

"But Doug," I pleaded, "this is the last job I would ever volunteer for. I'm a mom, a grandmother, a retired nurse, and I don't know much about finances."

"You don't have to. The committee does and they want you as chair because the church respects you and your communication skills." That made me smile. Doug was referring to my chairing the pulpit search committee—my first "whatever" and my first major act of faith.

God had blessed and used me to such a degree that I was now being asked to chair another committee and this was a real eye opener! I thought I was through with public speaking, but now I could see that God had helped me speak effectively so that He could use it to stretch my faith even further. Despite the knots in my stomach, I laughed and said, "God definitely has a sense of humor!"

Still, I failed to share Doug's obvious joy over his proposal, but he needed an answer and I felt absolute panic! The committee had prayerfully selected me, but had they misinterpreted God's sense of humor as divine direction?

If I was God's choice, I found that difficult to understand. God knew my simple faith and that I loved Him, but with no previous experience in capital financing why would God lead this committee to me? Others seemed so much better qualified.

I said I'd pray about it and I left, quite certain my answer would be no. But as I prayed, God reminded me that only a few weeks before, with a new year approaching and my term as deacon ending, I had asked God what He would have me do next. When I didn't get an immediate answer I repeated my "whatever" prayer, and suddenly I knew that God was giving me a new "whatever"! I would learn that this was part of God's unique and intimate plan to teach me His ways and draw me closer to Himself.

When I realized the committee was made up of very successful businessmen, even CEOs, my shyness and sense of inadequacy again challenged my faith. "God, how can I chair a group like that?"

Don't worry about embarrassment. If I ask you to do something, I'll help you.

Still trusting God to help me, I claimed the promises of Psalm 32:8:

I will instruct you and teach you the way you should go; I will counsel you with my eye upon you.

Specific, but Unspoken Direction

I met with Doug and the chair of the Building Fund Committee. We discussed what had happened at earlier meetings and I requested previous minutes. The next day they would introduce me to the Capital Fund Campaign Committee, and I would take over!

That evening I prepared opening remarks and an agenda. Having committed myself, the committee needed to know that the only way I could do the job was for all of us to totally trust God to direct us in everything we did.

The next morning I arrived in the conference room first. As I put my things on the table, I suddenly was compelled to go to the adjoining library. I had never experienced anything like that before, but I knew I should obey and although there were many books displayed, my eyes were drawn to one in particular. There was no question that I was to sign out Larry Lea's *Could You Not Tarry One Hour?* I didn't know why, but I did it.

At that point I wasn't about to question anything I felt "led" to do, and I use that word for want of a better one. God is in control and when He whispers I intend to obey. Although I didn't have a clue about what would be asked of me in the hours to follow, much less the days ahead, my contentment amazed me! Any fear of embarrassment or failure was gone. God had proved faithful before and even though this new "whatever" demanded even more faith than the first, I had no reason to doubt Him.

In addition to Pastor Doug, the committee of eight men and one woman were people of faith whom I loved and respected.

I opened our meeting by thanking God for our privilege of serving Him on the committee and I asked the Lord to give us His ideas because while our view was limited, He could see the whole picture. I asked the Holy Spirit to give each one of us a clear understanding of what we should do every step of the way. Needless to say, I prayed with all of my heart!

When I brought up previously discussed matters, the committee members were patient and generous in their explanations. I knew that the matter of hiring a professional consultant had not been resolved and so I raised the issue again. After discussing the great expense, and how God had brought people to our church with the talents needed at any given time, we realized that people with just the expertise and experience we needed were already sitting at the table. There was a unanimous vote not to hire a professional fund-raiser—God would be our chief fund-raiser!

This major decision was contrary to what professional fundraising is all about—even seasoned Christian fund-raisers raised their eyebrows. I found our choice exciting because I knew it was God's plan for us.

We talked about pledge cards, brochures, lead gifts (first approaching the top givers to our church for pledges), bulletin inserts, and the best way to approach the church. It was a good meeting and I thanked God for His direction.

Driving home and considering all that had happened a red flag went up, "LEAD GIFTS!" Much time had already been spent discussing what is generally considered the best way to secure the most funds, but someone had asked, "Is this in accordance with the by-laws?" Back at home I read the by-laws and learned that, "…the financial secretary shall…preserve at all times the confidential aspect of pledges and payments by contributors." If names of top givers were not available to us, neither was that fundraising approach, but some on the committee seemed determined about this.

Having trouble falling asleep, I prayed and then opened Larry Lea's book where I would find reassurance and encouragement throughout the campaign. That night I read:

> People heard God's voice yesterday…but it is also essential that we hear His voice today…God is calling His church to pray, and we had better listen because the bottom line on all that will take place from now on is: "Not by might, nor by power, but by My spirit," saith the Lord. (Zechariah 4:6)[9]

WOW! No wonder God led me to that book!

A Growing Trust

The next day the financial secretary confirmed my findings—I was headed in the right direction! When I asked God for further understanding, He said, *If you want to know what I think, talk to Me about it.* Beginning the next morning and every day for a week I awakened at 4:00 A.M. For many hours as I prayed and listened, God made it clear. We were not to use lead gifts. Our campaign was to be based totally on faith.

A Greater Stretch

I contacted two committee members who had already spent many hours preparing to solicit lead gifts. I wanted them to have time to think about it before the next meeting. Their responses were reserved, but also open to God's leading. Still, I wondered if they now questioned their choice of me as chair. Incredibly, I no longer did. God's presence was so real that I could confidently go forward in His power, believing that God would be glorified through our efforts. We only had to pay attention.

I placed "Lead Gifts" first on the agenda for our next meeting and included comments by Charles Stanley from his devotional magazine, *In Touch*. I had noted them earlier and now they were perfect for opening our next meeting.

> When God calls you to do something, He will take care of the details. When He opens a door of opportunity, He expects you to go through it, all the while relying on Him to provide the knowledge and strength you need to do the task.

> Don't be plagued by doubts and fears which can keep you from trying something new - something that could turn out to be a wondrous gift from God. There are times when fear strikes so that everything within us wants to pull back where it is safe, but in 2 Timothy we read that God has not called us to be fearful or afraid.[10]

My prayer included:

> Father, we know You are here with us and that You are listening. We're so grateful that You are bigger than our doubts and fears and we ask You to help us put our personal agendas aside and to seek only Your will.

Addressing lead gifts, I shared my findings and explained my conviction that God had closed a door because He wanted us to find a better approach. I suggested we cancel lead gifts and face our challenge purely on faith. I was convinced if we did that, the Holy Spirit would guide us each step of the way, and we could look to success with confidence.

Sometimes I was amazed at my thoughts, words, and insight about things I had never faced before. But knowing the Source, I whispered, "Thank You" and rested in the comfort of God's grace.

There was some discussion of other ways to select names for lead gifts, but God united our hearts and we voted to forget that approach and any house-to-house canvas. Our campaign would be totally based on faith!

Later, we arrived at what we called a "faith-sized goal." To calculate the dollar amount of our campaign goal, the guide book explained, "…multiply the church's base income from contributions in the past year by a factor of 2." Instead, because of the church's past generosity to budget needs and the support of missions, we decided to triple it! Our goal to be raised in three years by only about one hundred and thirty seven families was $750,000!

There was only minimal opposition to our goal or campaign of faith from a few who couldn't envision our success. Through frequent updates at services and in newsletters, we kept the church well informed so they could fully understand how we planned to run a successful campaign.

Our informational evening was well attended and we were open about our unconventional approach to fundraising. "We're putting our trust in God and demonstrating our confidence in the people of this church. Although the committee's faith in God is strong, the responsibility which we accepted is great, sometimes leaving us a little weak in the knees and so we're glad you're here…to make certain we're covering all the bases."

Our campaign brochures, titled "God's Challenge, Our Choice—Building on our Past for the Future," presented a comprehensive look at all aspects of our church life and campaign.

In it Doug said, "In every generation God has challenged people to act boldly in faith, going places they'd never been, attempting feats they never dared, pursuing dreams they couldn't imagine fulfilling. Throughout history the seemingly impossible has become reality thanks to God's power and people who responded to God's call in faith."

That sure sounded like a bunch of "whatevers" to me!

Acknowledging the significant amount of money we needed to raise, I focused on our privilege to show our love through sacrificial giving to the Lord, whose generosity we can never match.

Equal Sacrifice

On the four Sundays leading up to Easter we invited people of various generations to share their thoughts about the Lord, the importance of our church, their excitement about the church's ministry, and their support of the campaign. Many in the congregation were deeply moved by the tender remarks of a teenager, a young mother, a middle-aged gentleman, and a retired pastor and his wife.

On Easter our sanctuary overflowed with lilies, hyacinths, tulips, and hydrangeas, and despite an additional service, people still crunched together in too few pews! The need for a larger place to worship was demonstrated in a real way. I summarized our faith campaign and shared our excitement over being part of a growing church whose confidence was in God as our Chief Fund-raiser Who knew our needs, our future, and what we should plan for.

Although our pledges would vary according to each family's resources, we asked for equal sacrifice; suggesting that each person ask God what He would have us give. Challenging our church family was crucial to the campaign. Helping to raise funds through faith, they would also gain ownership in the success that we expected from God. If everyone asked God for direction and then trusted and obeyed Him, our church would grow closer to the Lord and make success even more meaningful. I closed with what had become for me the theme of my "whatevers"; the praise and faith-filled promise of Ephesians 3:20 (TLB):

> Glory be to God, who by his mighty power at work within us is able to do far more than we would ever dare to ask or even dream of—infinitely beyond our highest prayers, desires, thoughts, or hopes.

Campaign publicity featured a float in the annual Brewster In Bloom parade, and fundraisers included an auction, church cookbook sales, and events sponsored by various church groups. Excitement was contagious and many were delighted to be part of the campaign. Our Sunday school children collected their offerings in small church banks at home and then poured them into a larger clear plastic church that someone constructed for us.

God Touches Hearts

Our entire church was invited to a catered "Every Member Banquet." Doug suggested that generosity begets generosity and so we paid for it with already received gifts and pledges. Transportation and child care were also made available. The dinner would be followed by worship and the commitment of pledges.

The evening arrived; the tables set with linens, fresh flowers, and 'sand dollar' favors—perfect for a Cape Cod fundraiser! First on our program listing of those to whom we were grateful was, "God, without whom we have nothing to celebrate." There was an almost palpable excitement as we glorified God and celebrated His blessings, past and present, and our hope for the future.

I reminded the congregation that with the privilege of loving God, also comes the responsibility as stated in Luke 12:48, "From everyone to whom much has been given, much will be required." I suggested that we keep the eyes of our hearts focused on the Lord and give as sacrificially as possible so that we could make room for more of His children to know Him as Savior and Lord.

Doug gave a powerful message, "Giving Freely and Joyously," which was based on I Chronicles 29:17:

> I know, my God, that you search the heart, and take pleasure in uprightness; in the uprightness of my heart I have freely offered all these things, and now I have seen your people, who are present here, offering freely and joyously to you.

Sacred piano music played softly as prayerful commitments were made. Then, hearts and voices were joyfully raised to sing "How Great Thou Art" as we took our gifts and pledges to the podium where Doug dedicated them to be used for God's glory.

The next day Doug and I laughed with delight when we heard the results; later there would be tears of gratitude. Pledges and gifts of 137 giving units totaled $727,192. The $63,328.66 in pre-banquet contributions from those who couldn't attend the dinner brought the final total to $790,520.66, surpassing our first campaign goal by more than $40,000!

At worship services on the following Sunday, all eyes were riveted on Doug as he announced the results to an expectant congregation. There were gasps, laughter, and more tears as our hope became reality. Then, it was my turn. "We have a great God who is delighting in the joy He has given us. What a wonderful testimony this is to what God can do when we trust Him!"

A ground-breaking ceremony followed and as our new addition proceeded, excitement mounted. Once the roof was on, I couldn't stay away and almost every morning for several months, I walked to the construction site, knelt, and prayed before what would one day be our pulpit. To avoid being asked to leave by one of the contractors, I went early and when I heard the foreman arrive, I would brush sawdust and dirt from my legs and leave.

As partitions went up, I prayed in each room and for the people and ministries that would be housed there. The only rooms I didn't pray in were the bathrooms, but I should have—for the first several months we had major septic problems!

A Greater Stretch

Composing a letter of thanks to God, I asked for His blessings on our world, country, church, ministry, and my family and friends. On the day concrete was to be poured I gave my letter to Stefan and asked him to bury it in the pulpit area. He did his best to guess where that would be, but we later found that it's in the floor of the small room where the choir hangs their robes and so Stefan calls it "Shirley's Prayer Closet."

The dedication of our new building was a marvelous and emotional experience for all of us! Joy flooded my heart as I shared with our church, community, pastors, and leaders how God had blessed our faith campaign. It was definitely a time that reflected Ephesians 3:20 and it didn't end there!

In order to cover the full cost of our new facility, our fundraising continued and over six years we raised a total of just under $2,400,000! Less than four years after we began worshipping in our new sanctuary, our church was debt free! We're convinced that the best way to fundraise is to trust God for direction, to obey, and look forward with hope and confidence to what God will do.

Whispers from *Your* Heart

When have I worried more about embarrassing myself than disappointing God?

How do I trust God with something that makes no sense to me?

When I've ignored God or said "no" to Him, how did I feel?

I hope God has a sense of humor when I:

Chapter 4

Caring Ministries

"Like good stewards of the manifold grace of God, serve one another with whatever gift each of you has received."

—1 Peter 4:10

DURING THE YEARS of pastoral search and fundraising, the prayer chain and visitation teams, which also demanded my attention, were thriving. As a retired nurse I had compassion for the sick and shut-ins in our church family who were ill or confined to nursing and rehab centers. I welcomed opportunities to brighten their lives.

I remember the frustration of my nursing days when it was difficult to take even a few minutes to comfort frightened patients, but now I had a perfect opportunity to visit and comfort people who were hurting and afraid. However, my shyness and feelings of inadequacy threatened to short circuit my passion. I was comfortable with and experienced in patient care and medical crises, but on my first hospital visit to pray with a critically ill patient in a CCU, I got as far as the door and panicked. Retreating to an isolated hallway, I was disappointed by my lack of courage.

As I stood there looking out a window at the tarred roof of a nearby hospital wing, I remembered my decision several years earlier to learn how to pray in a group. Too timid to pray aloud in front of anyone publicly, I wanted to overcome my fears so much that I made myself join a prayer group at my church. I tried not to be conspicuous, but that was impossible as I was the only newcomer in a circle of ten. There I sat with friends and others I didn't know so well, and although I was warmly greeted, my focus quickly shifted from prayer to worry about embarrassing myself.

After sharing the needs and requests of our congregation and community, the others began talking to God as naturally as if they were talking to each other. Their beautiful heart-felt prayers rolled off their tongues so easily that I wanted to hide under my chair. *There's no way I can do this, God!* But I felt compelled to choose a name from the list of those needing prayer and silently asked God to help me.

Then I didn't hear anyone else's prayers because I was so busy rehearsing in my mind the three words I would pray, "God bless Ruth. God bless Ruth. God bless Ruth…" One would think I was just learning to talk, but I managed to say my whole prayer—all three words! At the end of the evening, I was relieved that no one commented on my prayer, but just accepted me as I was.

Clearly, the reason for the difference in my comfort level and that of the others is they could talk more freely to God because they knew Him intimately. They had taken time to develop a relationship with Him; to talk with Him and to listen for His answers. Deciding I needed practice, I started praying more regularly and out loud when I was alone, and soon I realized I was to talk *with God* and not for the approval of others.

My prayers had been sporadic, sometimes hurried, and with me doing all of the talking and not listening for God's response. After several months I did better, but my prayers never seemed good enough. I was relieved to learn that prayers don't have to be perfect. God not only accepts us at the level of understanding and ability we have, but He can work wonders through what we may consider the most inadequate of prayers.

God Help Us!

I found reassurance in David Roper's explanation of prayer in *Elijah, A Man Like Us:*

> As we pray, the Spirit of God directs our thoughts. We come with a list of petitions; he gently leads us from our list to his. We set out to express one concern; he interjects another. In the hours of waiting on him, he sorts out our misunderstandings, dispels our confusion, and shows us how he wants us to pray and what he wants us to do.[11]

I found strength in this piece by Chambers:

110

Oh, the bravery of God in trusting us! Do you say, 'But He has been unwise to choose me, because there is nothing good in me and I have no value'? That is exactly why He chose you. As long as you think that you are of value to Him He cannot choose you because you have purposes of your own to serve.[12]

If prayer-phobia isn't yours, you may be thinking *how hard can it be?* Many find it extremely difficult, but I've found that, like anything else I'm intent on doing, the more I pray and the more I trust God to show me how, the more He empowers me.

I no longer look for ease in praying, but consider it a privilege I want always to take seriously. As my love relationship with Jesus grows, I want more and more for the words of my mouth and the meditations of my heart to reflect what Jesus modeled. As Roper explains:

Prayer, for Jesus, was an expression of deeply felt need. It was the environment in which he lived, the air he breathed...the life of Jesus was continuous prayer, triggered by continuous need.[13]

I've learned that as Christians, we can have the assurance of the Holy Spirit living in us and be confident that He will help us pray or even pray for us when we can't. Sometimes in crises, we hurt so much that all we can say is, "Oh God." In Romans (8:26-27) Paul tells us:

The Spirit helps us in our weakness; for we do not know how to pray as we ought, but that very Spirit intercedes with sighs too deep for words. And God, who searches the heart, knows what is the mind of the Spirit, because the Spirit intercedes for the saints according to the will of God.

Henry and Richard Blackaby, in their book *Hearing God's Voice* say that we should begin our prayers by asking the Holy Spirit to control our thoughts:

Prayer does not come naturally...we do not know what to pray unless the Holy Spirit helps us. In fact, we are foolish to begin asking God for things before seeking what is on His mind. If we do, we will invariably ask God for the wrong things.[14]

I had not yet read Roper's book when I panicked on my first hospital visit to pray for a critically ill person and hid in a hallway. That patient was Esther, a sweet-spirited, elderly saint in every sense of the word, also known as a prayer warrior. Now in a CCU with serious heart disease, I believed she needed and deserved a really good prayer! Through the years we had delighted in happy times, but also endured and grew together through hurts, disappointments, losses, and the inevitable adjustments.

There was no doubt God had led me to my role in Caring Ministries and to Esther! I had learned that when we ask God to use us, He often chooses things we cannot do by ourselves because He wants us to rely totally on Him for direction, courage, and strength. I love Paul's assurance of this in Philippians 2:13: "For it is God who is at work in you, enabling you both to will and to work for His good pleasure."

I believed God would continue to empower me for His work, but at that moment my faith took a back seat to my fears. Paul's words provide quite a contrast to the picture of me shaking in my shoes that day! What could I possibly say to comfort Esther in the midst of her suffering? I didn't want to say the wrong thing and make a difficult situation even harder for her to bear.

God, can You really use me to bless Esther?

"Father," I whispered, "You know how much Esther loves You, and how faithful she's been in serving You. Now she's old and going through a tough time and I don't want to let her down, but what can I possibly say to make her feel better? What if I can't find the right words? I don't want to stress her further…"

I stood there quietly until I knew it was time to go to Esther, but not alone. I asked the Holy Spirit to transform my doubts and insecurities and to bless Esther. I wanted her not to see, hear, or feel me, but to know in a more real-than-ever way the love, grace, and mercy of Jesus through me. And God did that!

Esther's eyes were closed, but when I gently touched her arm her eyes opened and her face lit up with delight to see me. We talked about how much Jesus loves us and later as we prayed together, my shyness took a back seat to the Holy Spirit who fed my surprised mind with thoughts and words that were not my own!

Esther recovered and she continued to inspire many for several more years before Jesus took her to her heavenly home. I'll never forget Esther's blessings on my life or how God used me to minister to Esther that day in the hospital.

Learning to Trust the Holy Spirit Even More

When we pray for someone, we take that person into the presence of Jesus and trust Him in His wisdom to do what He knows is best.

Although Psalm 91 says that God is with all of us in our suffering, sometimes we hurt so severely we can't feel God. We may be in a fog of tragedy and our strength so depleted that we can't formulate words. In times like that, some say we need "God with skin on."

Any of us may be that person "with skin" whom God chooses to take a hurting brother or sister into His presence when he or she cannot get there by themselves. We can help them refocus on God and find hope for the future.

Through prayer we can find strength to open doors and trust God to open them wider or close them. Through prayers of praise and thanksgiving, we learn to love God more, and through prayers of petition (asking God for things), God enables us to do what is impossible without Him. Through prayers of intercession (praying for others), our Father comforts, strengthens, encourages, and gives His hope and peace through us. There's nothing quite so wonderful as seeing and feeling God at work after obeying and trusting Him to do so. We can take no credit for what God does, but we can rejoice over the privilege of being used by Him.

When a person asks us to pray for total healing we can do that, but we must trust God to define "total healing." That may be physical wholeness or spiritual maturity.

Almost always the people I visit are gracious, but when frustrated, frightened, discouraged, and even angry at God, some people can be resistant and even rude. I've found it helpful to remember the words of Frank Laubach: "I choose to look at people through God, using God as my glasses, colored with His love for them."

One man—a dear friend, but a bit of a curmudgeon, surprised me with his abruptness. When I asked if he would like me to pray with him before I left, he said, "Shirley, if it'll make you feel better, then, by all means do so." Hesitating only briefly, I told him, "Well, yes it will," and after finishing my prayer, he said tearfully, "Thanks, I appreciate that."

Sing to Her... Me...Out Loud?

Perhaps my most poignant experience of the power of prayer was with a young woman I'll call Susan. I had talked with her and her family a few times when they visited our church, and now Susan had attempted suicide. I went to the ICU and found her unconscious, restrained and receiving intravenous fluids. I wouldn't have known what to do, but I had asked God to help me.

Embracing her as best I could, I told her who I was, that I was from Brewster Baptist Church and that I loved her. Then I added, "More important, Susan, Jesus loves you and you're resting in His arms," but there was no response.

Then, looking at this beautiful young wife and mother, I knew I should pray for her—quietly, but out loud, and I did that until the nurses came to bathe her and I was asked to leave.

The next day I found Susan sitting up in bed. The restraints were gone, but she had a dazed look on her face as she rocked back and forth, back and forth. With no indication that she recognized me, I told Susan who I was and something must have touched her—perhaps my voice was familiar—and she leaned over to me.

As I stood there holding Susan in my arms, I felt compelled to sing to her and I didn't want to. I don't especially like my voice and I certainly didn't want to sing alone with only curtains separating the cubicles. But I had no doubt that was exactly what I was supposed to do, and the song was to be "Jesus Loves Me."

So I quietly sang, "Jesus loves Susan, this I know, for the Bible tells me so. Little ones to Him belong, they are weak, but He is strong. Yes, Jesus loves Susan, yes, Jesus loves Susan. Yes, Jesus loves Susan, the Bible tells me so." Susan didn't respond, but continued to nestle in my arms. For the next twenty minutes we stayed that way; my telling Susan about how much Jesus loves her, hoping she could hear and understand, and praying with her until once more the nurses needed to be alone with her.

The next day her bed was empty and my heart sank. *Had she tried again to kill herself? Had she been successful?* I found a nurse who said that Susan had been moved to a medical floor for a couple of days and then would be transferred to a psych center. Greatly relieved, I went to find her and through a glass hallway window, I saw her sitting squatty fashion on her bed talking on the telephone. As I entered the room, I heard her say, "Mom I love you—must go, I have company."

"Susan, it's wonderful to see you awake and smiling!"

She thought for a moment and then said, "I know you...you're from Brewster Baptist Church...you're Shirley Vogel."

Surprised that she knew my name, I asked if she remembered my visiting her in ICU. At first she appeared puzzled, but then smiling again, she said, "I remember you were one of those trying to get me to come back, and I remember your praying with me and singing "Jesus Loves Me."

Reader, I share this story for two reasons. First, because Susan was blessed by my prayers and my singing—simply because I made myself available to God, risked embarrassment, and invited Him to work through me. And, second, because this can be anyone's story. Yours may not be as dramatic, but it will be just as significant to the person God ministers to through you, and also to your personal relationship with the Lord as you experience the Holy Spirit working in and through you. God will provide all you need and more.

God Continues to Lead and Empower

As our church family grew and new needs became evident, I organized ministries to address them. With God's help I knew instinctively what to do; He whispered and I obeyed! With Caring Ministries multiplying at the same time I was chairing the pastoral search and fundraising campaign committees, there were many days when I didn't know what to do first. For several years it wasn't unusual for me to arise at 5 A.M. for my time alone with God and to have 12–14 hour work days before falling exhausted into my bed. Even at night and on weekends there were phone calls for prayer, encouragement, and support.

In addition to prayer, a writing by St. Francis de Sales proved to be a priceless resource for visitation. "Be at Peace" is a source of strength, reassurance, encouragement, hope, and peace for me and for the many hundreds of people with whom I've shared it. Countless times, I have read these comforting words to the sick and infirm, making sure of eye-to-eye contact, especially with the phrase, "God, whose very own you are."

Be At Peace

Do not look forward in fear
to the changes in life;
rather look to them with full
hope that as they arise, God,
whose very own you are,
will lead you safely through
all things; and when you cannot stand it,
God will carry you in His arms. Do
not fear what may happen tomorrow;
the same everlasting Father

> who cares for you today will take care
> of you then and every day. He will
> either shield you from suffering, or will
> give you unfailing strength to bear it.
> Be at peace and put aside all
> anxious thoughts and imaginations.
> St. Francis de Sales[15]

God blessed Caring Ministries and I was so busy that I simply went from one responsibility to the next, never considering the broader context of the ministries. I remember my amazement when I realized I hadn't seen—as the expression goes—the forest for the trees. When I finally got around to counting, there were fourteen ministries with about two hundred fifty people serving the Lord through them. By the final year of fundraising, the ministries would number twenty-five.

"Paper" ministries included our weekly *Prayer Concerns Lists* that were distributed at worship: one side for adults and the other for kids. Many hours of phone calls each week were needed to keep these lists current, but this worked hand in hand with the visitation ministry because in the process, I learned who needed repeat visits and this interaction reassured them of the love of their church family. The visitation team was highly organized and reported their visits on written forms, but the team contacted me or a pastor regarding urgent or special needs.

We had many support groups such as *Widows Might, Divorce Care, Encouraging Moms, Caregivers Support, Caring and Sharing* (for those with long-term illness), *Caring Heart to Heart* (bereavement ministry).

We had a *Parish Nursing* ministry run by nurses in the church. Using the town van, various men and women demonstrated their *Caring on Wheels* by providing transportation to worship services to anyone who, because of age, illness, or disability could not otherwise get there. Others, using private automobiles, provided *Transportation* for medical appointments and procedures.

Also well received was our *Sacred Music Tapes Ministry* which was provided and led by a gentleman who was helped through a time of excruciating physical pain by listening to inspirational tapes. He and his wife purchased supplies and assembled kits with Walkmans and sacred tapes which they delivered to those in hospitals and nursing homes. A special blessing was that this proved especially calming for those suffering from the confusion and even the violence of Alzheimer's disease.

Individual ministries included *Stefan's Bread Ministry* (homemade oatmeal bread delivered to those who returned home following hospital stays), *Shut-in Greeting Card List,* and *God's Promises* (handwritten packets of Scripture cards color coded to address various needs).

There was a three-fold goal for *Kids Kare Too!* First, one-on-one time was encouraged between a child and parent to do something together, such as baking cookies, picking flowers, or drawing a picture. Second, they brightened the day of a shut-in by taking their gift when they visited. Third, children were introduced at an early age to serving the Lord.

Some groups, such as JULIETs (Just Us Ladies Interested (in) Eating Together) and ROMEOs (Retired Outstanding Men Eating Out), met in restaurants for food and fellowship.

These are only some of the Caring Ministries. I've written about them in the past tense because many were not continued after God moved me in a new direction and I turned them over to other church leaders. This will be explained later on.

God blessed the growth of Caring Ministries in such a big way that when budget time rolled around each year, I not only asked for money to meet current ministry needs, but extra funds for "whatever" God would plant in my heart during the next year. Gratefully, the financial secretary agreed to leave the door open for God!

The Supernatural Provision of God

I could say the success of Caring Ministries was beyond my expectations, but I never had a vision for this comprehensive ministry and certainly no strategic plans. Clearly God did and as I went day to day and hand in hand with the Lord, praying for direction and trusting Him to provide and empower, He blessed my efforts as only God can—and, that continues.

In a supernatural way I know what to do and how to do it! That may sound simplistic, but when I trust God, He blesses my efforts in ways that demonstrate His power. Caring Ministries wasn't my idea, but I'm grateful for a heart that can hear God's whispers!

Brother Lawrence explains it this way:

When I have business to do, I do not think about it beforehand. When the time comes to do it, I see in God as clearly as in a mirror all that is needed for me to do.[16]

I have a small framed sketch that says, "A friend like you is a special hug from God". This characterizes the love of Caring Ministries - to reflect the love, grace, and mercy of Jesus Christ in such a way that God's presence is experienced in real and intimate ways. Our mission statement explains:

> Caring Ministries strive to meet the spiritual, physical, emotional, and social needs of our church family and those in the greater community. We do this by reflecting the love of Jesus Christ as we reach out and enfold them through the use of our spiritual gifts.[17]

Services are not limited to members of our church, but available to all. Reflecting to others the love of Jesus Christ and hoping they will pass it on, our joy is sustained because we know we're making a difference—temporal in time, but eternal in nature. Visiting and comforting the sick and lonely is a blessing wrapped in God's love and tied with ribbons of His grace for both the care receiver and giver.

Many stated their concern that I was working too hard. One friend encouraged me to establish boundaries; to divide each day into four parts: time for me and the Lord, time for me and Stefan, "alone" time, and time for the unexpected. I was reminded that Jesus frequently stepped away from needs in order to have time alone, and with His Father. If Jesus needed "down time," surely I do, but I don't earn high grades in setting boundaries.

Caring Ministries was a good fit for me, but one that cost a great deal on my husband's part, as well as my own, because I was not good at taking time for us. We sacrificed time together, visits to family, and time with friends. We missed entertaining and being invited to the homes of others. Stefan was patient when our home wasn't as neat as before, but this was frustrating for me. With my Dutch genes, I had always taken pride in a sparkling house.

When Stefan retired, he enjoyed more time for classical guitar, local theater, and his own ministries. Still, he offered to take on some of my responsibilities, drawing the line at cooking and ironing. Without his household help and editing my material, much of my ministry would not have happened. His support makes a huge difference and in that sense we share the ministries God gives me.

Many church members think I'm one of the salaried staff and upon learning that I'm not, some have expressed their disbelief that I "work for nothing." I've never looked at it that way because I feel so privileged that

God chooses to trust me with ministry that I can only do with Him. God's gift of Himself—of wanting to spend time with me—is a precious gift.

At one point when my pastor asked how I felt about being salaried, I said I needed to think and pray about it and I did. Although Stefan and I decided reimbursement would be helpful, I was never asked again. It's difficult for me to ask for things for myself so I never found the courage to bring it up.

GDI Degree!

I doubt that anyone feels more inadequate than I did initially with the "whatevers" God chose for me. I'm grateful I recognized my limitations and didn't go bumbling through on my own. God respected my fears and insecurities, and He used them to teach me that *with God all things are possible* (Matthew 19:26 NIV).

There's no joy like that of knowing God's love, and as I increasingly recognize and experience His generosity and faithfulness, I rely on Him and don't worry about what I don't know. Perhaps God chose to use me because I'm not an ordained pastor and because I've had no formal administrative training. Maybe God wants to demonstrate that He can use anyone with a heart to love and trust Him! God wants to use all of us to bless others and bring glory to Himself. Gifting each one of us according to His plan for our lives, God wants to spend time with us—showing us how, when, and what that is. How precious is that!

So the good news is, we don't all need theology degrees. I have a GDI degree and you can have one too! It stands for "God Does It!" It means that when we trust God and go forward in blind faith to do what He asks us to do, God Does it! GDI! His Holy Spirit guides and empowers us!

I may not be a seminary grad, but I'm learning from the best—the Master Himself through prayer, Scripture, and the written and spoken words of others directed by the Holy Spirit. Through faith I've earned an effective degree—the best—because I believe it was personally designed for me by Almighty God.

In the academic world where scholarly books and lectures are highly valued, our GDIs may not be impressive, but when we graduate to heaven and meet Jesus, it will speak volumes! Not because we're wonderful, but because He is!

I rely heavily on God's promises to help me, but when I get too busy, lose my focus, and just forge ahead on my own, responsibilities that weigh heavy and seem overwhelming remind me of my inadequacies. It's at those times that God gently whispers me back to my senses through Scripture, a Christian author, or perhaps a prayer being offered up for me; all significant to my ministry and spiritual growth.

God uniquely gifts us, and if we listen carefully we may hear God whisper, *Share my love. Use your spiritual gifts. Pass it on!* Let us not hide our gifts that show who we are and what we believe. In Matthew 5:14-16, we read:

> You are the light of the world. A city built on a hill cannot be hid. No one after lighting a lamp puts it under the bushel basket, but on the lamp stand, and it gives light to all in the house. In the same way, let your light shine before others, so that they may see your *good works and give glory to your Father in heaven* (emphasis added).

As I face new challenges, I find strength and encouragement in this anonymous quote: "God plus any one of us is a majority." Nothing is more exciting than sensing the work of the Holy Spirit in our lives.

God sometimes places us where we have to make a deliberate choice to trust Him totally, and even for the ability to keep on trusting Him one whisper at a time.

I wouldn't have chosen my "whatevers" because like most people, I don't want a job at which I know I'll fail. We don't want to embarrass ourselves and let down family and friends, but our primary concern should be about disappointing God who has promised to be faithful and always is!

In *Transforming Leadership* by Leighton Ford, Dr. Richard Halverson puts a little different slant on serving. In describing his first day as chaplain of the United States Senate, he says:

> I felt like a non-person, a mascot to one of the most powerful political bodies in the world. I wondered what I was doing there.[18]

That evening he read the words of Jesus in Matthew 28:18 (NIV):

> "All authority in heaven and on earth has been given to me…And surely I am with you always."

As he meditated on those words from Matthew 28, he realized:

> I am a garment which Jesus Christ wears every day to do what He wants to do in the US Senate. I don't need power; my weakness is an asset. If Christ is in me, what more do I need?[19]

Each of us is a "garment" that Jesus wears to visit the sick, to hold the hands of the dying, to embrace the grieving, to speak, to chair committees, to teach Bible classes—*whatever* God chooses to accomplish through our lives. Remembering that gives me courage, comfort, and peace and it's exciting!

God's Little Gal from East Pal!

Because I trusted God even when his choices seemed unlikely, God worked what I consider miracles! He took this little gal from East Pal, filled me with Himself, and transformed me into a person He can use as He will. God has taken the seeds of trust planted in my young mind so many years ago by God-fearing parents and Sunday school teachers, and has used adversity and challenges to grow them into a strong faith.

I've learned that if I say, "Father, I give You me for 'whatever,'" I had better mean it because God won't miss an opportunity to draw me closer to Himself! I take seriously the promises I make because God keeps His and He expects me to keep mine, and in God's grace He even helps me do that.

*Whispers from **Your** Heart*

How can I know my prayers are "good enough?"

How can I not get in God's way?

Do I serve God to please Him or to make myself look good?

When I serve God, who do I credit with my successes? Who do I blame for my failures?

Chapter 5

What's Next, God?

"Speak, for your servant is listening."

—1 Samuel 3:10

ONE EVENING AS I praised God, I declared naively, "Now there's nothing You can ask that would scare me."

Soon after, my close friend Maura phoned. Coping with a family crisis, she needed to talk, and someone to listen. That evening we met in a restaurant and later as I stood to leave, she said, "Wait Shirley, I want to tell you something. I believe God has a 'speaking ministry' for you."

Because I knew Maura prayed for me, I listened carefully. Was she right? The idea seemed so far-fetched. I wanted to make sure Maura's idea originated with God, and so I asked Maura not to discuss it with anyone. I confided only in Stefan, Pastor Doug, and a close friend because I didn't want anyone to manipulate events so that it would happen.

As I prayed, Satan put doubts in my mind. *Who are you to speak to others who may be more mature in their faith than you are...who undoubtedly know more than you do?*

However, if Maura was right, God would make it happen in a more wonderful way than I could imagine.

A few weeks later, I heard Jill Briscoe speak about an unexpected opportunity to address people in such a desperate situation that she felt inadequate in her own strength. Briscoe's prayer based on Jeremiah 1:9 is one that I've made my own, *Your words on my lips!*

"Oh God," I prayed silently, "if one day I'm to share my story, overflow me with Your Spirit...Your words on my lips!"

God's Promise of Hope

I'm always amazed by God's timing of events in my life; how He often propels me to pick up a certain book or devotional, or steers me to a Scripture with exactly what I need for that moment. This time it was the book of Jeremiah and immediately I could identify with his fears. Jeremiah 1:4-6:

> Now the word of the Lord came to me saying, "Before I formed you in the womb I knew you, and before you were born I consecrated you; I appointed you a prophet to the nations." Then I said, "Ah, Lord God! Truly I do not know how to speak, for I am only a boy."

Next to that verse, I wrote, "And I'm just a little gal from East Pal!" Then I read it aloud, "God, I'm just a little gal from East Pal—exclamation point!" But God wasn't into punctuation that day. Instead, He was beginning to whisper His future plans for my life. I didn't have details, but I was joyfully expectant, and laughing aloud I said, "God, You are such fun!"

I continued to read:

> But the Lord said to me, "Do not say, 'I am only a boy'; for you shall go to all to whom I send you, and you shall speak whatever I command you, Do not be afraid of them, for I am with you"
> —Jeremiah 1:7-8

In *Run With the Horses*, Eugene H. Peterson's reflections on the life of Jeremiah, God further enlightened me.

> We are practiced in pleading inadequacy in order to avoid living at the best that God calls us to. How tired the excuses sound! I am only a youth; I am only a housewife; I am only a layman; I am only a poor preacher; I only have an eighth grade education; I don't have enough time; I don't have enough training; I don't have enough confidence; or, with Biblical precedence, "Oh, my Lord, I am not eloquent"
> —Exodus 4:10 RSV

> Our ideas of what we can do or want to do are trivial; God's ideas for us are grand...promises that lead to fulfillment...God does what He says.[20]

Jeremiah 29:11 became a favorite verse and my email address.

"For surely I know the plans I have for you," says the Lord, "plans for your welfare and not for harm, to give you a future with hope."

I took a firm grasp of God's promises for good, and a future with hope, "whatever" that might be. If God's plans included a speaking ministry—well then, God bless me!

Invitations

Several months later I agreed to speak about Caring Ministries to a regional gathering of women from Baptist churches in Massachusetts. For the first time, I was comfortable before an audience. I loved sharing what God was doing and encouraged the women to also step out in faith—confident of God's empowerment.

That day, remembering Maura's insistence on my becoming a speaker, I wondered, *Is this the beginning?* Then I forgot about it until two months later when I received a phone call from a woman asking me to be the speaker for her women's retreat weekend. When I asked where she had gotten my name, she said a friend in her church had heard me speak about Caring Ministries and recommended me. She explained that I would be speaking at three sessions, each time for forty five minutes! *WOW,* I thought, *God doesn't fool around! Can I do this?*

I asked for time to think and pray and we agreed to talk again in a few days. Putting the phone down, I prayed, "Father, are You in this?" Over the next few days, God gave me the theme, "Joyful Expectancy" which pretty much described my attitude. Still, one day I awakened feeling inadequate and wondering if my material was good enough, and again God showed me that my fear of embarrassment was greater than my concern about disobeying Him. *Shirley, just share the stories and lessons I've given you over the past sixteen years; I'll take care of the rest.*

God was opening up a new "whatever" for me; one more step in growing me into the Shirley He created me to be.

I was encouraged by the faith of Abraham who clearly realized that Almighty God does not have to make "common sense." God had declared that Abraham would become the "father of many nations" and in Romans 4:19-21 it says:

[Abraham] did not weaken in faith when he considered his own body, which was already as good as dead (for he was about a hundred years old), or when he considered the barrenness of Sarah's womb. No distrust made him waver concerning the promise of God, but he grew strong in his faith as he gave glory to God, being fully convinced that God was able to do what He had promised.

I was inspired by Abraham's unquestioning faith in Hebrews 11:8:

By faith Abraham obeyed when he was called to set out for a place that he was to receive as an inheritance; and he set out, not knowing where he was going.

"Okay, Father, I will also go out not knowing where I'm going."

Agreeing to speak, I began praying for the women with whom I would share my testimony. I was still getting used to that idea when I was invited to speak at a second women's retreat in Rhode Island two weeks after the first. If I could do it once, I could do it twice!

Arriving at the first retreat, I was shown to my beautiful corner room with stunning views of Nantucket Bay and a beautiful marsh. That evening as I was introduced, I was somewhat nervous, but as I looked at the faces of the women for whom I had prayed, I was excited to be part of God's plan for them and me.

The women could relate to my challenges because most had known or were experiencing similar pain, doubts, and heart-wrenching situations. Providing stationery, I asked each gal to write a letter to God about whatever was on their hearts, and where they hoped to be in their relationship with God three months from that time.

The women found this a helpful tool in openly expressing themselves to God. I took the self-addressed and sealed envelopes with me to mail three months later. The women could then compare their hopes at the retreat with the reality of where they were as they re-read their letters to God.

On Saturday evening the retreat ended with all of us sitting around a large tray of sand in which we placed a candle we had been instructed to bring. The organizer of the retreat placed hers first and after lighting it, shared with the group a significant personal experience of the weekend. The others did the same, some talking about what God means to them, and some tearfully sharing how God had spoken to them at the retreat. Several said God had been nudging them into various kinds of ministry, but feelings of inadequacy had been stumbling blocks to their obedience and now they had courage to go forward in His strength.

When everyone else had taken part, it was my turn.

Not knowing the purpose for the candles, I had brought a tall taper while the others who were familiar with this tradition brought squatty fat candles or votives. At first I was concerned that my candle, towering over the others, would make the other gals think I felt superior. But as I got up to light mine, God fed me the perfect words.

Placing my candle in the middle, I explained, "Initially, I was embarrassed because my candle was different, but now I see that your candles surrounding mine reflect the warmth, love, and grace that has encircled and empowered me throughout the weekend. It wasn't until I was listening to your stories that I realized I had never even attended a women's retreat—certainly not as the speaker. Perhaps God led you to invite me to speak at this retreat because He knew He could trust you to encourage me as I stepped out in faith on my new journey with Him."

Not A+

At church the next day, Joanne, a gal in my small group who had been praying for me asked, "How'd it go?"

"I wanted my presentations to be A+, but even as I spoke, I knew there were things I could have done better. Sometimes I felt like a clay pot with all of my cracks showing!"

Joanne laughed and said, "That's wonderful, because when we're filled with the love of Jesus, our cracks permit His love to shine through to those around us!"

Isn't that wonderful? It takes a lot of pressure off to know that God can work through our weaknesses. We don't have to be perfect, because God is! Later, when I thanked Joanne she said her comments stemmed from having read Patsy Clairmont's book, *God Uses Clay Pots*.

I love knowing that I am and always will be a cracked clay pot, and as I prepared for my next retreat I asked God to shine His light through me.

The second retreat was a gathering of women from a mostly Afro-American Baptist Church, and culturally and spiritually it was a wonderfully diverse experience. Again I was welcomed with open arms, and hearts ready to receive what God had given me for them. But God's love also saturated my heart and soul through these women and I went home with beautiful new friendships, trusting that those gals had been blessed as richly as I was.

In the interval between the two retreats, I found great reassurance in Joshua 1:5, 9:

> As I was with Moses, so I will be with you; I will not fail you or forsake you...I hereby command you: Be strong and courageous; do not be frightened or dismayed, for the Lord your God is with you wherever you go.

And a few days later, John 15:16:

> You did not choose me but I chose you. And I appointed you to go and bear fruit, fruit that will last, so that the Father will give you whatever you ask him in my name.

I felt so blessed by God's timely encouragement that I wrote in my journal, "Abba—I love so much the way You speak directly to me through authors and Scripture. Sometimes it seems almost 'too good to be true.' When will I realize that You're not?"

Whispers from *Your* Heart

*I believe God has a unique plan for my life, but how can I know what He wants me to do?

*When God "stretches" me, where can I find courage and strength to obey?

*I claim and trust the promise of Jeremiah 29:11, "For surely I know the plans I have for _____(your name)," says the Lord; "plans for your welfare and not for harm, to give you a future with hope." This Scripture makes me feel:

*I can awaken each morning with "joyful expectancy" because:

Chapter 6

A Life-Threatening "Whatever"

"My soul is satisfied as with a rich feast, and my mouth praises you with joyful lips when I think of you on my bed, and meditate on you in the watches of the night; for you have been my help, and in the shadow of your wings I sing for joy. My soul clings to you; your right hand upholds me."

—Psalm 63:5-8

TWO MONTHS AFTER the retreats, I wrote a letter of encouragement to my friend, Thom, who had lost his job, and I shared with him the encouragement of Jeremiah 29:11:

"For I know the plans I have for [Thom]", says the Lord, "plans for your welfare and not for harm, to give you a future with hope."

I explained, "This is a promise that I've claimed for myself, and I awaken each morning with a sense of 'joyful expectancy'. It's exciting to look ahead and anticipate what God's going to do each day—even if it isn't what I would have chosen or what I have in mind. Sometimes I don't like at all what He chooses for me or what He asks me to do."

When I wrote those words, I had no idea of what was just around the corner. Only two days later, I was getting ready to attend our Sunday school Christmas program, and reaching for my mascara, my fingers suddenly froze in all directions. I screamed for Stefan who had returned from Vermont less than an hour before, and the next thing I knew was waking up in a heap on the floor with panic-stricken Stefan next to me. Thank God, I had the presence of mind to ask Stefan for aspirin and in

131

his haste to help me, I heard medication bottles scattering to the floor. Swallowing some pills I got up to walk, I think, just to prove that I could! When Stefan started to call 911, I said, "No, let's wait and see," but there was no waiting. My words were slurred and difficult to understand.

I was taken by ambulance to the ER where a CT Scan showed a blood clot in my brain and Heparin, a medication to thin my blood, was started intravenously. For six hours my speech vacillated between normal to very slurred; I had no control—it did its own thing. I had to tell my story to three of the ER staff and each time it became increasingly difficult to make myself understood. When I realized that the third person, a staff doctor, was going to ask me the same questions as the others, I asked if he could read the answers I had already given. He ignored me and persisted with question after question. My speech was getting more and more difficult to understand, and when I badly pronounced a word the doctor laughed at me. At that point when I became upset and couldn't form answers to his questions, he left the room clearly annoyed with me.

I heard him say to someone at the desk just outside my cubicle, "Mrs. Vogel went ballistic on me!" My nature is so far from being a trouble maker that I felt unfairly accused and I wept.

Pastor Doug came and although his concern was clear, he made me smile when he said that while driving to the hospital, he had told God, "This is not part of the deal!"

Later I was transferred to a post-stroke unit. My speech seemed to be improving and I encouraged Stefan to go home and get some rest, but shortly after he left, my speech deteriorated again. When the night nurse made rounds about 11:00 P.M., I expressed as best I could my discouragement. She explained that it takes 2-3 days for Heparin to reach a therapeutic level, and meanwhile my speech probably would come and go. When she returned just after midnight, although my thoughts were crystal clear, my answers to her three questions came out total gibberish—not one word made any sense!

Startled, frightened, and looking to the nurse for help, I saw compassion in her eyes, but she said nothing and I realized there was nothing more to say; we had to wait it out and the nurse went on to other patients.

I remembered what I had written to Thom just before my stroke. "Sometimes I don't like at all what the Lord chooses for me, or what He asks me to do. But I've learned that He's always right and I can trust Him." I also remembered stroke patients I had cared for; their sad, sad eyes reflecting the horrific fear that their lips could no longer express.

A Life-Threatening "Whatever"

Lying there fighting back tears, I decided I could either lie there all night and worry, or I could trust God. What came to mind was Psalm 4:8 that I had memorized to focus on before heart surgery twelve years earlier.

> I will both lie down and sleep in peace; for you alone, O Lord, make me lie down in safety.

I couldn't speak the verse, but I said it in my mind. Usually when I'm upset about something I don't sleep right away, but I must have fallen asleep immediately because the next thing I knew was waking up three hours later. I hardly dared to try talking, but I was able to say Psalm 4:8 almost perfectly, and my speech improved steadily after that.

At 7 A.M. I tuned in young television preacher Joel Osteen, and I could hardly believe how pointed his first comments were!

> Be happy where you are right now...don't let circumstances influence you...Don't worry about the future...take one day at a time...God has given us grace for today, but not for tomorrow...don't let Satan steal your joy.

I had no doubt that God was speaking to me through Osteen, and just in case I didn't get it the first time, he went on:

> God is directing you and you are exactly where God wants you to be today...Sometimes God allows difficult circumstances in our lives in order to use us to help someone else...God is stretching you and He sees your response...God has your best interest at heart...choose to be happy.

Reading Philippians 4:4 and 11, Osteen reminded me of Paul's response to adversity:

> Rejoice in the Lord always; again I will say, Rejoice...I have learned to be content with whatever I have.

Why, God?

I had been walking with God long enough to know that once again God was working in ways that I didn't fully understand. I loved the way God had spoken to me through Osteen. I felt the reality of God's love in healing my speech and because God, through Osteen, answered my questions before I formed them, I never thought to ask, "Why me?" Instead I looked for and learned a lesson. The Lord had a reason for setting me aside, and it was one of those times when we have to make a deliberate choice to trust God—no matter how difficult that may be! I believed that God, in some way, would use my experience to glorify Himself and that's what happened.

My role as a "caring minister" continued at the hospital! God brought five people into my life, three of them during the last day and a half of my stay; people new to me. I know the Lord did it because of the unique way each conversation and meeting occurred. I was given opportunities to share what God had done earlier in my life, and also about my stroke and healing. As Jesus filled me with His joy, facial expressions and verbal responses clearly showed that God was using me to encourage others, and I was reminded of a friend's advice, "Shirley, don't waste your suffering."

Four days after I was admitted, I was discharged, but the next day as Stefan and I were finishing lunch I suddenly had a prickling sensation around my mouth, fullness in my neck and a feeling of faintness. Stefan called 911 and back I went by ambulance to the ER for several hours. I would like to say I was calm through it all, but my physical and emotional exhaustion was taxed further when I began experiencing even more terrifying symptoms. I didn't know it then but that was the beginning of a series of panic attacks; something I never thought I would suffer from.

When the symptoms persisted, I wrote in my journal,

It's scary, Abba. Nothing seems right. My legs feel weak and all of these weird symptoms are frightening. In my heart, I know that You're enough; help me to know it in my head. Take my fears away; take my symptoms away.

Several days later the scenario was repeated. As the EMTs started an intravenous line, my weakness was overwhelming, but again the ER staff sent me home. I experienced bizarre and terrifying symptoms, sometimes for only a few seconds and, then, I was okay again. The most peculiar happening occurred when I was visiting my mother. At breakfast, I was eating cereal when suddenly my mouth seemed five or six inches to the right of where it really was. I couldn't eat more because I didn't know where my mouth was! Not wanting to startle my mother, I excused myself

134

and went to our bedroom and wept. It would take more than eighteen months for these debilitating neurological symptoms to stop.

wHispers!

About a month after my stroke, God planted the first seed that would eventually grow into "wHispers," the ministry explained at the beginning of this book. Planning this ministry required me to re-focus and eventually I learned to recognize and face the symptoms that could initiate panic attacks, usually when I'm stressed or over tired. Gradually, the signs lessened and most disappeared; the others I've learned to ignore.

I didn't understand why God would give me a new ministry when I clearly needed to cut back, but "wHispers" was God's direction for me; another "whatever." Needing God at a deeper level, I was determined to hold on and obey the directions I was confident He would give me, and trust Him for strength to endure.

Oswald Chambers wrote:

> God always instructs us down to the last detail. Is my ear sensitive enough to hear even the softest whisper of the Spirit, so that I know what I should do? He does not speak with a voice like thunder—His voice is so gentle that it is easy for us to ignore.[21]

I had experienced the truth of Chambers' words before, and as I developed plans for wHispers, I again relied on God for direction and strength. He knew my needs and those of the people we would serve before I could possibly understand.

If I had taken time to consider all that was happening, my head would have spun off my neck! But God set the stage; providing the resources I would need, and they were priceless gifts for this inexperienced little East Pal gal.

One morning during prayer, God whispered, *Shirley, you've always given me credit for successful "whatevers." Who are you going to glorify through wHispers?*

I was bewildered by the question because I believed God had given me "wHispers" to help women who didn't know the Lord, or wanted to know Him better. I decided to put wHispers aside and pray until God gave me clarity and peace to go ahead.

Early the next morning in my time with the Lord, He made it clear. *I want you to minister to women one on one and you know where to start!* And

I did! I was to heal a relationship with Joanna, a woman who seemed to dislike me, and I didn't particularly want to do this. However, I found it interesting that Dr. Cathy Kroeger, a good friend and mentor, had recently told me she thought God may be leading me into to a "restorative" ministry. Because I needed God's help, and perhaps because I hoped God would change His mind, I prayed for more direction.

The next day in a class on spiritual gifts, we listened to a tape of Ken Medema, a blind pianist, singing the story of Ananias in Acts 9. Medema relates in a powerfully dramatic way how God commanded Ananias to go to Saul who was blind. Because Saul had been persecuting Christians, Ananias was hesitant, but still obeyed. When Ananias called Saul "brother," Saul not only received his sight, but a new life in Christ and the new name, Paul. His ministry was so powerful that thousands of years later, we are still motivated by Paul's example.

But something else happened when Medema sang the part about Ananias calling Saul his brother. I was so strongly motivated to treat Joanna like the "sister" in Christ she is, that I had to leave the room, and outside I melted in tears. I felt so loved by God, grateful for the intimacy of that moment, humbled that He would speak so specifically to me, and privileged that again He would use me to make a difference in a woman's life. I didn't expect it to be easy, but I knew God would tell me what to do.

First, I was supposed to send Joanna a small gift to help open a door of possibility and because she had been going through a difficult time, I chose a "hope" rock and a small book about encouragement. A few days later, I received a lovely thank you note with meaningful words carefully chosen and handwritten. Clearly, God was working. I believe Joanna also had been praying because later that week as we shared a meal, God laid the groundwork for the healing that was to come.

Soon after that, I knew I was to proceed with wHispers. Because our church was being restructured to adapt to a growing congregation, I was required to write a four page developmental plan and brochure. I had no experience with this, but I sensed God feeding me ideas and words as I wrote, and I especially appreciated the Lord's direction when several roadblocks appeared that required insight and faith to continue. This brought to mind a Scripture I had come across earlier when our capital campaign efforts were threatened. I laughed as I re-read, Psalm 18:29, "...by my God I can leap over a wall."

A Life-Threatening "Whatever"

I was required to have three people in place before we could begin "wHispers" and when two of them withdrew for very logical reasons, I wondered if I had "misread" God's directions. Praying for wisdom, I soon had clarity about whom to invite into leadership roles, and they faithfully served as have the rest of the team that joined us.

Hurting women who continued to express to me their pain and frustration affirmed the need for a ministry like "wHispers". Ginny especially needed encouragement and after talking together about some of her experiences, I explained our wHispers acronym and ministry goals. Later that day, she emailed me about the fear, separation, and isolation she and many of her friends experience. She described it as feeling:

> …hard like a rock without a voice to sing…needing to be heard, but not knowing where my voice has gone or who would listen if I were to speak.

This is significant because I had not shared with her the Scripture which I had chosen as the theme verse for "wHispers," Ezekiel 26:36 (NIV):

> I will give you a new heart and put a new spirit in you; I will remove from you your heart of stone and give you a heart of flesh.

Also on our brochure is 1 Kings 19:11-12 (NIV):

> The Lord said, "Go out…for the Lord is about to pass by." Then a great and powerful wind tore the mountains apart…but the Lord was not in the wind. After the wind there was an earthquake, but the Lord was not in the earthquake. After the earthquake came a fire, but the Lord was not in the fire. And after the fire came a gentle whisper.

The goal of wHispers is to help women walk so close to the Lord that, despite the storms in their lives, they can hear, recognize, and understand God's most quiet whispers.

wHispers was God's idea and He chose to start it through me when I was at a very low point in my life, and I'm so glad I could trust Him. It's a privilege and humbling to have God work through us, and if God can use this little gal from East Pal—He can use anyone! Reader, I encourage you to be available and to trust God to complete His work in your life, no matter what He asks you to do. It will be exciting to see where God takes you and how He enables you to obey His plans for your life.

Sometimes Dying Brings Healing

I learned from my children that their father was dying of a rapidly progressing colon cancer, and my children's tears broke my heart. Never have I felt so helpless.

Although Con and I had remained friendly and Con's wife, Ann, and I very much like and respect each other, I didn't feel free to go and comfort my children, who were spending as much time as possible with them. As Con's condition rapidly deteriorated, I did what I could to support my children from a distance, but the ache in my heart reflected their grief.

One afternoon, Jim called and said that his father wanted me to call him. "Why?" I asked, but Jim didn't know. I agreed to call Con, but feeling so emotional, I worried that I would break down and make a tragic situation even more difficult for him.

Kneeling, I tearfully asked God for emotional stability and strength, for His thoughts to be in my mind, and His words on my lips. Con was always a man of few words and now being so close to death, I knew I would have to carry most of the conversation.

I was stunned by the weakness of Con's voice; barely above a whisper. I told him how sorry I was that he was ill, and he said, "Yes, there's nothing to be done."

"Jim said you wanted me to call you."

"Yes, I want to say good-bye."

That, of course, was a very poignant moment for both of us, and one in which God definitely fed me an unanticipated response. "Con, there's something I need to say and I believe you need to hear. Please know that I feel equally responsible for our marriage not surviving; I hope you have peace about that."

"Thank you. I appreciate your saying so."

"Another thing. I'm grateful to God for bringing you and Ann together. I respect her and I'm grateful for the love she shows our children."

"I've had two good wives."

I thanked him for that, and then we agreed we had done a good job of raising three wonderful children.

Any animosity or resentment between us was gone; God had brought healing as only He can. After we said good bye, I fell onto my bed in tears. I couldn't help but remember how he had left our marriage in such a hurry and without saying good-bye. Now he was leaving forever and none of us were ready.

I wasn't prepared for the days that followed. During Con's illness, I talked frequently with my children, listening and consoling them, but distance prevented the kind of intimacy needed. Now, words were totally inadequate to soothe their grief. I needed to embrace them and they needed for me to hold them, but it wasn't possible.

I asked their advice about Stefan and me attending the calling hours a day before the funeral service. Out of respect for Ann and not to create awkwardness for others, we reluctantly agreed we should not. Instead, Stefan and I went to care for our three youngest grandsons, so that Jim and Jody could stay with the others in Buffalo.

Following a favorite tradition, I took Jonathan and Nicky to choose their favorite donuts for breakfast, and on the way we listened to praise songs. Driving home, the music was not on and Jonathan said, "Grandma, will you put God back on?"

I turned "God back on" and later as we munched our donuts, I explained that God is always "on." I said that one of my favorite things about God is that He's omnipresent, and I explained that's a big word with a simple meaning—God is everywhere at all times—always with us no matter where we are. I added, "God is with your Mommy and Daddy right now and also with us.

Nicky, only 5 years old, quickly added with such assurance that it surprised me, "And even with Papa Con in heaven!"

Stef, my mother, and I went to the funeral, and the first time I saw my children and older grandchildren was when they, with Ann and all of her family, processed into the Catholic sanctuary. I could barely control my emotions when I saw their grief-strained faces. One empty pew separated us from my grandchildren, who, when seeing me, leaned over to embrace me, and we wept quietly together.

Shortly after the service began, the priest invited the congregation to greet each other and "pass the peace of Christ." My son made a bee-line from his front row seat and clung to me, his head on my shoulder and his large frame shaking in sobs. There were no words because neither of us could stop crying.

My children tearfully shared letters they had written for a book they compiled for their father's 70th birthday. It was a book about his life including pictures of his mom and dad and his early years, and letters from his children, grandkids, and wife. Sadly, Con never enjoyed reading the book as he was too sick by the time they finished it. I was proud of my children—their love for family, and lives that reflect their commitment to God as well as the gentleness of their father's favorite Scripture, Micah 6:8:

> What does the Lord require of you, but to do justice, and to love kindness, and to walk humbly with your God?

Whispers from *Your* Heart

When I have trouble accepting life events and get discouraged, how do I react? Do I, in anger, walk away from God or do I continue to trust His love and faithfulness?

In scary and sad times, how can I choose to be happy?

What can I do to prevent Satan from stealing my joy? Do I believe God is bigger than Satan?

It's wonderful to know I've made a difference in the life of someone. Describe.

Chapter 7

Jesus Still Walks on Water!

"I am with you always..."

—Matthew 28:20

MY HEALTH CHALLENGES didn't end with the stroke. Occasionally for just a few seconds, earlier symptoms reappeared and after our summer vacation, I was resuming plans for "wHispers" when Gina called, wanting to talk about how to pray. Although my explanation was simplistic, it touched her heart in a significant way and this was a direct answer to my frequent prayer:

> O God, help me to understand and retain what You know I'll need for the ministry You give me, and help me use the wisdom You entrust to me.

My joy in sharing with Gina was interrupted. Mid-sentence, for just a few seconds, I again felt as if I "wasn't there." Startled, I thought, *what was that?* Two weeks earlier I had experienced an episode of blurred vision, also lasting only a few seconds, but I knew both symptoms could indicate more blood clots.

When our conversation ended, I contacted my doctor who ordered more blood tests, and MRIs of my brain and brain stem to rule out further stroke damage. These were scheduled for Sunday afternoon and after that I would see a cardiologist in Boston to determine whether my symptoms were due to changes in my mitral heart valve. My doctor said this was a strong possibility, and if so, more heart surgery would be necessary to replace the valve.

Driving back to my church office with this possibility weighing heavily on me, I tried to remain calm, but my emotions somersaulted. "Why, God? What about wHispers—the ministry You gave me! What now?"

It was late afternoon when I returned to work, but unable to concentrate, I went to a nearby beach. I was glad Stefan was busy elsewhere because I needed to be alone with God. Breakwater Beach was deserted except for a few sea gulls, and it was low tide. Walking out on the ocean's bottom for almost an hour, I side-stepped tidal pools and occasional scurrying hermit crabs. I just walked and tried not to think, but when I returned to shore, I let God have it!

Sitting there in the sand, I complained. I wept and told God how disappointed I was—not so much afraid, but not ready to face yet another medical challenge. And as if God didn't hear me the first time, I cried out again "Why, God? I've worked so hard on this precious ministry and I finally have everyone in place—even a starting date! Why would You permit something to interfere? Father, You've given me a passion to help women and I want them to know You—Your love, grace, mercy, and faithfulness."

My tears and questions continued until finally I was exhausted and still. It was then God whispered again and this was one of His sweetest! *I still walk on water.* Instinctively, I looked out across the bay as if I might see Jesus. I didn't, but He continued to whisper, *Shirley, whatever waters come your way, I'll be walking on them.* And of course, I did what I do best when God reveals Himself in such a unique manner—I wept, but these were tears of joy.

Then I sat in silence, hardly believing what had just happened. Jesus had shown me in a very intimate way how much He loves me and cares about every detail of my life. My situation hadn't changed, but the frustration was gone. With all my heart I knew Jesus was walking with me and no matter how rough the waters became, He wouldn't let me sink in self-despair. He was my lifeline!

A quote from Donna Wallis describes my experience with Jesus at Breakwater Beach:

Sometimes God calms the storm, and sometimes he lets the storm rage and He calms His child.

I was reluctant to leave, but also eager to re-read Matthew 14:28-33 about how Jesus walked on water to his panic-stricken disciples in a boat on a stormy sea:

144

"Lord, if it is you, command me to come to you on the water." He said, "Come." So Peter got out of the boat, started walking on the water, and came toward Jesus. But when he noticed the strong wind, he became frightened, and beginning to sink, he cried out, "Lord, save me!" Jesus immediately reached out his hand and caught him, saying to him. "You of little faith, why did you doubt?" When they got into the boat, the wind ceased. And those in the boat worshiped him, saying, "Truly you are the Son of God."

Peter asked for a "whatever" and then he flip-flopped in the middle of it—not very different from us, is he? I was learning at a deeper level that sudden storms in my life can't overwhelm me unless I take my eyes from Jesus. When I focus on Him, the waves take second place to the calm reassurance I have in the Lord.

The Potter

Sunday arrived and I was determined at worship to focus on the Lord and not on the procedures scheduled for that afternoon or the possibility of more heart surgery. This proved difficult as we sang "We are an offering—all that I am, all that I have, all that I hope to be, I give it all to You," and I thought, *Yes God, that's what I want to do—just serve You.* Another song was, "Change My Heart, O God" and I silently prayed, *Oh God, please change it—heal it—heal me.* And with a sermon titled, "The Soil of Our Hearts," I had trouble forgetting my challenges.

Driving home I remembered an article about the Potter that I had never taken time to read. Based on Jeremiah 18:1-4, I'm convinced God brought it to mind because He knew I needed the reassurance of that particular Scripture:

The word that came to Jeremiah from the Lord: "Come, go down to the potter's house, and there I will let you hear my words." So I went down to the potter's house, and there he was working at his wheel. The vessel he was making of clay was spoiled in the potter's hand, and he reworked it into another vessel, as seemed good to him.

God was using my medical problems to *rework* me as it *seemed good to Him.* By medical definition God had not created my heart perfectly, but I know the full meaning of JOY because of an imperfect heart! The physical flaws led to open heart surgery which resulted in my "whatever" prayer.

I believe that God, who makes no mistakes, made my heart perfectly in accordance with His plans for my life. Psalm 139:13-16a says:

> For it was you who formed my inward parts; you knit me together in my mother's womb. I praise you, for I am fearfully and wonderfully made. Wonderful are your works; that I know very well. My frame was not hidden from you, when I was being made in secret…Your eyes beheld my unformed substance.

Jeremiah's words took me back to one of my first lessons on a potter's wheel: stay focused on the project, hands and eyes always engaged. It was a reminder I needed desperately at that moment. No matter the outcome, God—my Potter—would never take His loving eyes or grace-filled hands off of me. He never had and He never would.

Only a few hours later, I lost that focus as I walked into the radiology department feeling physically exhausted and emotionally drained. As the technician explained the procedure, I didn't think I had the strength to lie in the MRI "tube" for almost an hour, and not move at all for up to 7 minutes at a time. That may sound easy, but it would take more concentration than I thought I had at that time. Remembering the extremely loud banging and knocking of sound waves in previous MRIs, I wanted to leave. My head was the focal point and so earphones with music to cut the noise were not permitted. The only thing greater than my weariness, was my determination and assurance that I could do this in God's strength. Jesus was walking on these waves with me!

With a history of claustrophobia, I closed my eyes before being moved into the "tube" so I could pretend I was anywhere but there. As wedges were put in place to remind me not to move my head, I focused on the promise of Isaiah 26:3 (NIV): "You will keep in perfect peace him whose mind is steadfast, because he trusts in you."

That promise, and remembering that my Potter was using this event to remold me for reasons only He knew, helped me relax. Confident that God knew exactly where I was, I pictured myself lying in His protective hands and gradually I was so much at peace that, despite the racket, I almost fell asleep.

Test results showed no further stroke damage, but there was a difference of opinion between my cardiologist, who said he'd see me in six months, and my primary care doctor, who was not content to disregard the symptoms. He insisted on a second opinion and referred me to a cardiologist in Boston, but the first available appointment was two months away.

I wondered if God was permitting these challenges to help me redefine my boundaries. What did God want me to do about Caring Ministries and "wHispers," and what about my book manuscript? I enjoy writing and especially documenting the marvelous things God has done and is doing in my life.

Gradually, the wHispers ministry was becoming a reality as I sought and received advice and encouragement from Christian leaders of a similar program. Praying for direction about who to ask to serve through wHispers, God led me to ask women who were attending our church, but not yet serving, and that describes the majority of the women who eagerly responded. They not only would enjoy their new roles, but would grow closer to the Lord and each other as they demonstrated love for God in practical ways.

Our goal was to nurture and encourage the women of our church and surrounding communities with the love of Christ so that together we could find strength and courage for our journeys, and empowerment to share God's love, grace, and faithfulness with each other and with women who did not yet have a personal relationship with Jesus. We hoped to encourage love, respect, and unity with Christian women of all ages, all churches, and from diverse backgrounds. With God's help this came true.

Whispers from *Your* Heart

*When I bared my feelings and "let God have it," how did I feel?

*Why do I believe that God loves me enough for me to be "real" with Him?

*How has God reworked me as it "seemed good to Him?"

*How did I respond and how has it impacted my life?

Chapter 8

"wHispers" Becomes
a Reality!

*"O Lord, you are my God; I will exalt you and praise your name,
for in perfect faithfulness you have done marvelous things,
things planned long ago."*

—Isaiah 25:1(NIV)

AT OUR FIRST gathering there were ninety-five women representing nine denominations, twelve churches, and eight towns. Having prayed for God to touch the hearts of the women He wanted there, it was exciting to see the faces of those who would be blessed that evening. Many of them carried heavy burdens—working both in and out of the home, these women also assumed responsibility for meeting the needs of their extended families.

Wanting to pamper these women, our tables are always tastefully decorated with cloth table covers, candles, fresh flowers, and favors appropriate to the evening's theme. A special dessert and fellowship time is followed by devotional thoughts, special music, and an experienced and gifted inspirational speaker.

The gals are invited to leave their busy lives at the door along with any specific ways they worship God in their own churches, and for ninety minutes we fellowship and worship as sisters in Christ. (I like to think that "denomination" isn't even in God's dictionary!)

Instead of door prizes we have "grace gifts," which provide an opportunity to explain how God gifts us—or we could say graces us—with eternal life through Jesus Christ, and that we could never do enough to earn or deserve this. God's love is simply ours to receive. What are usually called "door prizes" we call "grace gifts" because, like God's gift of love to us, we have freely received gifts from friends and businesses in our communities which we pass on to them as reflections of God's unconditional love.

As these meetings continue, more than 200 women have requested prayer for spiritual direction by using our registration cards. To meet that need, we have twelve "Whisperers"—women who do not attend wHispers events due to reasons of age, health, or distance. Their prayers for the women as well as for our gatherings are vital to our ministry. Women leaders are available to meet with those who have questions regarding spiritual growth, and we also have Bible, CD, tape, and small group ministries to help them.

One of the gratifying aspects of wHispers is our demographics. We have welcomed as many as one hundred forty women who overall represent at least sixteen denominations, thirty two churches, and sixteen towns.

We have annual spiritual retreats at which numerous women have given their lives to Jesus, and Discovery Day Mystery Trips which are days of fun and fellowship for exploring new places and relationships.

We're grateful to God for whispering this ministry into place, and for the privilege of serving our sisters in Christ—especially women who do not yet have an intimate relationship with Jesus. It's gratifying to experience the joy and enthusiasm of women who desire to know the Lord better and also to fellowship with and support women from many backgrounds. Here are just a few comments taken from some of our registration cards:

"I look forward to these evenings of joyous renewal!"
"A lovely generous welcoming spiritual experience."
"These are beautiful events in my life. Thank God for all of you."
"Your programs are a blessing!"
"Wonderful. A great place to come. May God bless you."
"Thank you for this ministry!!! I'm grateful for the Lord's love."

Transition

After our first wHispers, God showed me in five different ways that I was to give Caring Ministries to church leadership so that others could be put in place to meet those needs. I was to focus on "wHispers."

Accepting an opportunity to tell our church that I would be stepping down from Caring Ministries, God gave me a message of glorifying

Him for what He had done! I explained my "whatever" prayer and how God had empowered me to recognize needs and establish ministries to address them.

I shared how God had given me "wHispers" and was now asking me to pass Caring Ministries on to others. Even as I spoke, it was difficult to imagine my life without these ministries which had dominated my life for eight years. I told the church how, on the day I gave Pastor Mary my resignation, a devotional for that morning was centered on Ecclesiastes 3:1, "To everything there is a season, a time for every purpose under heaven." That's confirmation!

Thanking my church for their prayers, I invited them as I now challenge you, reader, to offer a "whatever" prayer. God will hear you and I hope He asks you to do something you know you cannot possibly do on your own—something for which you too have to trust the Lord for direction and empowerment—something so special that you see one of God's dreams come true, simply because you obeyed.

Whispers from *Your* Heart

*When I'm hurting and confused about where God is in my heartache, how should I pray?

*When I was afraid, I knew Jesus was walking with me because:

*Here are three reasons why I love being the clay in my Potter's hands.

*How will I respond if God asks me to help make one of His dreams come true? Has He already asked? If so, how did I answer?

Chapter 9

A New Season

"He put a new song in my mouth, a song of praise to our God. Many will see and fear and put their trust in the Lord."

—Psalm 40:3

I'M GRATEFUL THAT our awesome Creator and Almighty God heard my "whatever" prayer, because He has used the "whatevers" to help me know Him better, and to love and trust Him more. I feel privileged that He chose to use me just as I was—inexperienced and without leadership training. And, if He can use me, He can use you.

In *Elijah, A Man Like Us,* Roper expresses his amazement over what God can do through us in His strength.

> God surrounds Himself with incompetents...It's not that he has to make do with a bunch of fools. He chooses them.[22]

I love being one of God's "incompetents," and I'm just "fool" enough to keep saying my "whatever" prayer because it's so exciting to see what the Lord will do next.

God wants to partner with us in His work, but sometimes we feel we're not worthy, or we're afraid, and so we do nothing. Being humble is not about self-degradation. It's about knowing that God can and wants to use all of us. I've heard humility defined as "letting God be God" and acknowledging our dependence upon Him. Being humble is about attitude.

I love this quote by Winston Churchill: "We are all worms, but I do believe I am a glowworm." I think all committed Christians are "glow worms" of the finest order! We can light up this world simply by reflecting the love and grace of Jesus to those God puts in our lives, and by letting God fulfill His plan for us.

God's Big Heart

When God asks what seems impossible and we have questions or fears, we can trust the Holy Spirit who lives in us to help, strengthen, guide, and empower us. We have a patient Father to whom we can go time after time, never having to worry that He'll complain, *Oh no—there's Shirley again! Won't she ever get it?*

When Jimmy was in first grade, the mother of a classmate called to say that her little boy no longer wanted to go to school. I had no problem with Jimmy, but one morning after we hugged and kissed good-by, Jimmy got to the end of the sidewalk, slowly turned, and came back. I expected that he also wanted to stay home, but instead, Jimmy said, "Can I have just one more?" Perhaps he was hesitant to leave, but he only asked for reassurance of my love before he did what he knew was expected of him.

Many years later, just after we moved to Cape Cod, Jim visited us for a few days and when he left, he hugged me and waved as he drove away. Then he came back, walked up the sidewalk, and said, "Can I have just one more?"

That's how God is with us. When we ask our Father for just one more blessing...will You help me do this...will You show me again how much You love me...He embraces us. God's love is greater than we can ever imagine and it's unconditional—not because we deserve it, but because of His grace and mercy!

God accepts our humble gifts of self and molds us into someone more and more like Himself. We can trust Him even when we don't have a clue about what He's doing. God will replace our fears with confidence, and transform our self-doubts into an overwhelming passion to trust and serve Him. And He'll reward our efforts with a deeper faith to keep on trusting Him, no matter how He chooses to stretch us.

Do you know there are "whatevers" in the Bible? Here's just one! In John 2:5 we read about a "whatever." It's the first miracle of Jesus. At a wedding in Cana the hosts ran out of wine. Jesus' mother, Mary, tells the servants, "Do *whatever* He tells you." (italics mine) Jesus asked the servants to bring Him water, and I think the servants must have wondered (as we would), *what good is this going to do?* But Jesus turned the water into a superior wine!

Jesus turned the ordinary into the extraordinary! He still does—and that's what He wants to do with all of us. When we do *with* God what He asks us to do, not only do we get it done, we do it Big Time! I repeat what Paul says in Ephesians 3:20 (TLB):

> Glory be to God who by His mighty power at work within us, is able to do far more than we would ever dare to ask or even dream of, infinitely beyond our highest desires, thoughts, or hopes.

Reader, are you trusting the Lord and listening for His voice? I hope so because God has something He wants to say *only to you,* but until you pay attention only God knows what that is. In His perfect timing, I hope the Lord gives you a "whatever" that will put you on the knees of your heart where you can hear Him. There's no better place to be!

The following quotation from Brother Lawrence describes my "whatever" experiences:

> I decided to sacrifice my life with all its pleasures to God. But He greatly disappointed me in this idea, for I have met with nothing but satisfaction in giving my life over to Him.[23]

Whispers from *Your* Heart

*Am I a "glow worm?" How do I reflect Jesus to those around me?

*How can I find courage to share Jesus with my family and friends who don't know Him?

*When I ran ahead of God, why was I sorry that I didn't wait for His timing?

*Do I have the courage to give myself to God for "whatever?" Why or why not?

Part Three

Strings

"I served the Lord with great humility and with tears, although I was severely tested."

—The Apostle Paul in Acts 20:19

"We develop what Thomas a Kempis calls a 'familiar friendship with Jesus.' Our unseen Friend becomes dearer, closer, and more wonderful every day until at last we know Him as 'Jesus, lover of my soul,' not only in song, but in blissful experience. Doubts vanish; we are more sure of Him being with us than of anybody else... It becomes easy to tell others about Christ because our minds are flooded with Him. 'Out of the fullness of the heart, the mouth speaks.'"[24]

—Frank Laubach

Chapter 1

Change My Heart?

"He put a new song in my mouth, a song of praise to our God. Many will see and fear, and put their trust in God."

—Psalm 40:13

WINTER ON CAPE Cod had been unusually mild, and on a crisp sunny February day I walked briskly as I did almost every day to keep fit. The weather was calm, but within me a storm was brewing because I knew God was more concerned with the condition of my spiritual heart than my physical well-being.

Through my Walkman, Roby Duke sang, "Change my heart, O God," one of my favorite praise choruses, using a theme God had used repeatedly to get my attention. The clay… me. The Potter… God. Change *my* heart? It was my prayer, but did I mean it? I was unsure and ashamed.

My heart ached as I struggled to love God more than my selfish desires. When I walked close and trusted Him, I knew the true meaning of joy. When I distanced myself and tried to design my own happiness, life was often confusing and even chaotic.

I thought of a college pottery class I enjoyed in my forties when I enrolled at SUNY Buffalo and earned a BS in Human and Community Services. I became adept at the wheel, but only after learning how to center a lump of clay and apply just the right amount of pressure equally on all sides. Until I mastered that, the clay repeatedly spun off to the floor, picking up dust and dirt. *So much like me,* I thought, *when I don't obey God's rules.*

God's commandments are clear and either I choose to live by them or I don't. God knows exactly how and when to remind me of His standards and my response demonstrates the depth of my love for Him. Or how superficial it is!

God knows I love Him, but the question He whispered that day was, *Shirley, do you love Me most? Turn your entire life over to me; your desires, hopes, weaknesses, strengths, temptations, heartaches, failures, successes, dreams, plans, fears, likes, dislikes—ALL that makes you My precious and unique child! Just trust Me with what is already Mine. You won't be sorry.*

Reading about Moses and David, I rationalized that if great God-fearing men like them could be afraid, could sin…but God wasn't buying my feeble attempt to distract Him from my own weaknesses.

Shirley, don't look at others. Look inside yourself. Do you love Me enough to trust Me with your ministry, your hopes for the future, your life—with everything that is you?

Although heart surgery was life threatening, and the "whatevers" intensely challenging, this time I felt stretched to the extreme. The Lord wasn't asking me to trust Him for health or ministry, but God was saying *I want ALL of you. No questions allowed. No answers given!*

"Okay, Father," I whispered, tears running down my cheeks. "I want to love You as You love me. I give You me—no strings attached!" But even as I promised, I knew I couldn't do it alone and it didn't seem right to rely on God to help me love and trust Him. "God, I should be able to do this on my own."

My precious child, no! I want you to need and trust Me; I want to help you. Take My hand and let Me teach you My ways. Let Me melt you and mold you.

"Oh, Father, you know that's one of my favorite songs!"

The next morning in my small group I shared my promise to God, and my friend Patti responded immediately, "No, Shirley! There will always be strings, but God will say, 'This is the string we'll work on today.'"

Patti was right. I was finally taking an in-depth look at my life and realizing that I'm not a puppet in God's hands, but His creation with a mind to recognize and understand His tugs at my "strings." Usually God's touch is gentle and all the direction I need, but sometimes my self absorption needs a firm jerk before I re-focus on the Lord.

I had promised God all of me, no strings attached, and He would show me that strings are very real fibers of character that interfere with our spiritual growth and loving God most! I would learn that some strings are more aptly called "hawsers," large diameter ropes used for towing or mooring a ship. As I struggled with mine—some knotted tightly in stubbornness—I would find them not easily destroyed.

To Know God Better

Time alone with God first thing each morning had become a priority and it set the mood for my days. I wanted to know my Creator better, to enjoy intimacy with Him unlike any other. Through prayer, Scripture and devotional readings, I was drawing closer to the Lord, listening more intently for His whispers, and trying harder to live according to His teachings. I was finally getting a handle on how vast the Lord's love and grace are. At first, my devotional time was only an hour, but then I was astonished at how quickly two or even three hours passed.

When I was still running Caring Ministries, there was often a Scripture or devotional that I thought would be helpful for someone who was hurting, and soon I had an email ministry that demanded even more time. I wasn't good at ignoring what I considered "God-whispers," and this added to the busyness of those days already dominated by capital campaigns and Caring Ministries.

As God put others in my life with theological understanding well beyond my own, I became a human sponge! I couldn't get enough and I had trouble walking away from any book that showed promise of helping me to know God better. Soon I had purchased more volumes than I had time to read.

A friend suggested two daily devotional books that explain Scripture and theology in ways I could understand and apply to my life. Along with the Holy Spirit, Oswald Chambers (*My Utmost for His Highest*) and Henry and Richard Blackaby (*Experiencing God Day by Day*) guided me to a better understanding of God's Word.

As time went on, God often led me to a particular Scripture or motivated me to pick up a book that I had walked past for months—even years; or a book I had started and then for some reason put aside for another time. Remarkably, where I had stopped reading earlier was often exactly what I needed that day to answer a question or help me deal with a current situation. I recognize God's hand and I'm still amazed by and will never take for granted God's personal provision and the depth of His caring. Clearly, my search for greater intimacy with God was not one-sided!

The more I've come to know God and recognize His goodness, the more I smile, but I wasn't aware of this until others began saying that I always look happy. I've found that true joy just happens when I feel God's presence and know His love, grace, and favor.

I had never worked harder or slept less, but I was doing what I believed God wanted me to do at that point in my life and it felt good. So good that it was easy to look away from the extent to which my ministry and studying were interfering with my life at home.

Late one afternoon Stefan asked, "Shirley do you think you could clear off just one flat surface in this house so we can eat dinner?" The kitchen table and counter, as well as the dining room table were covered with one project or another. I did as he asked and promised my patient husband I'd try to do better.

The next day, the Scripture on my desk calendar was Ecclesiastes 3:1, 5: "There is a time for every activity under heaven…a time to scatter stones and a time to gather them."

I couldn't resist sharing that with Stefan, and especially Chuck Swindoll's comment regarding it:

> Not many really creative people—in the process of creating—keep everything neat, picked up, and in its place.[25]

Stefan laughed and his love was clear in his continuing support, but my intentions were short-lived. As ministry and study continued to occupy a major part of my life, I had a new string to deal with. I needed to establish boundaries, but it was difficult to untie myself from the demands of growing responsibilities and my passion to know God better.

Then a friend recommended Charles Swindoll's new "Profiles in Character" book series and I purchased all eight of them. *Moses* and *David* became "textbooks" for me as Swindoll explained truths about the Old Testament prophets and lessons that I had never learned. It took me several months to get through each of them as I searched related Scriptures and took notes. Up to that point my Bible reading consisted mostly of the New Testament, the Psalms, and Proverbs. I came to love and know books of the Bible I had previously avoided, thinking they were better suited to pastors and Bible scholars.

I learned that Abraham, Moses, David, Jeremiah, and other paragons of faith had experienced fears and inadequacies similar to mine, but still God used them in significant ways. In particular, I could relate to the "whatevers" of Moses and Jeremiah; to their questions and doubts about their ability to speak effectively! I was in good company! God had blessed them and He was transforming my strings of fear and inadequacy into a greater faith. I delighted in a calm assurance of God's power, and my curiosity about what else God might have in mind evolved into an even deeper commitment to live my life according to His plan.

To Know Jesus Better

In the spring of 2000, I was disheartened to find I had a new string needing attention. Each time we celebrated the Lord's Supper, it seemed something was missing for me. Why wasn't my Savior's immense sacrifice more heart-wrenching; why didn't His cruel suffering and death impact me at a deeper level? I began praying for a more heart-felt understanding of the Jesus I accepted as Savior in my teen years, having made that declaration with whatever understanding and faith I had at that time.

My childhood home in East Palmyra, NY was at the end of a lane which began at the Christian Reformed Church, to which we walked twice every Sunday for worship and Sunday school. On Saturdays, my brothers and I attended Heidelberg Catechism classes. Our Christian faith wasn't discussed very much at home, but the foundation of my parents' lives was obedience to the laws of God and they made certain we knew them at a very young age.

My father always thanked God before our meals and afterward read a devotional and prayed again. We also prayed at bedtime and one of my favorite childhood memories is seeing my six foot father kneeling in prayer, his head covered with the bed sheet to keep out distractions. Mostly, my parents left spiritual training to our pastor and Sunday school teachers and I never thought to question what I was taught. Confirmation of my faith was expected and I was happy doing that.

Although our church did not permit dancing, my parents allowed me to learn in high school gym classes. Attending movies was also unacceptable; my first was "Ivanhoe" as a high school senior and by the time I celebrated my sixtieth birthday, I probably had seen about forty movies. With the exception of some quality films (a favorite is *Shadowlands*), they hold little fascination for me. With so much sadness and despair in life, I have no interest in using precious hours to view fictional accounts of violence, extramarital affairs, etc. And I could care less about fantasy! That makes me smile because many say the story of Jesus is too supernatural to believe, yet I have no trouble accepting the miracle that we call Jesus!

Now, many years later, I was asking Jesus to help me better understand the immensity of His sacrifice. The summer months passed and when fall arrived, communion still didn't hold more relevance for me. So with advent approaching, I asked God not only for a better understanding of the death of Jesus, but also His birth.

A few weeks later, at the Women's Christmas Communion Service, we sang, "A Communion Hymn for Christmas." The words caught my attention and as the service continued I made a mental note to study them at another time. Three days later, on Saturday, December 16, 2000, I went to the piano and sang the song God would use to change my life. One line celebrates the birth of Jesus and the next grieves His death, and this pattern is repeated throughout the song. For example:

Gathered 'round Your table on this holy eve,
Viewing Bethl'hem's stable we rejoice and grieve.
Joy to see You lying in Your manger bed;
Weep to see You dying in our sinful stead.
Prince of Glory, gracing heav'n ere time began,
Now for us embracing death as Son of Man.
By Your birth so lowly, by Your love so true,
By Your cross most holy, Lord, we worship You![26]

The meshing of the birth and death of Jesus was exactly what I needed. My heart rejoiced with Mary over the birth of her Christ Child. I grieved as never before for the suffering and death of Jesus in my place. I delighted with those who celebrated our Lord's resurrection, and then I melted in grateful tears because through a song, God had explained Jesus to me! My Savior was more alive for me at that moment than ever before. Never had I known such joy!

In reflection, what touched my heart most was not the words of the song, but again God's personal answer to my prayers. I had prayed to know Jesus better and the meshing of the birth and death of Jesus in the words of that song was exactly what God knew I needed.

I learned my experience could be called an epiphany which is defined in Webster's as, "a moment of sudden intuitive understanding; flash of insight."

When I explained excitedly to Stefan what had happened, he asked, "Shirley, are you going to ascend?" Then laughing, he winked and added, "I don't understand what you're experiencing, but I'm very happy for you."

New Understanding of Childhood Truths

I can't remember not knowing who Jesus is and although I had accepted Him as my Savior, I never knew the defining moment of great excitement or joy that many Christians describe. My love for God had grown gradually, but this was such a powerful experience I thought *this must be how people feel when they say they're "born again!"*

All my life I had gone to worship services; faithful in singing songs of praise, saying my prayers, attending worship and Sunday school, and memorizing Scripture, creeds, and commandments. I was a good girl who did what was expected, but I didn't fully comprehend the significance or power of the precious words of Scripture and the old hymns of faith.

Although sincere, I didn't know how to have a personal relationship with God. Undoubtedly, my Bible teachers walked close to the Lord, but I wasn't shown how to do that in a way I could understand. I also didn't realize how much God desires intimacy with me—with all of His children. James 4:5 says, "God yearns jealously for the spirit that he has made to dwell in us."

I've heard Joyce Meyer say that just as sitting in a garage doesn't make us a car; going to church doesn't make us a Christian. Faithful church attendance and superficial worship didn't make me a growing, vital Christian who yearned to love God more. When I finally understood, I wonder if God breathed a sigh of relief. *Finally, My precious little East Pal gal—now you've got it!*

With God's help in untangling my strings of confusion and ignorance, I became passionate to love Jesus in a greater way and to interact with Him more constantly.

My understanding of God as Triune—God in three persons—Father, Son, and Holy Spirit—was also limited and I had no idea how precious each person of the Trinity would become to me.

I was comfortable praying to God the Father because that was what I had done all my life. At worship we celebrated Jesus as Savior and recognized the Holy Spirit, but I don't remember ever hearing anyone pray to Jesus or the Holy Spirit—not until I heard Hector Cortez's prayer that I mentioned earlier. I wanted to know the Holy Spirit as Hector did and as my friend, Carol, had expressed—to love the Holy Spirit so much! God was about to nurture the seeds my friends had planted.

Praying and searching to know the Holy Spirit more intimately, I was especially moved by John 13:33 where Jesus tenderly addresses His beloved disciples as "little children" and prepares them for His return to the Father.

"Little children, I am with you only a little longer…Where I am going, you cannot come."

165

And in John 14:18-19, 25-27:

"I will not leave you orphaned: I am coming to you. In a little while the world will no longer see me, but you will see me; because I live, you also will live…I have said these things to you while I am still with you. But the Advocate, the Holy Spirit, whom the Father will send in my name will teach you everything, and remind you of all that I have said to you. Peace I leave with you…Do not let your hearts be troubled, and do not let them be afraid."

I embraced a new passion to learn about the Holy Spirit's activity in the life of Jesus even in His virgin birth. In Luke 1:35 we read:

The angel said to (Mary), "The Holy Spirit will come upon you, and the Power of the Most High will overshadow you; therefore the child to be born will be holy; he will be called the Son of God."

And in Matthew 3:16, about the baptism of Jesus:

And when Jesus had been baptized, just as he came up from the water, suddenly the heavens were opened to him and he saw the Spirit of God descending like a dove and alighting upon Him.

How marvelous to learn that the Spirit Jesus trusted in His divine humanity, is the same Holy Spirit who wants to live in and help all of us to know Jesus better. And for all of us who have accepted Jesus as our Savior, Jesus is also our brother—we share the same Heavenly Father!

I accepted an invitation to be part of a small group that would study *Devotional Classics* edited by Richard J. Foster and James Bryan Smith, and use *A Spiritual Formation Workbook* by James Bryan Smith with Lynda L. Graybeal. At the end of the sessions we each chose one exercise on which to focus for the next week. The most meaningful one for me was inviting the Holy Spirit to read the Word with me; to bring to my attention a particular verse or word and help me reflect on why that verse or word was significant; what lesson I needed to learn. When I do this, familiar Scriptures suddenly have new meaning and so I continue to invite the Holy Spirit into my study and life situations.

A Grace-full Incarnation

Several days after my spiritual epiphany, I received a Christmas greeting that affirmed my communion experience.

Change My Heart?

> This year when you gaze in wonder at the miracle in the manger, see behind it an old rugged cross, and surrounding it all an empty tomb.

The joy, tenderness, and promise of the manger became even more intertwined with the grace-filled love and painful sacrifice of the cross. As a result, I began to know in my heart and not just my brain, the magnificent hope that is ours in a resurrected Jesus who lives within us if only we open our hearts to Him.

I asked friend and artist Fran Geberth to draw the Christmas greeting for me, and the resulting sketch is exquisite. "A Grace-full Incarnation" ties together the birth, death, and resurrection of Jesus in a unique way that further clarifies my understanding. Never again will I see the manger apart from the shadow of the cross under which our Savior was born.

In the radiant light that emanates from the empty tomb, a cross is suspended which indicates the ascension of Jesus to His throne until He comes again. But there's more. The shadow of the cross falls across the manger in front of it, and that deeply touches me. Jesus who was born in the shadow of a cross, would later willingly lower his bleeding and lacerated spine to the hardness of a cruel cross, the likes of which we will never know. Our Lord modeled a life of perfect submission to His Father even to the point of dying an excruciating death for us.

Now when I celebrate Holy Communion, I visualize Jesus standing in front of me holding the elements out to me. I picture Him showing me the nailprints in His hands and side, and then pointing to the crown of thorns piercing His brow. In my heart I hear Him say, *Shirley, I did this for you, you are forgiven, you are Mine, go now in peace to love and serve Me.*

The bread remains bread and the juice the same, but in some mystical way I experience a union with Christ that causes me to grow in His grace. I have a greater heartfelt love and tearful appreciation for Jesus who made Himself the sacrificial lamb. Holy Communion is not just a ritual for me, but a precious interactive remembrance and recognition of the most costly sacrifice and love gift of Jesus for all of us.

When I think of my sins and consider those of everyone who ever lived, I can't begin to grasp how immense the Father's love is; how extensive the grace of Jesus, and how powerful the Holy Spirit! This has brought me to a place where, instead of describing my negative behavior in such benign terms as a mistake, slip-up, or shortcoming, I call it what it is—sin! I own my disregard of Jesus and His sacrifice and that is more and more convicting for me.

When I realize how frequently I'm on the receiving end of the Lord's amazing grace, I weep. Tears! All my life I rarely cried, always thinking I had to be strong for those around me; my parents, who worked hard and did without personal things in order to provide for my brothers and me, my first husband, who suffered deeply when his mother died, my children because that's how moms are, my patients, and so on.

Experiencing the immensity of God's love during corporate worship or while meditating before Holy Communion can bring tears of humility and joy; but my most intense times of intimacy are when I'm alone with God. That's when I can truly worship.

Most precious is when God unexpectedly graces me with a whisper, mind image, or a very specific and direct answer to prayer. I'm totally awestruck over how much He loves me and grateful beyond words for His amazing patience; for gracing me with ministry despite my sins!

Tears of Joy

At first my tears embarrassed me, but now I realize they are part of God's unique gift to me; symbolic of my growing deeper in love with the Lord. As I experience the Holy Spirit in new ways, my heart cries.

In *Prayer*, Richard Foster devotes a chapter to "The Prayer of Tears." He says:

> *Penthos* is the Greek word for it...It sounds a bit depressing, at least to those of us who have been raised on a religion of good feelings and prosperity. The old writers...saw it as a gift to be sought after...deep joy.[27]

> Through the Prayer of Tears we give God permission to show us our sinfulness and the sinfulness of the world at the emotional level. As best I can discern, tears are God's way of helping us descend with the mind into the heart and there bow in perpetual adoration and worship.[28]

My tears of "deep joy" occur most often when I'm in close proximity to God, inviting Him into my experience of that moment; a time of focused worship, adoration, and repentance. As I write this book or other material, I trust the Holy Spirit for His thoughts and words; to help me know what to include and what to leave out. When I write or say something I know is not my own, I am in awe of the Holy Spirit's presence and His power to help me accomplish God's plan for my life.

168

Change My Heart?

This is a margin note I made in my copy of *Prayer*:

The Holy Spirit has become so precious to me. When I'm alone with God, especially in the mornings, when I kneel to pray and call God by name; Father, Son, or especially Holy Spirit, I weep; overjoyed to be in His presence, to know without a doubt that He's there—in and around me. I'm awed and overwhelmed by how much God loves me—no strings attached!

No strings attached! Unconditional Love! That's how God loves us—and that's how God wants us to love Him! I asked God to change my heart and He's doing that. He wants to make all of us more like Himself and this is a life-long process.

Whispers from Your Heart

How can I know Jesus better and love Him more?

Time alone with God is crucial to knowing God better and loving Him more. How can I make certain this takes first place in my life?

What "string(s)" do I need to focus on?

* Do I love Jesus enough to trust my life to Him? ALL of me—no strings attached?*

Chapter 2

Regrets and Complaints

"A cheerful heart is good medicine, but a downcast spirit dries up the bones."

—Proverbs 17:22

A FRIEND IN my prayer group gave me a copy of Bruce Wilkinson's, *The Prayer of Jabez*. I didn't have a clue who Jabez was, but I was curious about the now famous prayer attributed to him in 1 Chronicles 4:9-10 (NKJV) and surprised to find that the essence of Jabez's prayer was what I had asked God for Caring Ministries!

> Oh, that You would bless me indeed, and enlarge my territory, that Your hand would be with me, and that You would keep me from evil, that I may not cause pain![29]

I smiled as I connected these words of Wilkinson to God's work in my life:

> Your Father longs to give you so much more than you may have ever thought to ask for...when was the last time God worked through you in such a way that you knew beyond doubt that God had done it?[30]

And then I laughed aloud!

> When in faith, you start to pray for more ministry, amazing things occur. As your opportunities expand, your ability and resources supernaturally increase too. Right away you'll sense the pleasure God feels in your request and His urgency to accomplish great things through you.[31]

Amen! God was blessing me and Caring Ministries to the point that I reverently suggested, "Maybe You could ease off a bit until I catch up!" But that wasn't about to happen. As our church grew, God showed me how to develop even more ministries to address the increasing number and variety of needs of a growing congregation. Compared to any nursing position in my life, volunteering 40-60 hours a week in ministry was more intense, but I enjoyed it so much more.

Reflecting on all God had done and was doing, I marveled that He had chosen to work through me. So often I still felt like that little East Pal gal! *God,* I wondered, *are You using me to prove that if You can use me, You can use anyone?* I didn't know where the Lord was taking me, but I was certain He knew, and my growing faith in Him was a divinely stabilizing force in my life.

Although my days began early and I rarely went to sleep before 10:30 P.M., there never seemed to be enough time for fund raising, caring ministries, and physical exercise. There was little time for housekeeping and not enough time with Stefan, or to visit our children—all of whom lived at a distance. My excessive passion for ministry and my unquenchable thirst to know God better had become a hawser that interfered with my life and Stefan's. I knew I should deal with it, but I didn't know how or where to cut back and so I tied a knot and held on! Gratefully, Stefan held on with me!

God continued to encourage and empower me. I only had to ask, and I did—not because God wouldn't remember, but because I needed to feel close to Him. A prayer in my journal from that time is:

> Oh God, help me walk so close to You that I recognize and understand Your very touch; I don't want to miss opportunities to serve You. And if they scare me, help me trust You again and again for courage and strength to obey.

But as I fell more in love with the Lord, I had yet another string to deal with. I began faulting Him!

> God, why didn't You draw me closer to You when I was young? Why didn't You let me go to Calvin College as I wanted to? I would've had a wonderful Christian education and my years of serving You could have been more significant. Why did You wait until now to give me this passion to know You better?

These questions were reminiscent of my discontent when my father died suddenly at fifty-nine. It was only after working through my grief that I finally found some resolution. I had not questioned God's gift of a loving father, so how could I fault God's permitting my dad to die earlier than I wanted or expected?

Although my new complaints were different, the underlying problem was the same—self-focus and forgetting that God never makes mistakes. Agonizing over life choices and grieving over what might have been, I was angry with God for allowing me to make decisions that now seemed wrong.

God's answer was clear: *Shirley, if you continue to center on your regrets, you cannot soar with Me!* I couldn't fully participate in God's plan for my life as long as I was reaching back and stumbling over myself! I purchased and displayed in a strategic place a small print that says, "Don't trip over the things behind you."

I was determined to follow Paul's example in Philippians 3:13, 14:

Beloved, I do not consider that I have made it on my own; but this one thing I do: forgetting what lies behind and straining forward to what lies ahead, I press on.

All that I was learning about God was precious to me and the more I knew, the more I understood. The more I discovered, the more I loved the Lord. The more I adored Him, the more I wanted to obey Him. The more I tried to live as Jesus lived, the more I was aware of my failures. The more I could identify my sins for what they were, the more miserable I was in my grief and guilt, until I finally understood at a deeper level how immeasurable are Jesus' love and grace!

I needed to center God in all of my life; mind, heart, soul, thoughts, words, love, and actions. I had a long way to go, but I was on the right track. I wrote in my journal, "Dear God, Help me not to miss the blessings of today and the promises of tomorrow by letting regrets blur my vision of You."

Walking with God

We vacationed with family at Black Butte Ranch in the Cascade Mountains of Oregon where stately Ponderosa Pines, some blackened by fire, surrounded our vacation home. Steve, our son-in-law, explained that in order for these trees to propagate, the officials allow periodic supervised controlled fires.

I found this explanation analogous to our relationship with God. We grow closer to God when He permits flames of pain, loss, fear, and devastation to threaten our lives because it's then we go to our knees pleading for His help, restoration, and peace. My spiritual growth is always most dramatic when I opt to trust God to manage what seem to be "uncontrolled fires" in my life. That's when I learn to trust the Almighty at a deeper level. It may not be until later when I can look back more objectively that I find God's ways are perfect.

Each day while my family slept, I arose early for my study and devotional time, followed by a magnificent four mile walk. With the exception of a few other early risers, the place belonged to me and many deer who often allowed me within a couple of feet, occasionally glancing at me while calmly munching their breakfasts. When I saw them at streams I was reminded of my mother's favorite Scripture, Psalm 42:1 (NIV):

> As a deer pants for streams of water, so my soul pants for you, O God.
> My soul thirsts for God, for the living God.

More than ever before, I knew the reality of God's presence and peace as I walked through isolated areas. I had no fear—just an eager expectation about spending time alone with God in this new place.

I'll always remember my delight the first morning at Black Butte Ranch. Rounding a bend, there suddenly appeared an enormous meadow with many trees and wildflowers, a bubbling brook, and about fifty horses grazing in the distance—all of this against the magnificent snow-capped Three Sisters Mountains!

But even that exquisite beauty couldn't compare with the joy of praising God in this breathtaking setting that He had created. Every day I sat on a large wooden stile to worship and sing praise songs, to talk with God and listen for His responses.

These experiences, as well as incredible sunsets that often filled the entire sky with varying shades of aqua, pink, peach, red, and yellow were splendid reminders of God's majesty.

I was at a spiritual high that week, but when we returned home my regrets were waiting and again my heart was heavy. Clearly, my string of regrets had evolved into a hawser!

The depth of my guilt was surpassed only by frustration over my inability to get rid of these complaints once and for all! Eventually, I realized that blaming myself for bad choices and faulting God for not making me do things differently was irrational. My confusion was starting to give way to acceptance.

I received more clarity from a retired pastor who corrected me after I shared my discontent in an email:

> In actuality you were then exactly where God wanted you to be…no less enlightened then than you are now. And you could not have loved God more than you did because your love for God is not your doing. It is God's grace given to enable you to love Him. And you could not have served God more effectively in the past. Whatever services you rendered others was not your doing. It was Gods grace "doing" in and through you…

> Wondering about the past is always secondary to living the present in anticipation of the future…the first and basic question is who does God want me to be where I am now…at this moment? Life then becomes a most interesting, mysterious, agonizing and delightfully surprising journey of attempting to live the answer, as God gives us Light.[32]

Thinking that I had beaten my strings of discontent and regrets, I rolled them into a small ball that I called *Successes*—obsessions that had interfered with my spiritual growth for far too long. Thanking God for a healthier perspective on life, I trusted Him to continue to help me identify strings that still needed attention so that I could add them to my ball of victories.

Hawsers!

A few months later we visited my mother near the town we lived in when I made the life choices that now seemed so wrong, and back they came! I unwound those strings of discontent and regret!

Why, I wondered again, *did I so easily accept what seemed my only choice; why didn't I ask for help from my pastor or guidance counselor?* More important, I couldn't remember asking God for direction! I had no reason to be angry with God; I made the decisions and I needed to own them!

That evening as I knelt to pray I grieved more than ever for what might have been, and what in my mind "should" have been! In my confusion, the compassion I so easily feel for others, enveloped me and I was crushed in despair and self-pity.

The next day I awakened with a heavy heart for friends who were dealing with difficult and threatening health issues, but even as I prayed for them, God whispered. *Focus on your own problems, Shirley! You've pulled away. Your concern for personal desires and plans, your manuscript, the needs of others and even your ministry have gotten in the way of your drawing closer to Me. I don't want any of that until after I have more of you!*

God made it very clear! I needed to re-center on Him and despite my incessant whining and disobedience, God continued to demonstrate immense love and patience. I was further encouraged and directed by Henri Nouwen's comments in *Here and Now: Living in the Spirit*:

> When we look back at all that has happened to us, we easily divide our lives into good things to be grateful for and bad things to forget. But with a past thus divided, we cannot move freely into the future. True spiritual gratitude embraces all of our past.[33]

When my friend, Patti, was going through a tough time a friend told her, "I love you and I'm willing to walk through the muck with you in order to pick the flowers on the other side."

God was walking with me through the "muck" of my confusion, and although I anticipated a day when we would pick our bouquet, my stubbornness went on! It was several more months before I realized what I was doing and I was ashamed. It was as if I were slapping God in the face and saying *Your gifts aren't good enough! Why didn't You wrap them this way instead of the way You chose, and why didn't You use this kind of a ribbon instead of that kind of bow?*

As this continued, God's whispers became more intense. *Shirley, we've been over this before. Center Me in your life now and trust Me. Don't continue to waste time—just do it!*

Tired of repeated failures, I determined to focus on the future and thank God for my gift of life—just as it was and for "whatever" God would bring my way. As I re-wound those strings I anticipated the wonder of unwrapping each new day to see what God had in store!

Remember my sampler that impressed Stefan when we first met? *What we are is God's gift to us; what we become is our gift to God.* I want my life to be a gift treasured by God—a life of adoration and faith wrapped in the assurance of His constant love and secured with ribbons of His never-ending grace, peace, and joy. Those ribbons are the kinds of *strings* to aim for!

Regrets and Complaints

Amy

Earlier I mentioned hawsers, and the ultimate one was owned by Jesus. Because He loved and trusted His Father, and because He loves us, Jesus stretched Himself to the extreme of His earthly self to die on a cross for our sins.

When my friend Amy faced a severe hawser, she also centered on her Father. For over eighteen months, this young wife and mother suffered from cancer which relentlessly invaded many of her major organs. Healing of one site would be followed by the discovery of a new tumor elsewhere. How agonizing it must have been for Amy to think about leaving behind a loving husband and four little girls–7, 5, and 2 ½-year-old twins. Still, Amy had great faith and never complained, but looked to Jesus for courage and strength. Amy lived and died claiming the promises of God, and the supernatural peace that she reflected as she rested in the Lord's arms inspired many others to trust God at a deeper level.

At Amy's memorial service, her pastor said:

> Our resolution to all the issues surrounding Amy's illness, our prayers for a miracle, and her ultimate healing through translation to Heaven is explained in Psalm 138:8 which Amy had written on a note stuck on her mirror: "The Lord will fulfill His purpose for me; your love, O Lord, endures forever."

> God has fulfilled His purpose for Amy, and that may have been different from our purpose for her. We must rest with knowing that the love of the Lord endures forever.

Because I couldn't attend Amy's service, some of my thoughts in a letter to Amy's husband, Wayne, were read:

> In our last conversation Amy was very honest with me: "The human side of me wants to stay with Wayne and our girls, but most of all I want God's will to be done."

> Amy showed us how to trust God despite the most trying of circumstances, and how to die with dignity. The first four verses of Psalm 34 embody Amy's faith:

> "I will bless the Lord at all times: his praise shall be continually in my mouth. My soul makes its boast in the Lord; let the humble hear and be glad. O magnify the Lord with me, and let us exalt his name

177

together. I sought the Lord, and he answered me, and delivered me from all my fears."

Amy has reached her goal and is experiencing greater joy with her Lord than we've ever known. Our loving God answered Amy's prayers. Reaching down, He took her hand and suddenly heaven became even sweeter.

Abraham

God also taught me through Abraham's hawser. Abraham was asked by God to sacrifice Isaac, his precious promised son for whom Abraham had waited until he was very old. His response was stunning! Abraham rose early the next morning to obey God! No argument! No complaining!

Genesis 22:1-3, 9-10:

God tested Abraham. He said to him, "Abraham!" And he said, "Here I am." He said, "Take your son, your only son Isaac, whom you love, and go to the land of Moriah, and offer him there as a burnt offering"…So Abraham rose early in the morning, saddled his donkey…and set out and went to the place in the distance that God had shown him.

When they came to the place that God had shown him, Abraham built an altar there and laid the wood in order. He bound his son, Isaac, and laid him on the altar, on top of the wood. Then Abraham reached out his hand and took the knife to kill his son.

Abraham's "hawser" was one of monstrous proportions, but in God's grace-filled strength, Abraham found courage to obey and God provided an alternate sacrifice!

Verses 11-12 state:

The angel of the Lord called to him from heaven, and said "'Abraham, Abraham!" And he said, "Here I am." He said, "Do not lay your hand on the boy or do anything to him; for now I know that you fear God, since you have not withheld your son, your only son, from me."

I can only imagine this devoted father's relief at that moment; his elation, gratitude, and tears as he hurriedly released and embraced his son. God was delighted with Abraham and promised to bless him.

178

Regrets and Complaints

In *My Utmost for His Highest*, (April 26) Chambers writes:

> A person's character determines how a man interprets God's will. Abraham interpreted God's command to mean that he had to kill his son…If the devil can hinder us from taking the supreme climb…he will do so; but if we keep true to God, God will take us through an ordeal which will bring us out into a better knowledge of Himself…The great point of Abraham's faith in God was that he was prepared to do anything for God…he remained true to God, and God purified his faith.[34]

Although God has chosen less severe ways to stretch my faith, I need the courage of Jesus, Abraham, and Amy to do *whatever* God asks. If God asks me to sacrifice an *Isaac* in my life, I need to obey regardless of what that is—money, material things, a relationship, ministry, and even family! And often we need to do this before God will draw us closer.

Carol Kent, in her book, *When I Lay My Isaac Down*, says:

> Our "Isaacs" are the heart sacrifices we make when we choose to relinquish control and honor God with our choices even when all seems lost. We have to decide if we will let go of our control over a person, situation, or event, or if we will hang on for dear life and refuse to relinquish something we cherish.[35]

Whispers from *Your* Heart

*How has God used me in His service?

*What strings have I ignored that are now hawsers?

*Where do I need to establish boundaries?

*What is God asking me to sacrifice? Am I willing to obey? If not, why not?

Chapter 3

New Pain, New Repentance

"He heals the broken hearted and binds up their wounds."

—Psalm 147:3

I DUSTED OFF my GDI degree, and as God empowered me to do more ministry well beyond my own capabilities, I continued to hunger for a greater intimacy with Him. My intentions were sincere, but I was about to learn a very hard lesson; how devious, subtle, and powerful Satan is.

2 Corinthians 11:14 warns us, "Satan disguises himself as an angel of light."

Always on the lookout and ready to attack every opportunity he gets, I find Satan most active when I'm tired or discouraged, and especially when I'm walking close to the Lord and doing my best to serve Him. Suddenly I had a new string to deal with!

Tempted in an area where I had felt safe, my vulnerability surprised and disappointed me. I learned that everyone is susceptible to Satan's clever and camouflaged deceptions. My understanding of who God is had broadened, my love for Him had deepened, and my ministries had thrived, but even so, when the Holy Spirit whispered warnings, I tuned Him out and permitted Satan to feed my self-centeredness.

A Bible story that convicted me at this time is found in Luke 22 where we read about Jesus telling Peter that Satan had asked for him, to sift him as wheat. But Peter said (v33-34):

"Lord, I am ready to go with you to prison and to death!" Jesus said, "I tell you, Peter, the cock will not crow this day, until you have denied three times that you know Me."

181

What follows is Jesus in the Garden of Gethsemane; His prayer, betrayal, and arrest. And after the arrest, Peter followed at a distance. The story continues (v55-62):

> When they had kindled a fire in the middle of the courtyard and sat down together, Peter sat among them. Then a servant-girl, seeing him in the firelight, stared at him and said, "This man also was with him." But he denied it, saying, "Woman, I do not know him." A little later someone else, on seeing him, said, "You also are one of them." But Peter said, "Man, I am not!"

> Then about an hour later still another kept insisting, "Surely this man also was with him; for he is a Galilean." But Peter said, "Man, I do not know what you are talking about!" At that moment, while he was still speaking, the cock crowed. The Lord turned and looked at Peter. Then Peter remembered the word of the Lord, how he had said to him, "Before the cock crows today, you will deny me three times." And he went out and wept bitterly.

Like Peter, my tears were bitter and I was ashamed, but that was not and never will be enough because that's about me. When we sin we also need to make it about Jesus—we need to repent of our sins and thank Him for dying for us and then do our best to live our lives according to the life Jesus modeled for us.

In the Luke 22 passage, the phrase that most pierces my heart is, "The Lord turned and looked at Peter." (61a) No words; the look was enough. I don't think Jesus' face reflected anger, but rather His disappointment, hurt, tenderness, and concern for Peter. Jesus knew Peter loved him and He knew how devastated Peter would be as a result of having denied his Savior and best Friend.

Many of us know how it feels to have someone we cherish make a wrong and pathetic choice; an option that could even put their own life or that of someone else in severe jeopardy. Any anger or disgust we feel is tempered by love, compassion, and worry over what this may mean for our loved one's future and maybe for our own, simply because we care.

We also may know what it's like to be let down by a best friend; the hurt and sadness of having someone we love and admire deny the value of our relationship because of their personal needs of that moment. Fear, envy, a lack of self-worth—any emotion that is given free reign in our lives can cause us to react in ways that are not beneficial to our lives or those of people we care about.

New Pain, New Repentance

Peter's fear of being known as a friend of Jesus, who had just been arrested, led to three firm denials of Jesus whom He loved! Peter's string had quickly become a hawser and there was no going back, so "Peter went out and wept bitterly." (verse 62)

Luke 22:61a could also read, "The Lord turned and looked at Shirley," or you can insert your name. To envision Jesus turning and looking at me in my guilt is very painful and upsetting. I want to obey God, not because I'm afraid of what may happen if I don't, but because I adore Jesus and don't want to despise Him. Ironically, I need God's help to do that and in His grace He does.

We're all at risk of ignoring God's rules for our lives, and sometimes we rationalize by saying we're just bending them a little. But there is no grey area; either we obey the Lord or we don't! Either we love God most, or we don't!

Sometimes God lets us dig a deeper and deeper hole until we can't get out, and sometimes the walls collapse and we're buried in embarrassment and pain. Gratefully that isn't my story. Instead, God graciously put me on my knees where I could hear Him and where He could convict me through Scripture, including Isaiah 53:3, 5b:

> [Jesus] was despised and rejected by others; a man of suffering and acquainted with infirmity; and as one from whom others hide their faces he was despised and we held him of no account...upon him was the punishment that made us whole, and by his bruises we are healed.

This poignant Scripture about Jesus' intense suffering to save us had previously brought me to tears many times, and now I too had deliberately despised and rejected my Lord. I knew shame and humility as never before, and my tears were bitter. Chambers expresses it this way: "When God wants to show you what human nature is like separated from Himself, He shows it to you in yourself."[36]

Now I have a greater understanding and compassion when others face temptation because I've been there, and knowing the disappointment and guilt that can accompany human weakness I can encourage them.

I've found a very simple way to deal with recurring temptations, but it demands persistence—I guess, forever! When even a potentially problematic reminder enters my mind, I immediately whisper, "Thank You, God, for helping me to love You most." If necessary, I repeat it until I believe it again.

Gratefully, the Almighty is a God of second chances. Taking great pleasure in saving us from ourselves, God sees through His love and grace what we can become. He wants us to serve others and help each other. In 2 Corinthians 1:3-4, the apostle Paul speaks to this.

> Blessed be the God and Father of our Lord Jesus Christ...who consoles us in all of our affliction, so that we may be able to console those who are in any affliction with the consolation with which we ourselves are consoled by God.

As God continued to bless my efforts, I felt so privileged that I asked a pastor friend why God would choose to use me. He straightened my thinking with this candid response:

> To ask the question "why me" is to focus more on what we perceive to be our own unworthiness and not on the miracle of how God puts His treasure in earthen vessels...Instead, we are to view ourselves according to the measure of faith God has given us; to accept our specialized giftedness and unhitch it from a sense of worthiness. As we gratefully view ourselves in the light of the measure of faith which God has given us, we continue to serve with humility, joy, gratitude and confidence.

Whispers from *Your* Heart

Do I believe Satan is a real threat to me?

Have I deliberately "despised and rejected" Jesus? How?

How did I repent and why do I believe Jesus heard me?

How did I change my sin—my behavior?

Chapter 4

Finding God in Each Other

*"We ought to support such people, so that we may become
co-workers with the truth."*

—3 John: 8

REVIEWING MY DAILY prayer journals, I'm reminded of how often the Holy Spirit has led, strengthened, and empowered me not only through Scripture, Christian authors, and speakers, but also through many friends who pay attention to God's whispers and take time to affirm and encourage me and others in their lives. Here are a few examples.

The first time I was invited to speak at a retreat:

What a wonderful opportunity and open door for ministry! I am so very proud of you and I know God will make His will clear for the theme you are to use. Go for it, BIG TIME!

Affirmation for Caring Ministries:

When the universe gives people a crash course in vulnerability, that's when they discover just how crucial and life-preserving good friendship is. Thanks to God for sending you as a faith-filled and true friend to so many of God's needy people!

After I spoke to the church about resigning from Caring Ministries and going forward with wHispers:

God must have been screaming in your heart, not only whispering! What a resounding success you have made out of your inspiration. You surely have the gift of communication on top of the gifts for caring. We thought that you put the use of ourselves in a wonderful perspective which will be so encouraging for people to try using their gifts with the confidence of God's leading.[37]

Barbara, a member of our church, was clearly someone the Lord had anointed as one of my chief encouragers. When I felt nervous and inadequate just before leading the first Caring Ministries workshop, Barbara came rushing in at the last minute, hugged me and whispered, "I'm so glad you haven't started; I don't want to miss anything you have to say."

Several years later when I visited her in a hospital where she was dying, we embraced and with still sparkling eyes, she asked, "Shirley, have you gone to "Reverend School" yet?" Seminary was Barbara's dream for me, but I didn't sense it was God's plan. I told her about my GDI degree and she smiled her agreement.

God-given support and affirmation through other Christians humbled me to the point that I wrote in my journal, "I fear that I will not live up to Your expectations, God; help me be as good as people think I am!"

It's awesome to know God has made each of us unique for a particular ministry and sometimes it's that of encouraging others who also serve Him. Some people seem to think pastors and others in ministry don't need prayer as much as others. But I believe it's just the opposite. Satan will attack anyone and especially those who are dedicating their lives to serving Jesus.

Affirmations of my ministry are significant, but even more precious are prayers offered for me. Many I'll never know about, but here are just two by email that have encouraged and given me strength to go on.

Regarding ministry:

My prayer is that the Spirit will surround you, fill you, and empower you so that in everything you think, do and say you will be a personal embodiment of our Lord Jesus Christ.

And Patti's prayer for me after my stroke:

Dear Abba, I lift Shirley into Your healing presence this morning. May the perfect blood of Jesus flow through every artery and vein; clearing out any and all blockages that are present. May her body be warm with Your presence and her heart alive with Your love. Speak to her in a "gentle whisper" a message more powerful than she has ever heard before. And we give You all the glory and honor forever. Amen.

Pray for Those Who Persecute Me?

Despite the encouragement and support of friends, I was not prepared for the unjust criticism and attacks by some co-workers in ministry. Is it totally naïve to think that Christians with the same goal of serving God can lovingly work together? Surely, if our attention is God centered, we can see our need for each other. Sadly, not true! Sometimes we can't see beyond our own agendas. While unwarranted criticism and verbal abuse might seem more likely in a secular setting, I was stunned to learn first hand and from dedicated servants in other places, this demoralizing conduct is not uncommon in churches.

Here is Dietrich Bonhoeffer's view of the church:

We are created, Bonhoeffer believed, to be in relationship with one another in all that we are and do; we were made for community. Our social relationships are grounded in our relationship with God, who is essentially a relationship as well–the relationships of Father, Son, and Holy Spirit. Our most important experience of such godly relationships for Bonhoeffer was the community of the church which he understood to be God's way of continuing to exist throughout history in the midst of human life...The wonder of the church, however, is that if we allow ourselves within that community to be formed into the image of God becoming the body of Christ, we will learn there to see Christ in one another.[38]

Wanting to heal my situation, I looked to the Bible for direction and found encouragement in Exodus 14:14: "The Lord will fight for you, and you have only to keep still."

And instruction in Matthew 18:15-16, where Jesus says:

If another member of the church sins against you, go and point out the fault when the two of you are alone...if you are not listened to, take one or two others along with you, so that every word may be confirmed by the evidence of two or three witnesses.

When I confronted the first individual who had repeatedly verbally attacked me, he owned it, but said he had no plans to change and walked away. Another time, deciding to follow God's instructions, I arranged a meeting with a person who had treated me with deliberate hostility. I hoped and prayed for fairness, integrity, and healing, but it ended with more loud, bitter accusations and me in tears. Needing someone in leadership who would keep us both accountable, I arranged a second meeting, but even with a third person, we were like water and oil. I had prayed for both of us to be open to the Holy Spirit's direction, but instead, more inaccuracies, exaggerations, and hurtful accusations were fired at me.

I shared the words of Jesus in John 13:20: "Very truly, I tell you, whoever receives one whom I send receives me; and whoever receives me receives him who sent me."

And Blackabys' paraphrase of that Scripture: "Whenever you meet another Christian, you come face to face with Christ."

That phrase had penetrated my heart and as a result I was trying to be more careful in my approach and response to others. I often see Jesus in others and I hope they can see Jesus in me, but in misunderstood and hurtful situations it's more common to feel frustration and sadness because we don't feel loved by the other person. And if we aren't considered lovable, how can we be Jesus to them? I asked that question in our meeting, but my question was ignored by both parties and no one found courage to take a stand and help me.

My hopes dashed, I left the meeting and went home to one of my favorite places for reflection—our hammock under a canopy of trees. Recalling a story about Moses being supported by his friends, I re-read Exodus 17. Amalek is coming to fight with Israel at Rephidim, and Moses tells Joshua to fight with Amalek. In verses 9-13, Moses says:

> I will stand on the top of the hill with the staff of God in my hand. So Joshua did as Moses told him, and fought with Amalek, while Moses, Aaron, and Hur went up to the top of the hill. When Moses held up his hand, Israel prevailed; and whenever he lowered his hand, Amalek prevailed. But Moses' hands grew weary; so they took a stone and put it under him, and he sat on it. Aaron and Hur held up his hands, one on one side, and the other on the other side; so his hands were steady until the sun set. And Joshua defeated Amalek and his people.

Gratefully, it's been rare that instead of supporting my hands, it feels more like someone is hanging from them, trying to drag me down. That day I needed to remember positive experiences when God and others had graced me with love and encouragement; where I could again find strength and even desire to love those who mistreated me.

That evening, as I reached for a book on my bedside stand, my eyes went instead to a Discipleship Journal. In "The Fragrance of Love," Anne Graham Lotz writes about Mary showing her deep love for Jesus by breaking her alabaster jar and pouring its precious contents on Jesus. Lotz connects Judas' criticism of Mary to our experiences.

> Attacks on your sacrifice for Jesus—and mine—may also be based on a hidden motive...jealousy because one's relationship with Jesus is intimate and the other person's is distant...the person feels threatened by the reality of our relationship with Christ and the impact our sacrifice makes on others...(or) resentment over the attention we receive as a result of the fragrant blessing that our sacrifice bring into the lives of others.

> Whatever the motive might be, Jesus sees right through it today, just as He did then. He silenced the criticism with a scathing rebuke: "Leave her alone." (John 12:7)[39]

In her book, *My Heart's Cry,* Lotz asks:

> When have you shared (Jesus') cross? When have you ever entered into the fellowship of His suffering? Just because you love Jesus, when have His tears of pain and rejection been on your face?

> When you love Someone with all of your heart, His grief is yours... His joy is yours...His love is yours...His pain is yours...His blessing is yours...His tears are on your face.[40]

Except for God's presence and Stefan's encouragement, this was a lonely time and I didn't feel free to talk about it with anyone except them and a close friend. My spirit was crushed; my heart heavy with unresolved hurt, a lack of support, and an unfulfilled desire for peace. But, if I was sharing in the suffering of Jesus in even a small way, that put a new slant on my despair.

God Answers

I asked God to help the others see how unfair they had been. Instead, God showed me I was to obey His teachings in Matthew 5:44 where Jesus says, "Love your enemies and pray for those who persecute you."

I cared about these friends, but my frustration outweighed my love for them. I had prayed for our relationships to heal, but not for God's blessings on them. I was not obedient to God's Word.

191

The Lord took me a step further through Isaiah 50:6-8a where we read about how Jesus responded to persecution of the worst kind.

> I gave my back to those who struck me, and my cheeks to those who pulled out the beard; I did not hide my face from insult and spitting. The Lord God helps me; therefore I have not been disgraced; therefore I have set my face like flint, and I know that I shall not be put to shame; he who vindicates me is near.

Even when dying on the cross, Jesus reached out compassionately to the thief at his side and gave him the greatest gift of all—salvation! And in Luke 23:34, after Jesus was nailed to the cross, His response was:

> "Father, forgive them, for they do not know what they are doing."

I'm to love those who don't love me and I'm to pray for and forgive them even if I think they don't deserve it—just as Jesus forgives me in my unworthiness!

Satan does not want us to love and serve God and he'll do whatever he can to discourage us, to sap our strength to go on. We're most vulnerable when we're struggling with our own issues and lose our God–focus.

Criticism, politics, and backbiting are some of Satan's favorite ways to confuse and mess up our lives. I pray to be free of those sins so that Satan cannot use me to interfere with God's plans for my life or that of someone else.

Hopefully, I won't know the pain of more verbal/emotional abuse, but if it happens I'll re-read these words of Lotz to remind me to examine myself and clarify my perspective.

> Instead of avoiding those with whom we are incompatible or just tolerating them, Jesus commands you and me to love them. And as we obey His command, He will use that person to grind off our sharp, impatient, un-Christlike edges.[41]

MY *sharp, impatient, un-Christlike edges*! Ouch! Loving them means to love them as I love myself!

In *Whispers of Hope*, Beth Moore says,

> Over and over David trusted people who let him down...Surely nothing compares to dashed expectations involving a person of God...Because he poured out his heart to God, David's experience with shattered

expectations did not produce bitterness, it produced a lifelong benediction: God alone…

Every one of us is hanging on to something or someone for security. We hold a knotted rope and depend on whatever is on the other end to keep us from falling…close your eyes and imagine looking up the rope…who or what do you see?…If it's someone or something other than God alone, you're hanging on by a thread…[42]

A few days later, God convicted me further through this profound and life-changing statement by Oswald Chambers.

God never gives us discernment so that we may criticize, but that we may intercede.[43]

I saw that an end to this distressing time was within my grasp, but it was up to me. I had not forgiven my friends and my earlier prayers were not sincere. Instead I had foolishly and prematurely wound my twisted strings of pain, confusion, bitterness, and sadness onto my ball of successes; distorting it so that it wobbled back and forth in my mind between trusting God and focusing on my pain; between God-centeredness and self-focus.

I had to unwind and deal with each one. I began praying *with love* for the people who had been unkind, and I needed to forgive them for their weaknesses—their strings! After a while I no longer needed the understanding I expected would never be mine. And as God resolved my pain and frustration, the relationships were healed in what seemed an almost miraculous way.

God knows what's going on and He knows how to fix things. When others are wrong, He shows them, and when I'm mistaken God corrects me. Trusting God to deal with each situation gives me freedom and peace. Sometimes doing all for God's glory means to look away from what seems best for me and even my ministry, and to love others and adopt a willingness and desire to be part of God's plan for someone else.

1 Peter 1:22 says:

Now that you have purified your souls by your obedience to the truth so that you have genuine mutual love, love one another deeply from the heart.

Whispers from *Your* Heart

How has God affirmed me or my ministry through Scripture and/ or other people?

Has God asked me to affirm and encourage someone in their faith and/or ministry? What did I do? How did it make me feel?

If someone criticizes me, why do I find it difficult to pray for them?

How can I learn to forgive as Jesus forgives?

Chapter 5

Ribbons of Grace in Disguise

"Where can I go from your Spirit? Or where can I flee from your presence? If I ascend to heaven, you are there; If I make my bed in Sheol, you are there. If I take the wings of the morning and settle at the farthest limits of the sea, even there your hand shall lead me, and your right hand shall hold me fast."

—Psalm 139:7-10 (NKJV)

BECAUSE OF A persistent burning sensation in my ankle I was examined by an orthopedic surgeon. He prescribed a "walking boot" and immediate surgery, followed by six weeks on crutches with a leg cast, and then six to twelve months of physical therapy! Concerned about the added risk of stopping my Coumadin, a medication to prevent more blood clots, I asked for a second opinion. This specialist said surgery was premature because there was a 50-50 chance of recovery without it. Because I didn't think he factored prayer into the equation, I believed my prospects for healing were even better.

For three months, I was to wear the boot that housed my leg from toes to knee and I wasn't a happy camper! Worried that my early morning walks would have to end, I was delighted to learn I could do anything I wanted as long as the boot was in place. Later, I would begin five months of physical therapy, wearing the boot between sessions.

Continuing in ministry and working on my manuscript, my already busy schedule became even tighter with physical therapy sessions. As the burning persisted, more doubts crept in. I knew God could heal my ankle without surgery, but would He? I had gotten good at whining and

195

with disappointment and self pity threatening to overwhelm me, I could hardly hear God.

But God is patient, not only putting up with our nonsense, but sometimes using what we consider unreasonable challenges to mold us into people He can use. Sometimes He works in unusual and unexpected ways to help us get to that point.

A Book

A short time later, I went to a book sale and with only a few minutes to shop, my eyes went directly to a small book by Wirt, *Not Me God*, which God used to take me to the next step of intimacy with Him. Through this fictional dialogue between a nameless man and God, Wirt demonstrates the importance of talking to God and *listening* for His response. I was especially impacted by how this man greeted God each morning. "Good morning Father, I love You very much."[44]

At first I thought, *I can't talk to God that way,* but I've found it to be a very tender experience; a unique closeness to God. In the first and greatest commandment (Matthew 22:37-38), we are told:

> You shall love the Lord your God with all your heart, and with all your soul, and with all your mind.

When we fall in love we can't hold our feelings back; we're passionate about being with and pleasing that person as much as possible. Our Heavenly Father, who loves us most, wants our love returned just as we desire for loved ones to respond to us. If we love God with all of our hearts, it's easy to express devotion and we don't want to be apart from Him. In Romans 8:38-39, Paul assures us that nothing can separate us from God:

> For I am convinced that neither death, nor life, nor angels, nor rulers, nor things present, nor things to come, nor powers, nor height, nor depth, nor anything else in all creation, will be able to separate us from the love of God in Christ Jesus our Lord.

A Bush

Whenever I could, I grabbed a few minutes to work on my manuscript, but it was difficult to accomplish much. Frustrated and wondering if a book was what God wanted, I offered Him the manuscript I had started fifteen years earlier. *Father, I don't want to waste Your time or mine. What do You want me to do?*

As I sat in stillness, I sensed God's peace washing over me, and in the quietness of the moments that followed, God gave me an image! In my mind's eye there was a bush with branches blowing gently in the breeze; no leaves or flowers—just bare branches. For me, that symbolized the spreading of my story of God's love and hope by a few readers who would in turn *branch* it out to others. The gentle wind symbolized the Holy Spirit whispering this book into reality.

Then came the inevitable tears that accompany my encounters with God. Once more God had reminded me of how He meets us personally wherever we are; that He had heard my question and reassured me that I was in His will.

The following Sunday I was one of five women in a class on prayer. Patti, as leader, asked us to share something that had happened to us in the previous week; something we might have missed out on if we were not attuned to God.

Last to share, I eagerly told the group about my having prayed for clarity about God's will for my book, the vision that God had given me, and what I thought it meant. As before, Patti immediately expressed her insight, affirming my understanding and adding that leaves and flowers would appear on "my bush" as God used the book to bless readers and bring them closer to Him.

Blackaby's devotional for that day validated my experiences.

> Hope in the Christian's life is not wishful thinking. It is confident expectation…If God has indicated to you that He is going to do something, you can be absolutely confident that He will do it.[45]

I was learning that when God asks me to do something I must go ahead and do it even, and I would add, *especially* if I don't know the outcome. Sometimes we need to step out in faith and *then* God will bless us. This was true not only regarding my book, but for me physically.

"Donkeys"

God was silent about my torn tendon. Healing was slow and physical therapy sessions were extended. I wanted to pray with confidence, but had trouble. *Why can't I believe that You'll heal me, Father? I know You can, but will You?*

Reading in Mark 9:23-24 about the father of a son with convulsions, I could identify with the father whom Jesus told:

> "All things can be done for the one who believes." Immediately the father of the child cried out, "I believe; help my unbelief!"

I wanted to believe God for healing without surgery, but what if God planned to stretch me further through surgery with the added risk of stopping my anticoagulant therapy? I didn't know if I could handle the disappointment. After so many years of medical issues I'd had enough and wanted only the good stuff God had to give!

But remembering my *whatever* prayer, I decided to trust the Lord to define what that would be. If surgery was required, God would give me strength to endure.

Preparing to attend the annual Christian Writers' Conference at Gordon Theological Seminary, I again anticipated fellowship with other writers and hearing their stories as we assessed and critiqued each other's efforts. Most of all, I relished just holing up in the library and having hours of uninterrupted writing time.

I couldn't drive while wearing the boot, and so Stefan drove me to the hotel and saw that I was settled in. But soon after he called to say he had arrived home, my heart began racing, skipping, and pounding! I phoned Stefan, who insisted on making the three hour trip back, but I persuaded him to wait, "Most likely my medication will work and I'll be fine. I just wanted to talk."

Hanging up the phone I wasn't so sure. Wondering if God was permitting yet another problem, I complained. *"I already have a foot problem and now this! Please God, quiet my heart. I can't do this right now! I just want to write the story You've given me—our story!"*

In *Donkeys Still Talk*, Virelle Kidder writes about "donkeys" in our lives; such things as difficult people, illness, and even ourselves! It seems *donkeys* is Kidder's word for *strings*. She writes:

> I'm learning that God sends His donkeys into my life exactly on schedule whether I'm ready for them or not...Our donkeys remind us to listen for God's voice, to focus on Jesus, and to trust Him to give us everything we need for the journey. They carry us places we never would have imagined.[46]

Only the evening before, I had read:

> Your donkey's name may begin with "If only…" (I knew all about those!)
> Can you name the thing that discourages you most, frustrates you, and
> maybe even threatens to crush your spirit or break your heart? There's
> no better place to hear God's voice than on your donkey's back.[47]

*Oh God, that describes me right now—my spirit is crushed and my
heart is breaking! I've tried to do what You ask. Why do You let all of this
continue?*

I named my donkeys "Heel" and "Heart," and with an erratic 160
beats per minute, "Heart" sure had my attention! I took three prescribed
medications over the next two hours, but still, as I sat on the bed facing
a full length mirror, I could see my pulse pounding in my neck, and my
torso actually shifting from side to side. This was scary stuff and I wished
I weren't alone. I didn't know who was attending the conference or if
anyone besides my friend Linda had arrived early, and she was at dinner
somewhere with the other instructors.

Calling Stefan again, I heard his concern, but I still didn't want him to
make the long trip back. He prayed for me over the phone and I decided
to rest and give the last medication time to work. Lying on my bed, I
picked up a book and out of it fell a sheet of paper with three songs on
it from the old Psalter Hymnal of my childhood church.

Just that morning, I had been motivated to go to the piano and open
the Psalter to "My Jesus, I Love Thee." I found with it two other songs,
"May The Mind of Christ, My Savior" and "Be Thou My Vision." When
I sang them, I noticed a progression. First, I'm to love Jesus as my Savior
and Redeemer, second, to ask Jesus to overflow me with His mind, peace,
and love and last, to live with a vivid awareness of being in the presence
of Jesus. I copied the songs for future reference and tucked them into
one of the books I would be taking with me.

As I focused again on these songs, my fear gave way to God's peace,
and my resolve to trust the Lord was strengthened, but my heart was as
stubborn as a donkey. Despite the medications, it continued to pound
erratically at 160 and more beats per minute. I did not want another
ambulance trip to a hospital, but when I called Dr. Mac, my cardiologist,
he insisted I dial 911 and go to the nearest ER.

When the paramedics gave me a choice of two unfamiliar hospitals,
I asked, "If I were your mom, where would you take me?" They weren't

supposed to say, but compassion overruled and I was grateful to go to a trusted hospital.

Caring and skilled ER professionals listened carefully as I explained my unusually rapid response to the intravenous medication of choice, and the doctor ordered half strength. As the young nurse administered it, she saw my blood pressure dropping rapidly and stopped after only half of the prescribed half-dose. She returned with the doctor who was amazed at my reaction. Surely that young nurse was one of God's answers to our prayers for my protection and wisdom for my caregivers.

Exhausted, I rested and focused on memorized Scriptures that had been so strengthening during earlier challenges, such as Proverbs 3:5,6 and Psalm 4:8, but God seemed to whisper, *I have another Scripture for you.* I didn't understand, but I knew from experience God would bring clarity.

The nurse returned, handed me the television control and said to relax. Instead I asked for one of the books I had hurriedly thrown into my bag. She handed me Henry and Richard Blackaby's *Experiencing God Day-By-Day,* and the devotional for that day was titled, "A Loyal Heart" based on 2 Chronicles 16:9 (NKJV):

> For the eyes of the Lord run to and fro throughout the whole earth, to show Himself strong on behalf of those whose heart is loyal to Him.[48]

It was a timely reminder that God watches over those who are committed to Him, or as a friend explained:

> God is constantly aware of where we are, what our circumstances are, what our needs happen to be, where we are weak, and how He can strengthen and enable us.

During the next two hours, I memorized 2 Chronicles 16:9 and reclaiming God's promise to be with me always, I vowed to stay loyal to God and to leave the reins of my "donkeys" in His hands.

God knew I was in that ER bed and He knew my needs. With additional medication my heart eventually converted to a normal sinus rhythm, and after conferring with Dr. Mac, the ER doctor ordered a new medication and I was discharged at 2 A.M.!

Because I had no car, a cab was called to transport me back to my hotel and although I was assured the taxi company was reputable, there can be exceptions and I didn't want to be one! It was the middle of the night and having no idea in which direction we should go, I felt vulnerable.

I was exhausted, and although a new string—more like a hawser—threatened to tie me in knots, I gave my fear to the God of 2 Chronicles 16:9 who "never sleeps" and "constantly" knows where I am—even defenseless in a taxi!

As the cab pulled up, I was startled to see two men in the front seats. Having shared my concern with Stefan, I did what he asked—to call and give him the name of the company as soon as I entered the cab, and to call again when I arrived at the hotel.

I felt very alone, but when the driver introduced the second fellow as a trainee, I sensed the driver was aware of my concern. Because both gentlemen talked with me, I relaxed, but still I was delighted to pull up in front of the hotel twenty minutes later!

Kidder says that donkeys:

> ...show us how much we need God, that life's journey is too dangerous to handle on our own. Donkeys will carry us to places we never planned to go, where we yearn for God to lead us to safety. The rub is, first we must hand Him the reins, which anybody knows is definitely not for sissies.[49]

I spent the rest of that day taking it easy. The next morning as my friend Ruth and I sat down to eat breakfast, my donkey returned in a gallop! Deciding to finish my meal, I hoped "Heart" would calm down, but that didn't happen. When I again hesitated to call 911, Ruth's concern was evident in her plea, "Shirley, please think like a nurse!"

As I dialed 911, my heart pounded violently, and as I was lifted into the ambulance Ruth's eyes met mine and I knew she was praying.

As before, the paramedics were efficient and compassionate, but the routine of oxygen, intravenous lines, and heart monitors was getting old. I was grateful for good medical care, but it was also a nuisance for which I had no time!

In case God had forgotten, I reminded Him that I wasn't getting any younger and there was so much I still wanted to do—for Him! There it was—another string—this time, doubt! *Oh God,* I agonized, *why can't I just leave it with You?*

I knew God was monitoring my thoughts which could best be categorized, *Why God? Are You allowing these interruptions to provide more material for my book, or don't You want it written at all?*

This time Stefan insisted on coming to the hospital and when he arrived a few hours later, my heart had converted to a normal rhythm. I was discharged and Stefan drove me back to the hotel, encouraging me to salvage what was left of the conference. I agreed, but only ten minutes after he left I phoned and asked him to return and take me home. Our days on campus were long and if I had another attack, I didn't want to interfere with my friends' schedules. It was the right decision because the new medication significantly lowered my blood pressure and I was glad to be where I could rest when I needed to.

"You Go Girl!"

According to Oswald Chambers, (August 3, 06) "Jerusalem, in the life of our Lord, represents the place where He reached the culmination of His Father's will."[50] *Oh God,* I wondered, *where is my Jerusalem?"*
Chambers explains further:

> Nothing ever diverted our Lord on His way to Jerusalem. He never hurried through certain villages where He was persecuted, or lingered in others where He was blessed.[51]

I prayed to be so one with God that I wouldn't question His purpose for what He was allowing in my life, but try to learn the lessons God had for me on my journey to the Jerusalem He chose for me. As I desired more of God, I was getting closer to the end of self. I found it exciting to anticipate what God would do next and to wonder about how He might do it.

God again blessed me through Patti; this time in an email of encouragement:

> I'm so sorry that you didn't get to stay at the writers' conference, but I've prayed that going through this experience will give you more clarity and the "fuel" to put into words whatever might have been missing...I feel really good about how God is going to use this event in your life, writing, ministry, and your relationship with Him...that you will experience a richness that you could not have otherwise.

My response:

> Thanks so much for your caring, affirming, and loving note... I'm so comforted to know God is in control of everything that happens and

Ribbons of Grace in Disguise

I've claimed for myself the wonderful promise of Psalm 138:8, "God is perfecting that thing that concerneth me." No matter what!

Patti's next email is so gracious that out of modesty I'm tempted to omit it. However, I'm including it because God has often affirmed me and my ministries through another person, and I'm hoping you will also take time to encourage friends and colleagues.

From Patti:

"God is perfecting that thing that concerneth me." No matter what! Shirley, that's it! That's the conclusion of your book, isn't it! You told God that you would do "whatever" He asked of you. You have been faithful to everything He has put before you. He has grown and matured you to accomplish every one of the "whatevers," and you have been equal to the task by God's good grace and your own willingness to be obedient.

But now there are two who are conspiring to shut you down: the world (call it growing older, bodies marked by deterioration, a lack of medical knowledge to completely cure these problems, etc.) and the enemy! But you keep pressing. Shirley, don't you know (as your enemy knows) that people who face what you've been facing are supposed to get mad, give up and tell God to go take a hike! After all, you've been faithful, you've done His work with love, grace, eloquence and fruitfulness—and this is the thanks you get!

But no! You look at the odds and say, *"Some might look at my situation and think the odds are even, 2 against 2, not too good. Who's going to win—the world and the enemy, or God and His precious daughter?"* Then *"Ha!"* you say, *"Is this a trick question?" It's a no-brainer! No matter what—we will win! So take that you evil conspirators! We have already won, no matter what!* Your "whatever" has ripened into the plump, seed-bearing, others-nourishing fruit of "no matter what!"

You are my inspiration Shirley. I am not saying that glibly. I love how you love God, and how you have served Him "no matter what!" Proverbs 31:25-26 comes to mind when I think about you: "She is clothed with strength and dignity; she can laugh at the days to come. She speaks with wisdom, and faithful instruction is on her tongue"...and in her book! (Uh...just a little paraphrase there ☺)

So Shirley, thank you for being the kind of woman I want to be. Thank you for giving me an image and an example of what it means to love

203

God so much that serving Him is a part of your every breath...no matter what!

My response to Patti:

As I read your letter, I wept—not because of your words, but because I feel the Lord's love so strongly through them—and I so much needed to feel His presence in a very real way this afternoon. The Holy Spirit truly has given you insight regarding my needs and that demonstrates once more how much God loves me; that He is in control and uses even our disappointing situations for His glory.

In the moments that followed I could almost hear God whispering a Patti-phrase, *You go girl!*

A New String

A few weeks later, I was delighted to learn that God had healed my foot without surgery. However, "Heart" continued to be relentless, and despite the use of three different medications over a period of several hours my heart would pound irregularly for up to 8 hours. I was scheduled for a cardiac ablation to end the frequent lengthy episodes of disabling rapid heart beats. In this process, catheters would be threaded into veins in both groins and then into my heart where, with an electrode, the surgeon would attempt to replicate my erratic heart activity as captured on EKGs. When they found the trigger point, a tiny area would be killed with either extreme heat or cold delivered by another cathether.

First, I needed to transition to a different anti-coagulant, and for the last twelve hours I would not be allowed any blood thinners at all. This wasn't easy to accept. Do you remember Linus from the Peanuts comic strip with his little blanket? I felt like Linus without his security blanket and I needed to focus on God—my security blanket! I needed to remember that God is bigger than anything we can ever face.

Two days before the ablation, I was watching a Gaither's TV program filmed in Jerusalem; a place I long to visit and I was riveted to scenes where Jesus had lived. Then someone sang, "I walked today where Jesus walked...I knelt today where Jesus knelt...I prayed today where Jesus prayed...," and I ached for those experiences to be mine.

It was then God whispered a unique blessing. *Shirley, I've done even better for you. Jesus lives in you and He walks where you walk, He kneels where you kneel, He prays where you pray, and on Monday morning when you lie on the operating room table, Jesus will be with you!* Marveling over God's compassion and personal attention, I could only whisper, "My God, how great Thou art!"

Later, as I reflected on how fragile life is, I remembered an image God gave me early one morning during my time alone with Him at my mom's kitchen table. It was only a couple of weeks after my stroke and I was physically and emotionally drained. In my mind's eye I saw two strong hands which I knew were symbolic of God's hands, and resting in them was what appeared to be a fragile iridescent puffy glass heart—as delicate as a soap bubble.

My Father was showing me He knew how fragile I was and that He's always ready to hold and protect me. The circumstances may not change, but I've learned as many have, that when we trust God, there's a new sense of going forward in His strength. We can have the joy of knowing the joy of God's presence and the peace that follows.

At worship the next day when we celebrated the Lord's Supper, my mind recaptured the now familiar image of Jesus showing me His hands and His feet, and whispering, "Shirley, I did this for you." My tears of regret and repentance were real and recalling my prayers for a better understanding of the birth and death of my Savior, I could pray, *Jesus, now I do know You better and I love You with all of my heart!*

The next morning, Stefan's anxiety was evident even as he prayed for me. As we drove to the hospital, I realized I was humming the song, "He Who Began a Good Work in You...will be faithful to complete it..." I laughed and told Stefan, "God has such a wonderful sense of humor! I've been wondering if I'll survive this procedure, be able to continue with wHispers and finish my book—and He gives me this song!"

I smiled as I remembered the Danish proverb, *What you are is God's gift to you; what you become is your gift to God.* I felt like a gift wrapped in God's faithfulness and tied with ribbons of His love and peace, and I marveled again at God's love and His interest in the details of my life.

During the ablation, my heart was stimulated to beat so fast and hard that I felt it might burst! I could quiet my fears only by remembering that Jesus was there with me, and that God would help me complete the good work He had begun in me!

The cardiac ablation went well, my physically fragile heart is stronger, and I thank God for taming my "donkey." The debilitating hours of rapid and irregular heartbeats ended and now I have only rare and brief episodes. I'm grateful for more time to share lessons learned through my fragile heart moments, and I know the joy of hearing women say how God is blessing them through wHispers and my story about God's faithfulness.

It reminds me of Pastor Doug's words a few years before: "You have a significant ministry—you are a proven person—one with influence and authority, a stabilizing factor." My unspoken response at that time was a resounding, *Who, me? This little gal from East Pal?*

When I think back to that moment, I remember being stunned and almost disbelieving of Doug's affirming comments about me in ministry, but at the same time warmth washed over me and I knew God was blessing and encouraging me through Doug. I noted in my journal that day, "God, I'll never take Your gifts and power for granted. What a wonderful and undeserved ride with You!"

Now it's humbling and gratifying to know that God is blessing my efforts and using me to make a difference for Him. I praise God for the challenges He uses to melt and mold me into someone He can use for His glory. And I thank God for Pastor Doug, who prayed for direction and then found courage to obey, inviting me into a crucial role even though I must have seemed an unlikely choice.

Ribbons of Grace in Disguise

Whispers from Your Heart

*How can I walk close enough to God to hear His whispers?

*How have I shown God that I love Him with all of my heart?

*How has God demonstrated His love and care to me?

*What does God treasure about me?

Chapter 6

Really, God?

"For we are what (God) has made us, created in Christ Jesus for good works, which God prepared beforehand to be our way of life."

—Ephesians 2:10

IN JANUARY 2006, in wHispers' third year, God began showing me in various ways that it was time to complete my book. Hardly daring to acknowledge that, I wondered, *Am I reading God wrong? Is it wishful thinking? I'm so busy with wHispers—how can I find time to write?* But there were too many special happenings for it to be anything but God.

Lin Bourie, our next wHispers speaker said:

God gives us seasons of change—don't wrestle with them, but embrace them. Be like a leaf that drifts along in the current provided by our Creator. At times we wait on the side of the bank as that current encourages us to pause and wait for the timing to move on. (in my journal I wrote, "Yes, God—Your river!")

Wonderfully affirming Scriptures appeared in devotional readings:

"Neglect not the gift that is in thee."

—1 Timothy 4:14 KJV

"Who knows? Perhaps you have come to royal dignity for such a time as this?"

—Esther 4:14

Chambers:

> Allow (God) to be the source of all your dreams, joys, and delights, and be careful to go and obey what He has said...Daydreaming after God has spoken is an indication that we do not trust Him.[52]

A month later at Congress, an evangelical conference sponsored by Vision New England, God guided me through the words of two speakers in particular. Carol Kent, popular speaker and writer: "Say yes to the burden God puts on your heart—and no to everything else."

Barry Black, Chaplain to the US Senate, quoted Ecclesiastes 11:4: "Whoever observes the wind will not sow; and whoever regards the clouds will not reap."

Black's comments:

> Tragedy is waiting for the perfect time, and waiting for the perfect time is an insult to God...don't become preoccupied with life's obstacles—move ahead for Jesus anyway! Move ahead by faith—don't let obstacles distract or interfere. Leave it to the Holy Spirit and you'll serve in unlikely places!

I believe God was telling me, *Shirley, for almost twenty years you've put your manuscript aside in order to do the ministries I've given you. Now it's time to complete your book—the time is now!*

In Job 42:1, 2, and 12, I found affirmation and encouragement:

> Then Job answered the Lord: I know that you can do all things, and that no purpose of yours can be thwarted...The Lord blessed the latter days of Job more than his beginning.

God, I prayed, can I take these verses literally? They seem so relevant and too good to be true—but so are You! Thank You for all that You've done, are doing, and will do. But God, what about wHispers?

Barry Black's words echoed in my mind, "...waiting for the perfect time is an insult to God."

After more praying, I decided to explain to the wHispers team what I believed God was asking me to do, and at the same time, Satan put doubts in my mind. *What if you're wrong? If you tell others and it doesn't happen, you'll look foolish.*

I decided to ignore Satan and tell my team. They all understood and we adjusted our program to give me more time to write while keeping the integrity of our program. Wrapping up that season and finding speakers for the next year occupied the rest of that spring, but I anticipated a wonderful summer of writing.

I attended the April Festival of Faith and Writing at Calvin College in Grand Rapids and registered again for the Writers' Publishing Workshop at Gordon Conwell Theological Seminary in August.

Feeing well and making progress with my writing, I didn't think life could get much better! I was further inspired by this hope-filled insight from Chambers: "Every God-given vision will become real if we will only have patience…Ever since God gave us the vision, He has been at work."[53]

WOW!

"Oh God…"

Just into summer, I began to have the same unsettling symptoms I experienced during my stroke recovery three and a half years before. For a few seconds, I felt as if I "wasn't there;" no warning and afterward I would think, *What was that?* If I was talking with someone, it never lasted long enough for the other person to notice, but it was disturbing to me.

I had adapted to unsteadiness at times, but this was different. Now I actually felt as if I was going to tip over—almost as if someone had pushed me. Because these events occurred infrequently, about a week apart, and lasted only a few seconds, I was tempted to ignore them. I was weary of doctor's exams and coping with physical ailments, but I didn't dare ignore the symptoms.

The next day, I was examined by Dr. George who said that the part of a brain affected by stroke can be particularly susceptible to seizure disorders. He ordered an MRI of my brain for that evening.

Dr. George went on vacation the next day, and Stefan left for his week-long guitar seminar. I focused on writing, and with no further symptoms I forgot about the MRI results, and a week later, my friend Amy and I drove to Gordon Theological Seminary for the writers' conference. I was symptom-free until the fourth evening, when on my return to the hotel, my left hand tingled, but as soon as I mentioned it to Ruth, who was driving, the symptom subsided.

An hour later, I was surprised when Dr. George called, his concern immediately clear in his question, "Shirley, has anyone talked to you about your MRI results?"

When I said no, he explained that I had a small hemorrhage in the right temporal lobe of my brain. He was particularly worried because I was taking Coumadin and aspirin—both strongly contraindicated with hemorrhage.

I told him about the tingling in my hand and that I had taken my Coumadin about an hour before that. He said the symptoms in my left hand were in line with the hemorrhage in my right brain. Clearly, I was at risk, and he urged me to go to a hospital immediately for a CT Scan and blood work. Only three hours from home, I chose to return to doctors who knew me rather than go to a nearby ER.

I called Amy and told her I needed to return to Cape Cod, and then went to Ruth's room and explained Dr. George's phone call. Ruth's face mirrored my concern, but taking my hands she said, "Shirley, let's pray," and as she entrusted me to God's care, we were led from fear to a serene assurance that God was with me and would protect me.

As Amy and I drove back to Cape Cod, I realized how fragile my health was at that moment. I began to panic until I remembered that Jesus could calm even these waters! God had already protected me for two weeks following the hemorrhage not known to me, even though I had continued to take Coumadin and aspirin every day.

My doctors would later agree there was no explanation other than God's protection for my not having suffered a major bleed, which could have led to extensive paralysis or even death. God's immense love and peace washed over me and put a smile on my face. One of the blessings of this situation would be opportunities to share with believers and non-believers how God had protected me.

Instead of a steady uninterrupted ride along Route 3 near Norwell at 11 P.M. on a Thursday, we suddenly found ourselves in bumper to bumper traffic lasting for at least an hour. I was grateful that Amy shared my faith in God. Surely she realized her responsibility for getting me to the ER as soon as possible, and also what a time bomb I might be! However, I wasn't the only one with explosive attributes at that moment!

When it was our turn to merge into the left lane, orange cones were on our right and a huge semi-trailer truck on our left. Amy signaled and the driver seemed okay with our merging, but then she began revving her engine. Perhaps she was annoyed because her schedule was delayed, or because the stop and start traffic only permitted us to merge slowly. Whatever the reason, we tried to ignore her "growling," but when we were kitty-corner in front of the semi, the driver, from a stopped position, gunned the truck's engine and plowed into the left rear panel and bumper of our car! Amy and I were stunned victims of road rage!

There was a police car ahead and we continued forward until we reached him. I explained the incident as well as our concern over confronting this aggressive woman and exchanging operator information with her. The officer couldn't leave his site, but called a trooper who helped us and we went on our way to the Emergency Room, shaken but okay.

About midnight I was admitted to the ER where a CT Scan showed no hemorrhage. The doctor explained this did not mean the hemorrhage was gone, but that it had not grown despite the anti-coagulants I had ingested. I was discharged to the care of my physician.

My Rock

That was not an easy time. Feeling very fragile, I needed God "with skin on;" I needed hugs and smiling faces reassuring me of their prayers. A few days later, our wHispers small group met and these women not only reflected Jesus' love and compassion as they listened intently to my concerns, but then laying their hands on me they prayed for my healing.

Stefan and others continually reassured me of their prayers; their faces, voices, and written comments all making my "load lighter" as they helped me bear it. It was reassuring to hear from many to whom I had ministered, that they were now carrying me to God in their prayers. Sometimes in my most difficult moments, I couldn't find words to pray, and other times the Lord seemed so close I felt no need. Could it be that the prayers of others were keeping me in His presence?

The next week, my doctor ordered a repeat brain MRI. A radiologist again said it showed no hemorrhage, but I was to remain off aspirin and Coumadin. I found it very difficult to shift from earlier instructions, "You need to take Coumadin to prevent further strokes," to "No more Coumadin or aspirin because brain hemorrhage is worse!"

I felt as if I were *between a rock and a hard place*—a trite expression, but appropriate for me at that time. The hemorrhage was bad enough, but now I was also at risk of another stroke. Knowing that kind of thinking would only lead to discouragement, I read Scriptures about the Rock, such as Psalm 40:1-2 where David thanks God for divine help:

I waited patiently for the Lord; he inclined to me and heard my cry…set my feet upon a rock, making my steps secure.

213

And David's song in Psalm 18:1-2a after he was delivered from his enemies:

> I love you, O Lord, my strength. The Lord is my rock, my fortress, and my deliverer, my God, my rock in whom I take refuge.

I was not between a rock and a hard place, but rather God *is* my Rock! When stormy waves of sickness and fear threaten to overflow me, I can stand on the Rock as David did! I can find rest in my Rock, and miracle of miracles, the Rock lives in me—not weighing me down, but miraculously lifting me to the freedom of a greater peace and joy.

I found great comfort in the words of a song, *Rock of Ages,* written by Augustus M. Toplady in 1776. "Sir William Henry Wills, in a letter to Dean Lefroy, published in the [London] *Times* in June, 1898, says:

> Toplady was one day overtaken by a thunderstorm in Burrington Coombe, on the edge of my property, Blagdon, a rocky glen running up into the heart of the Mendip range, and there, taking shelter between two massive piers of our native limestone rock, he penned the hymn, Rock of Ages, cleft for me, Let me hide myself in Thee. There is a precipitous crag of limestone a hundred feet high, and right down its centre is the deep recess in which Toplady sheltered.[54]

All of my tests would be re-evaluated after I was examined by a neurologist. Trying to think positively, I fell asleep at night knowing I was safe in the cleft of the Rock of Ages, and whispering the promise of Psalm 4:8 that had strengthened me so many times before.

> I will both lie down in peace, and sleep, for You alone, O Lord, make me dwell in safety.

I received a greeting card with the following quote by Dorothy Bernard, "Courage is fear that has said its prayers." My father knew that courage and in his former church hangs a framed sampler I embroidered in my Dad's memory. It says, "Fear knocked at the door...faith answered...no one was there."

Whispers from Your Heart

Am I neglecting a gift that God has given me?

How would I respond if God guided me in a way that seemed too good to be true?

Is God my Rock and if not, why not?

When fear knocks at my door, how do I respond?

Chapter 7

Renewal

"The Lord is good, a stronghold in a day of trouble;
he protects those who take refuge in him..."

—Nahum 1:7

STEFAN AND I celebrated our 20th wedding anniversary with a two-week vacation on Deer Isle, Maine. Because it's a remote area and our rental home isolated, my doctor was at first reluctant, but with two tests negative for hemorrhage, he gave his permission to go.

Our vacation was marvelous; a cabin on a small cove near Warren Point, and huge blackberry bushes heavy with my favorite fruit! We ate handfuls every time we walked past and still had more than enough for two delicious pies. We even purchased freshly dug clams from fishermen as they walked past our deck.

The deck, only fifteen feet from the water, provided a blissful place for my time alone with God each morning. I often listened to Carol Cymbala's song, "He's Been Faithful," the powerful lyrics reminding me of how many times and for how many years God had already blessed me. Continually encouraging, leading, teaching, providing for, and empowering me through challenging and sometimes fear-filled times, the Lord had drawn me closer to Him and for that I loved Him more deeply than ever.

Every evening Stefan and I enjoyed reading some of the hundreds of greeting cards and letters which we had sent to each other; beautiful reflections on the life and love with which God has gifted us. The verses on two cards not only describe our love for each other, but also the love of God for each of His children. One says, "If you ever need a hug—my arms are always open. Always is forever!"

And the other is indicative of the smile Stefan puts on my face, as well as the joy I feel whenever I sense God's presence or talk about Him.

There's something special about you that makes me smile each and every time I think of you...OOPS...there I go again!

Some cards and notes, more intimate than we wanted our children to find one day, are now part of the landfill in Stonington, ME!

The morning we left Deer Isle, we got up at 4:30 and went outside to enjoy a sky alive with brilliant, sparkling stars of all sizes; some seemed so close they invited our touch. It was one of those times when the astounding beauty of God's creation leaves one almost breathless. This striking display capped off two weeks of oohing and aahing over God's stunning creation; islands bursting with hemlock, pine, and spruce trees, the tides and power of the ocean, magnificent sunrises we could see from our bed each morning, and glorious sunsets from nearby beaches.

That evening, back at home, we were sitting on the sofa watching a Christian television broadcast. Stefan's arm was around my shoulders, and later when I realized he had gently placed his hand on my head, I asked, "Are you praying for God to heal my brain?" Nodding yes, he said that through the years of medical challenges when he held me in his arms he had often silently asked God to heal me.

Stefan knows I'm not afraid to die and although we don't often discuss that, we frequently express our love for each other and know at a deeper level how precious our life together is. But because we do talk about faith and our relationships to God and each other, Stefan knows that as much as I love him, I love God most. Stefan however insists, "No, Shirley, I love you most."

I'm continually amazed by how unconditionally Stefan loves and supports me. He reflects to me the love and grace of Jesus more than anyone else in my life; always ready to listen, forgive, and to support me with "whatever" God permits in my life. For example, when I said something unkind that I immediately regretted, Stefan accepted my apology without hesitation, "Its okay—that wasn't the real you!" Stefan reminds me of Jesus, who not only forgives us, but sees our hearts and what we can become. But, as much as I treasure Stefan's love, I pray for him to love Jesus most.

Enough Already!

Stefan, who has supported me for twenty years through many crises, can't comprehend why God permits me to suffer. "You shouldn't have to, Shirley; you're so faithful in serving Him." I said I don't understand either, but God permitted even Jesus to die a most horrendous death that He didn't deserve—because He loves us so much.

I want to be well so I can share my testimony of God's faithfulness and make a difference for Him in the lives of others, but I know God loves me and I trust Him with my life.

The Apostle Paul had a great passion to serve Jesus, and in 2 Corinthians 12:8 we read about Paul asking the Lord to remove a "thorn" in his flesh, but instead Jesus says in 12:9, "My grace is sufficient for you, for power is made perfect in weakness."

And Paul's response in verses 9b and 10:

So I will boast all the more gladly of my weaknesses, so that the power of Christ may dwell in me. Therefore I am content with weaknesses, insults, hardships, persecutions, and calamities for the sake of Christ; for whenever I am weak, then I am strong.

I found encouragement and hope in Paul's words, but when a new dimension came into play, I struggled to live Paul's response. Larry Crabb's comforting comments in "Going Deeper With God," gave me insight and even acceptance of my inability to rejoice in devastating circumstances. And it encouraged me to keep on keeping on.

In some ways, I think the Christian who is disappointed with the Christian life is on the way to true maturity. Paul in Romans 8, talks about groaning. I think if we met the Apostle Paul, he might say, "Yes, the power of Christ moves through me, but don't assume that is an ecstatic experience. I've seen the risen Lord, but my life right now is this: I'm in prison. I'm lonely. I'm cold. This is really hard. But I'm deeply content in any circumstance."

The word "content," however, doesn't mean feeling good. If you look at the Greek for the word, it isn't an emotional word. It is a purposeful word that says, 'I have the resources within me to persevere, no matter what.[55]

A neurologist found my negative MRI results confusing. Insisting that a hemorrhage would not dissipate that rapidly, he ordered yet another

MRI. Thanks to his persistence in consulting with the radiologists and demanding they review my test results together, it was agreed that earlier tests were read incorrectly. The hemorrhage was evident on all! On the positive side, the hemorrhage had resolved to a point where my doctors felt it safe for me to begin taking a baby aspirin daily again.

I was disappointed and disgusted with the inaccuracies, and confused by doctors who expressed concern for my well-being if I didn't take blood thinners, and then in their next breath insisted I never take Coumadin again. That, on top of physical weakness, led to apprehension which I believe caused more symptoms of panic attacks—emotionally I was at my lowest.

How far short I had fallen from where I wanted to be; how easy it was to forget that Jesus was walking with me on these rough waters. I decided to re-focus on God's promises and the next morning I was encouraged through Numbers 11:23:

> The Lord said to Moses, "Is the Lord's power limited? Now you shall see whether my word will come true for you or not."

Or as it says in the NKJV, with a rather sarcastic slant that makes me smile, "Has the Lord's arm been shortened?"

I memorized that verse to focus on when I became discouraged, but God sometimes beat me to it. A neurologist at Boston's Mass General Hospital confirmed the hemorrhage and suggested it may be one of several. Asking for repeat MRIs in six months, he assured me of his availability at any time if I had more symptoms. The possibility of more hemorrhages was worrisome and six months seemed forever.

And the Lord whispered, *Isn't my arm long enough?* Knowing it is, I reached determinedly for God's strength and tightened my grip on His promises for my future. I didn't understand what God was doing, but I knew He was in control.

One of my favorite Bible stories is in Daniel 3 about Shadrach, Meshach, and Abednego's unyielding determination to worship only God Almighty—no matter what! When King Nebuchadnezzar erected a golden statue about ninety feet high, one of the king's heralds proclaimed:

> When you hear the sound of the horn…you are to fall down and worship the golden statue…Whoever does not fall down and worship shall immediately be thrown into a furnace of blazing fire.
>
> —verses 5-6

Because Shadrach, Meshack, and Abednego were relentless in their refusal to worship the idol, the furious king asked, "…who is the god that will deliver you out of my hands?"

Their brave and powerful declaration continues to inspire me.

> O Nebuchadnezzar, we have no need to present a defense to you in this matter. If our God whom we serve is able to deliver us from the furnace of blazing fire and out of your hand, O king, let him deliver us. But if not, be it known to you, O king, that we will not serve your gods and we will not worship the golden statue that you have set up.

The enraged king ordered the furnace to be heated seven times hotter than usual, the guards to bind Shadrach, Meschak, and Abednego and throw them into the furnace of blazing fire. The raging flames killed the guards, but Shadrach, Meshack, and Abednego, who fell into the fire, were seen walking unhurt in the midst of it, with a fourth person whom King Nebuchadnezzar described as having "the appearance of a god" or according to the NKJV "…like the Son of God." Following the king's command to leave the fiery furnace, they came out totally unharmed and "not even the smell of fire came from them."

What if God permitted the heat of my "fiery furnaces" to escalate even further? Could I trust Him to protect me? Could I hold on when common sense whispered, *Shirley, you're never going to finish that book, and how can you share your testimony when you're sick and weak? Now you're at risk for another stroke or hemorrhage, and you're not getting any younger, you know!*

God's Answers

God doesn't always make common sense to me, but I've learned that God is not common. Our God is awesome even when I don't understand. Many times I've found refreshment in the comforting words of Isaiah 43:18-19:

> Do not remember the former things, or consider the things of old. I am about to do a new thing; now it springs forth, do you not perceive it? I will make a way in the wilderness and rivers in the desert.

I love knowing how well God knows my head and my heart, and how often He knows when I need to be reminded of even the most simple truths. I rarely miss corporate worship, but the next day I stayed home because I couldn't face people who loved me; friends whom I knew would ask questions for which I had no answers. And quite frankly, I was discouraged and questioning God again. How could I speak and write a book when I felt so crummy?

I tuned in Dr. Charles Stanley's televised sermon and he was already preaching; his first words after I tuned in were, "Are you going to obey God or are you going to spend the rest of your life wondering what marvelous things God may have done?"

Stunned by Stanley's question, I haven't looked back since! When doubts come, I reflect on the many times God has made Himself known to me in remarkably intimate and mysterious ways. Humbled and encouraged by the wonder of it all; my trust is reinforced in our God who walks with us in the fires of our lives!

The very next day, my friend Donna emailed me a piece by Sheri Rose Shepherd, "His Princess—Love Letters from your King." Shepherd's words were so pertinent to my situation that I wept for having received them at my precise moment of need.

Wait on Me My patient princess. My timing is always perfect. I know you're anxious about many things and I see your passion for all the plans I put in your heart and I know that you long to fly. However, just as a vinedresser nurtures the vine and waits patiently for the right moment to harvest the grapes, so too am I working tirelessly to prepare you to bear fruit. Don't run ahead of Me or try to fly before I am done with you. Your strength will fail you and your dreams will wither away. Trust me that My dreams for you are greater than you can ever imagine. You will run farther and soar higher when you patiently wait for the season of My blessing. Draw close to Me now and I promise, this season of waiting will bring you the sweetest of rewards.
Love,
The Lord of all strength."[56]

This reminded me of Bruce Wilkinson's *Secrets of the Vine* that I had read several years earlier, weeping as I saw my need for discipline and change. Based on John 15, Wilkinson focuses on Christ as the "true vine," our Heavenly Father as the "vine grower," and all of us as "branches" who can bear fruit only if we "abide" in Jesus.

This time when I opened the book randomly, it was to the chapter, "Flourishing Under the Shears." I found hope in bittersweet statements about pruning in maturity.

Mature pruning is about your values and personal identity. God moves in close for more intensive pruning because by now you are ready to really produce…the pruning will intensify as God's shears cut closer to the core of who you are. God isn't trying to just take away; He's faithfully at work to make room to add strength, productivity, and spiritual power in your life. His goal is to bring you closer to the "perfect and complete" image of Christ.[57]

I could see how the teachings of this book dovetailed with Shepherd's comments and although spiritually eager to comply, I didn't have the strength to take much more. Even though I slept well, I was physically exhausted and unsteady much of the time, emotionally stressed, mentally fatigued, and my memory compromised.

Whispers from *Your* Heart

*I have experienced God's "hugs." Here are three examples of His faithfulness to me in disappointing times:

*What do I do when "furnaces" in my life heat up beyond my control? How do I counteract my fear?

*How has God pruned me?

*I have trouble waiting for God's timing because:

Chapter 8

Mom

—

He will cover you with his feathers, and under his wings you will find refuge; his faithfulness will be your shield and rampart. You will not fear the terror of night, nor the arrow that flies by day, nor the pestilence that stalks in the darkness, nor the plague that destroys at midday."

—Psalm 91:4-6 (NIV)

ABOUT A WEEK later, on a beautiful late fall day, Stefan was horseback riding with a friend and I had decided to work on my manuscript at Breakwater Beach. Before leaving, I talked with my brothers, both of whom live near our mother in New York state, while Stefan and I live more than four hundred miles away. We were all increasingly concerned about our ninety-one year old-mother who had started repeating comments and questions several times within brief conversations. That day with workers replacing the roof of her house, Mom seemed worse; unusually stressed and not coping well with the interruption in her usually quiet life.

We all tried to create a healthy balance between heart and mind regarding Mom, but the panic in Don and Larry's voices over Mom's deteriorating memory and her confusion that day surprised and saddened me. They were always strong and even though I was the eldest, I relied on their support.

I called Mom who immediately described the noise and the mess of having her roof replaced. She said not to worry and then began repeating all that she had just told me, and for the first time Mom didn't sound like my mother. There was a strange shrillness to her voice.

I hurriedly changed the subject to the weather and encouraged her to sit outside and enjoy the sunshine. She responded with what had become an oft repeated phase. *It's important to enjoy these beautiful fall days because there won't be many more.* Promising to call her again later, I ended our phone call and wept.

At Breakwater Beach I found it difficult to focus on my manuscript and soon gave up. The day was gorgeous; the sun delightful and the bay a vibrant blue, but my thoughts about Mom saddened me. Then I realized I was sitting near the place where Jesus whispered, *I still walk on water and Shirley, whatever waters come your way, I'll be walking on them with you.*

"Oh Jesus," I prayed, "not only my waters, but Mom's…."

I read and reclaimed God's wonderful promise in Deuteronomy 31:7-8:

> Be strong and bold…it is the Lord who goes before you. He will be with you; he will not fail you or forsake you. Do not fear or be dismayed.

Jesus would never leave me alone, or my mother.

Medication has not brought improvement for Mom, but it may have slowed and stabilized the process. Stefan and I have adjusted our schedules to spend more time with Mom and my brothers and, uniting to help Mom, we've all grown closer.

We pray for God to permit Mom to stay in her own home until Jesus comes for her and so far that is happening. Best of all, Mom's faith remains secure. She loves to worship with Larry and her church family, but most important is her intimacy with God. Over the years of traveling with her, I would hear her whispering her prayers from the back seat of the car or in the other bed of a motel room we shared. When we visit her—even now—I often see her lying in bed on her tummy, head up and hands folded in front of her, praying for her family and others.

We've hired Mom's niece to help with Mom's care, housework, and medications each morning and my brothers visit her frequently and help her a great deal. Because she lives alone I've assumed the responsibility of phoning her and walking her through the latter part of each day when we're not there. I call her at 5 to remind her to eat the bag lunch brought with her hot noon meal by the *Meals on Wheels* people, at 8 to take her medications, and at 9:45 after she's in bed, I read a devotional to her. She loves this; asking questions at times about the content and she always adds, *Thanks for reading to me.* Before we say goodnight, I pray with her and she often adds her "Amen. That was wonderful."

Reading to Mom and praying with her at bedtime was not my idea, but a precious whisper from God that blesses both of us, and Stefan too, who fills in when I'm unavailable.

Sometimes when we visit Mom for a week or longer, I get weary from repeating, from grieving the loss of the Mom I've always had, and even her meekness when I have to ask her to re-dress herself or repeat some other simple chore. One evening after repeatedly trying to explain something to Mom, she asked, *Shirley, why do I get so confused?* I told her it was part of being ninety-one and she let it go, but I was tired and couldn't.

Sad, frustrated and wishing I were more patient, I wept as I knelt next to my bed. I asked Jesus to help me, but then I thought, *You don't know how it hurts to see your mother get old and suffer.* And almost immediately, in my mind I saw Jesus on the cross and nearby, His mother, whose feeling of helplessness and despair I can't even imagine.

I've often become emotional when considering the intense agony and humiliation of Jesus as He was repeatedly tortured and then crucified, but never had I thought about how agonizing it must have been for Jesus to look down and see His mother. Knowing her grief and wanting to comfort her, Jesus could have reversed the whole thing, but our Lord did what He had to do for all of us—including His mother.

Whispers from *Your* Heart

*Why can I trust Jesus to walk on the waters of my life with me?

*Why is it sometimes difficult to trust Jesus with those I love most?

*Sometimes I have trouble believing that Jesus understands what I'm going through. Explain:

*Whose prayer life has been a strong example for me? Why?

Chapter 9

Stretching Even Further!

"Keep on doing the things that you have learned and received and seen in me, and the God of peace will be with you."

—Philippians 4:9

A NEW YEAR arrived, and with it more unanticipated direction concerning wHispers. I was to remove myself from the leadership role, complete my book, and be more available for inspirational speaking! I was concerned about disappointing my team and the other gals who made wHispers happen, as well as those who expressed their delight in attending our programs. Would they think I was being selfish, concerned only with myself? Wondering about who would run the program, I realized it was my responsibility to obey God and leave the rest to Him.

I decided not to tell my team until God affirmed my thoughts because I wanted to be certain I understood God correctly, and I also needed to get used to the idea! God had asked me to resign from coordinating Caring Ministries, and He now wanted me to do the same with wHispers. Again it didn't make sense, but I had been through enough *whatevers* to trust Him again. On the other hand, the prospect of having time to share my testimony through my book and speaking excited me.

The next month at a conference for women in leadership, God clearly confirmed His earlier instructions. It was such a clear revelation of God's plans for me that when I knelt to pray I wept out of pure joy. The specifics were unknown to me and I felt like Abraham in Hebrews 11:8, "By faith Abraham obeyed… and he set out, not knowing where he was going."

God did not say when I was supposed to step down, but after more praying I knew I was to continue through the already scheduled events for fall. The last one would be in November—a celebration of wHispers and the women who had served; rejoicing in what God had given and where He was now leading us, even though we didn't have a clue where that was! This would be a powerful testimony of how personally God blesses us when we trust and follow Him one step at a time. Gratefully, the women did not consider me selfish. Instead, they thanked me and spoke of their confidence in my walking close enough to God to know His will for my life and wHispers.

But first, there would be another string to deal with. I was so weary of still more trips to doctors' offices and diagnostic centers, that when I became lightheaded again and experienced twitches in the left side of my mouth, I was tempted to ignore the symptoms. Yet the last time I felt that way, I had had a brain hemorrhage and so I returned to Mass General where an extensive series of MRAs confirmed the neurologist's first suspicions. There were more small hemorrhages, but again no cause was given or suggestions for how to prevent another. The neurologist said I might have amyloid angiopathy, a disease where amyloid (a protein) builds up in cerebral blood vessels, thinning the walls and causing them to break down. Later a specialist in that field would determine that because of a lack of specific evidence, it was only a possibility.

When the unnerving symptoms continued, requiring still more examinations and tests, I made a firm commitment to praise God anyway. I was tired of unsteadiness when I walked and also in the shower where I had to brace myself against the wall with one elbow. A twitching in my lip, although not visible, was a worrisome nuisance. Sometimes my discouragement was so great that I could only be still and trust Jesus to intercede for me. I refused to complain, but again I wondered if I had misunderstood God. A book and a speaking ministry—how could that be? I was barely coping with each day!

I needed something to counteract my weakness and I found it in these words from a friend:

> In Deuteronomy 33:25 (NIV) are these very comforting words, "...and your strength will equal your days." God's grace is custom-made for each day and for each person. It matches precisely the person, the circumstances, and the needs. So each day becomes a day of full strength to follow as the Lord leads.

In *Secrets of the Secret Place*, Bob Sorge gives insight about the joys, and even the privilege, of what he calls "The Secrets of Confinement."

> When you've been troubled by circumstances that twist and press your soul, be assured that your Lord is closer than ever!…When the lights of understanding go out and you're plunged into emotional darkness, you are actually being issued an invitation into God's secret place. It's in the darkness where God meets in secret with His chosen ones.[58]

That reminder of how many times God had met me in my emotional darkness brought comfort and reassurance of God's faithfulness. And as I re-read the following advice from a friend after my stroke, I was directed in a very specific way.

> As you have been the loving and caring minister to so many, now it is time to give that same ministry to yourself, as proof that your ministry really works. Shirley, you have a beautiful opportunity right now to give a strong witness and a striking example of who you are in Christ. Don't waste your suffering.

God is showing me how to use my suffering for His glory, and I think hand in hand with that is the reality of Romans 8:28, "We know that all things work together for good for those who love God, who are called according to his purpose."

I've continually been given opportunities to share my faith and the marvelous peace I have in God. For example, one of my doctors is brusque and rude, interrupting me even when I'm answering his questions; nodding as if he already knows what I'm about to say. At the end of one visit, however, he seemed different and closing my file, he quietly said, "Just continue taking a baby aspirin."

His eyes, however, seemed to say *I wish I could do more for you,* and so I said, "I'm not afraid, but I have a wonderful peace! God is so good to me! He keeps on blessing me and healing me; He puts joy in my heart and a smile on my face. What more can I ask?"

It was the first time that doctor ever seemed to listen intently to anything I had to say. His eyes met mine, he returned my smile, and the visit was over. Leaving his office, I wondered if he was thinking, *That poor woman has lost her mind…she's in denial…does she really know she could die at any moment?*

Instead, I hope my comments caused the doctor to reflect and want to know more.

Fragile Heart Moments

What I call *fragile heart moments* are situations that put us on our knees; events through which we can learn how much God loves us. That's when having an intimate relationship with the Lord is most precious because believers know that when our life here ends, we're with Jesus forever! I've already given Jesus my heart and He's promised me eternal life with Him—that's reciprocity at its best! It just doesn't get any better than that!

I'm not unique—just an ordinary person with a very extraordinary God, Who while carrying me through many challenges and crises, is making me more like Himself. The Scriptures I share, the promises I claim, the Jesus I know and love—they are gifts from the Father for ALL of us. In addition Jesus sent His Holy Spirit to live in and guide us in our walks with Him.

Reader, I hope you are on this journey with me. You may know the deep love of a husband, parent, child, or friend, but no one can love you as much as God. Perhaps you have trouble believing that, but this is clear in John 3:16 (NKJV):

> For God so loved the world that He gave His only begotten Son that whoever believes in Him should not perish, but have everlasting life.

If you don't know Jesus, I believe you're cheating yourself of the most precious relationship you can ever have. There's no better time than now to thank Jesus for dying for your sins and to invite Him to live in your heart. It's so simple that some think it's too good to be true. Somewhere I read this quote by Billy Graham:

> You don't have to do some wonderful thing to be saved. All you have to do is accept the wonderful thing Jesus has done for you.

Some say there's no hurry, but life is unpredictable and one thing is certain—at some point, our life on earth will end and what happens after that is our choice. If you were to die today, do you know where you would spend eternity?

I've taken a close look at death, and in John 14:1-3 (NIV), Jesus says:

> "Do not let your hearts be troubled. Trust in God; trust also in me. In my Father's house are many rooms; if it were not so, I would have told

you. I am going there to prepare a place for you. And if I go and prepare a place for you, I will come back and take you to be with me."

My father was only fifty-nine-years old when he died suddenly of a heart attack, but he died with a smile on his face. My mother and I find comfort in believing that Dad was smiling at Jesus Who had come to take him to the place that He had prepared for my father. Not everyone receives this blessing of a smile; Jesus makes Himself known in various ways, but one day Jesus will come back for all who have invited Him to live in our hearts.

Meanwhile we can go forward, knowing that when we have "why" questions, we can pray "God, I know You're always with me, but today I could sure use a sign that You are."

God will answer, but we need to stay so close to Him that we can hear even His most quiet whispers. We still may not understand and there may be times when we wonder if God has deserted us. Even Jesus had fragile heart moments.

On the night before he was crucified, Jesus asked His Father to take the cup from Him, but later Jesus said, "Your will be done." And the next day, while dying on the cross, Jesus said, "My God, my God, why have You forsaken me?" Subsequently, His question became a statement of trust when Jesus said, "Father, into Your hands I commit my Spirit," and Jesus died.

Gratefully the story doesn't end there. Christians know the profound joy of celebrating Easter—Jesus lives! He lives in our hearts and we look forward to a wonderful future with Him where there'll be no more fragile heart moments! Meanwhile, if my faith falters, I repeat this anonymous prayer, *My God, here I am—all yours. Make me according to Your heart."*

I understand the severity of the risks with which I'm living and I choose not to let fear dominate my life. God is bigger than any situation I can ever encounter! Trusting His promise to never leave me, I can sleep at night without fear of not seeing another day and I awaken with a fresh appreciation of how much God loves me. My future has a happy face on it!

Not long after God promised me more opportunities to share the story He's written for my life, I was invited to speak at a Women's Communion Breakfast at First Baptist Church in Hanson, Massachusetts. I was blessed as eighty women listened intently, some weeping quietly at times. As the program ended, each woman came to me for a small glass heart magnet which I explained was a reminder that God loves them and is bigger than any problem they can every face. They were visibly touched and thanked me for coming, but what affirmed my ministry most were the many expressions of reclaimed hope in their words, "Now I feel that I can go on."

My friend's words echo in my mind, "Don't waste your suffering." I love encouraging women and I hunger for new opportunities, but I've learned to wait for God's timing. I find immense freedom in opening doors and trusting God to open them wider or to close them, confident that His choice is always best. That kind of freedom brings peace as I wait for God to reveal more of His plan for my life.

I'm reminded of the image of a bush God gave me several years ago—the branches blowing gently in the breeze—no leaves or flowers—just bare branches. For me, that was a promise that one day my story of God's love and hope would be spread by a few believers who would in turn *branch* out their love for and faith in God to others. I'm delighted this is happening—leaves and flowers are appearing through the work of the Holy Spirit! May the branches be heavy with blossoms that symbolize a growing love for God.

Whispers from *Your* Heart

How has God stretched me?

If God asked, could I go out like Abraham—not knowing where I was going? Explain.

When I was in darkness, I knew God was there with me because:

When have I experienced the truth of Romans 8:28? Did I share it with someone?

Chapter 10

Life Puzzles

"The ransomed of the Lord will return. They will enter Zion with singing; everlasting joy will crown their heads. Gladness and joy will overtake them, and sorrow and sighing will flee away."

—Isaiah 51:11 (NIV)

ON MY 60th BIRTHDAY, when I asked God for new experiences for the next decade, He gave me what I asked for and more! Some I made happen, such as horseback riding with our children and grandchildren at Black Butte Ranch in Oregon, and later that summer I boogie-boarded with friends in Nantucket Sound. Stefan and I also enjoyed a European River Cruise and other new travel experiences.

I delighted in successful *whatevers;* being used by God and learning to trust Him for direction and empowerment, and for being part of God's amazing plans. It's a lot of work, but I've come to know God so much better.

Heart disease, stroke, torn tendon, and brain hemorrhages were not what I had in mind for my 60s, but when I see Jesus, I'll be too full of gratitude and praise for the blessings received *through* those challenges to even think of asking why!

As I near completion of this manuscript, I've just celebrated my 70th birthday–a new decade and another new experience - with Stefan and all of my children and grandchildren in rented cottages on a lake in Vermont! A few weeks before, a close friend asked, "Do you dread the day you will turn 70?" I could honestly say no.

My 70th was my best ever—not because of the love we share as a family or their thoughtful and generous gifts, but because of God's immense love and faithfulness. Early the next morning as I walked downhill on a dirt road winding through dense woods with the sun shining through in spots, I felt like a million dollars—my foot, my head, my heart—all behaving themselves! Even the little twitches in my mouth had stopped. As I walked, praising and thanking God for healings and for the depth of His love, I knew pure joy!

Reflecting on God's promises for my book and more speaking opportunities, I was surprised by a wave of great anticipation for my next decade that seemed to wash over me. I was so wrapped in the wonder of it all that I laughed aloud! "Oh God," I exclaimed, "Thank You for what You are going to do!"

In light of my health history that may sound far-fetched, but my confidence in God's faithfulness and His power overflowed my heart that morning and still does.

I love this comment by Sorge:

> "When the life of God begins to flow into your world of impossibilities, this is the stuff of miracles."[59]

About a month later when I flew to visit my daughter in Virginia, I felt as I did the first time I flew to York, Maine, to meet Stefan—greatly favored by God and confident of His divine protection. I'm eager to see how God keeps His promises and I look forward to a growing intimacy with Him in the process.

I'm so grateful the Holy Spirit lives in me as teacher, comforter, guide, strength, enabler, protector, conscience, and so much more. He helps me center on God when I'm tempted to self-focus. And, as my life editor, the Holy Spirit critiques the story I'm living. He shows me where I'm doing fine, what areas need revision, where to expand my efforts, and what needs to be deleted. Where God puts a comma, I know I need to pause and reconsider my choices, and sometimes a period is God's choice for that time in my life. Whatever, I no longer need answers to questions that seem to have no answers. As I mature spiritually and experience the reality of God, question marks are being replaced by exclamation points of delight!

I love to recall how God used the "Communion Hymn For Christmas" to help me better grasp the miracle of Jesus. I can only imagine His joy when I finally received that pivotal piece into what I call the picture puzzle of my life.

Life Puzzles

The pieces of my "life-puzzle" reflect the many strings with which I have struggled, some more easily untangled than others and no longer an issue while some are still knotted in stubbornness. Other pieces are faded by doubts and fears that questioned the hard times, or streaked by tears of sadness and the bitterness of regret, while a number are so warped by my self-centeredness that only through persistent prayer and God's grace can they fit into His plan for me. Henri Nouwen a great advocate of prayer says:

> Praying is no easy matter. It demands a relationship in which you allow someone other than yourself to enter into the very center of your being, to see there what you would rather leave in darkness, and to touch there what you would rather leave untouched.[60]

Nouwen likens a resistance to praying to that of "a desire to cling tightly to yourself, a greediness which betrays fear." Using an image of an elderly lady in a psychiatric crisis who refused to give up a small coin in her tightly clenched fist, Nouwen says, "It was as though she would lose her very self along with the coin."

This analogy to coins, I believe, can also be applied to the *strings* in our lives. We want to keep them—we like the status quo and even if we feel guilty, it's easier to hold on than to open our fists and release them to God. Nouwen explains:

> So you fill your hands with small, clammy coins which you don't want to surrender. You still feel bitter because people weren't grateful for something you gave them, you still feel jealous of those who are better paid than you are, you still want to take revenge on someone who didn't respect you, you are still disappointed that you've received no letter, still angry because someone didn't smile when you walked by. You live through it: you live along with it as though it didn't really bother you... until the moment when you want to pray. Then everything returns: the bitterness, the hate, the jealousy, the disappointment, and the desire for revenge. But these feelings are not just there; you clutch them in your hands as if they were treasures you didn't want to part with. You sit rummaging in all that old sourness as if you can't do without it, as if in giving it up, you would lose your very self.[61]

The Lord is in the business of saving those who aren't living according to His rules. Through redemption Jesus Christ renews our broken strings and frayed hawsers, transforming our darkness into the glorious color of joy-filled moments with Him. God brings beauty out of ugliness, good out of evil, joy out of grief, forgiveness out of pain, acceptance out of doubt, and hope out of despair by continually and patiently renewing and readjusting the pieces of our lives. I'm so glad He re-shapes us to fit His design. One day our puzzles will be complete—including the pieces we didn't think would fit at all!

God does His part and we have to do ours. Once we are one with Jesus, we must be willing to give up our *strings*—anything not in accordance with Jesus' teachings.

In 1 Peter 5:10 we are promised:

> And after you have suffered for a little while, the God of all grace, who has called you to his eternal glory in Christ, will himself restore, support, strengthen, and establish you.

My prayers for Divine help have progressed from simplistic selfish pleas for God's help to those of praise, hope, and joyful expectancy—not only for *whatever* God chooses, but *however, wherever,* and *whenever* the Lord wants to use me; and that He is glorified in the process.

Whispers from *Your* Heart

Have I grown more in love with Jesus? How do I know?

How can I have anticipation, and even excitement, for what God wants to do in my life—despite not knowing what that may be?

Am I willing to obey God and put a period where He says to put one? Why or why not?

How would I feel if God asked me to give Him myself for whatever, however, wherever, and whenever He wanted to use me? What would my answer be?

Chapter 11

Satisfied!

"...because of what Christ has done we have become gifts to God that He delights in, for as part of God's sovereign plan we were chosen from the beginning to be his, and all things happen just as he decided long ago."

—Ephesians 1:11 (TLB)

DEAR READER, I'M honored that you're reading the story God and I have written for my life this far. If you didn't have a personal relationship with Jesus before you started reading this book, I hope you are now passionately exploring this most precious of gifts. If you already loved Jesus and were serving Him, I trust that *wHispers* has given you even more reason to rejoice in God's immense love and faithfulness and to anticipate the *whatevers* He has for you and how they will impact your walk with Him.

May we all say together with a humble heart, a willing spirit, and an ever broadening and more deeply rooted trust, *My God, Your will be done in my life. I give You ALL of me—no strings attached!*

Patti was right. Each one of us, with God, will always be working on *strings* and may we welcome them because in the process we become the persons God created each of us to be.

Many years ago in a psychology class, we studied Erik Erickson's Eight Stages of Human Development. I was most intrigued by the last one which I made my goal, *Integrity Versus Despair* or, as it was labeled in our class, *Ego Integrity*. According to Erickson:

> If the other seven psychosocial crises have been successfully resolved, the mature adult develops the peak of adjustment: integrity. He trusts,

he is independent and dares the new. He works hard, has found a well-defined role in life, and has developed a self-concept with which he is happy.[62]

For me, that meant in the later years of my life I would be able to look back with acceptance, contentment, and genuine joy at how my life had played out. As a satisfied and naive young woman, there was no doubt I could accomplish that. But as years passed, divorce occurred, and my health deteriorated I found that life is not perfect and I wondered if it would ever be possible to look back with satisfaction and a grateful heart for the way my life had unfolded. Could I ever trust God with my unfulfilled desires and poor choices?

Jenny sent me a Mother's Day card that says, "You've picked me up, calmed me down, cheered me on, helped me out...and loved me through it all."

Because God has done all of that and more, I do have ego integrity and I've learned that life is not just about the journey, but how close we stay to God and what we learn along the way. God has patiently walked me through my confusion and self-doubts; my *show me again* moments, and those times of tearful repentance when I whispered, *Father, can You really love me that much?*

God really does love all of us that much; in fact, more than we can ever know. I can't even imagine our Heavenly Father's despair in watching Jesus, His only Son, being persecuted and crucified for all of our sins. Our stories, no matter how tragic, cannot begin to compare to that of Jesus on the cross—stretching out His arms and dying because He loves us that much. And still God listens to our gripes, and loves and graces us again and again.

When I was totally broken, I turned to God whom I had always believed loved me, but now I clung to Him and God began answering my prayers for help in surprising ways. Then as I began trusting Him at a deeper level, God's love became more real than ever before and once I knew God more intimately and experienced His answers in real ways, there was no going back. Perhaps God had been whispering to me for a long time, but it wasn't until out of deep need that I put my listening ears on and could hear Him.

Overwhelming pain and tears continued, but underlying it all was a vital sense of God's peace which has continued to flow in my life like a river—God's river! Looking back, I see that my broken marriage was the jumping off place for my faith to mature. And praise God, He also allowed another great love to flow into my life—Stefan. The love and sincere acceptance I found in this second marriage, along with Stefan's supportive care and validation continue to encourage me as possible obstructions to my growing faith continue. But rather than blocking the course, God's peace has flowed in and around, over and under, and through all kinds of them.

As a result I now have no doubt about how much God loves me; that He's always with me and has a reason for permitting crises in my life, or that He will bring good out of every one of them. God does this despite my strings and hawsers—my sinfulness which, because of my humanity and despite my sincere efforts, will continue until I die. That's called God's mercy.

Doubting God is not an option for me. Even when facing heart surgery or in recovery from the stroke or brain hemorrhages, I never thought to ask God, *why me?* Rather, I choose to thank God continually for working in my life even when I don't have a clue what He's doing; even when I can't feel Him near. I have a refrigerator magnet that reads, *I believe in the sun even when it's not shining. I believe in God even when He's silent.*

I've claimed God's promises always to be with me and to be all that I need—even when His answers are long in coming or not what I would choose. He's proven Himself repeatedly and only in His strength can I continue to defeat *strings* in my life that interfere with my loving Him most. When I trust God to help me unknot my *strings* of fear, envy, resentment, regret, pride, or other sins, my struggles become less burdensome.

I'm not surprised by the number of *strings* I've faced in my life because I know my tendency to sin, but I grieve over how many have grown into *hawsers* simply because I chose to ignore their impending stranglehold on my heart and look away from God. I've struggled with and successfully beaten many of them and I rejoice in the growing ball of strings that I've defeated—hopefully for good, but dear reader, I've learned that no string is irretrievable. One weak moment—one self-centered weak moment, and I can soon be entangled again by a string that draws me away from Jesus and His best for me. Ridding my life of sin is more impossible than unsnarling the ribbons on a large cluster of balloons when an unexpected breeze takes them in many directions. Those knots are nothing compared to the tangled confusion that sin can bring into our lives. I go forward in God's strength, knowing He will equip me for any struggle.

Reader, I hope learning about my strings encourages you to avoid being bound by cords of sin that not only can ruin your life, but more importantly interfere or prevent intimacy with our Savior. Today's culture through multi media continually and blatantly attempts to entice all of us into ungodly situations and sadly, more and more Christians opt for the gray area of just a little sin, but they eventually lose control or are found out. Statistics now show about the same percentage of divorces in the church as in secular society. What I said earlier bears repeating: either we love God most or we don't. We live as Jesus taught us or we don't. It's up to us!

No one else hears what God whispers to us. His personal thoughts are unique and known only to the Father and His child who is paying attention. But once God has whispered, He is often still until we obey and that silence can be deafening.

I'm grateful to God for giving me spiritual eyes to recognize my strings for what they are—blatant disregard of God's will for my life. And I thank God for a heart to love Him most. Reader, I hope you can do the same and that together we can echo the words of David in Psalm 16:6,9,11:

> The boundary lines have fallen for me in pleasant places; I have a goodly heritage…Therefore my heart is glad, and my soul rejoices; my body also rests secure…In Your presence there is fullness of joy; in Your right hand are pleasures forevermore.

The following quote by Frank Laubach expresses so eloquently how I feel about my life:

> To be able to look back and say, "This has been the finest year of my life"—that is glorious! But anticipation! To be able to look ahead and say, "The present year can and shall be better!"—that is more glorious!

> If we said such things about our achievements, we would be consummate egotists. But if we are speaking of God's kindness and we speak truly, we are but grateful. And this is what I do witness. I have done nothing but open windows—God has done all the rest. There have been few if any conspicuous achievements. There has been a succession of marvelous experiences of the presence of God. I feel, as I look back over the year, that it would have been impossible to have held much more without breaking with sheer joy. It was the lonesomest year, in some ways the hardest year of my life, but the most glorious, full of voices from heaven.[63]

Satisfied!

I'm so grateful I can hear even God's most quiet whispers. I can trust Jesus to continue walking on *whatever* waters come my way. Regarding my passion to share Jesus with others, I claim the truth and hope of Jesus' words in John 7:37-38:

> "Let anyone who is thirsty come to me, and let the one who believes in me drink. As the scripture has said, 'Out of the believer's heart shall flow rivers of living water.'"

I'm encouraged by Chambers' words regarding this.

> In essence, (Jesus said), "He who believes in Me will have everything he receives escape out of him."...If we believe in Jesus, it is not what we gain, but what He pours through us that really counts...and we cannot measure that at all.[64]

My personal dream is to share a profound oneness with Jesus; to live the prayer of Hannah Whitall Smith who prayed to be content in the Lord alone—without any of His gifts or blessings; just Jesus.

I still have much to learn, but I know I'm getting closer when I kneel and can't find words big enough to express my love and praise for God. Instead there are only tears—not of grief, fear, or frustration, but of purest joy flowing from a full heart still stretching to grasp how great God is.

My sincere wish, dear reader, is for you to know this same joy.

Psalm 40:1-5, 8 (NLT)

I waited patiently for the Lord to help me,
and he turned to me and heard my cry.
He lifted me out of the pit of despair,
out of the mud and the mire.
He set my feet on solid ground
and steadied me as I walked along.
He has given me a new song to sing,
a hymn of praise to our God.
Many will see what he has done and be amazed.
They will put their trust in the Lord.
Oh, the joys of those who trust the Lord,
who have no confidence in the proud,
or in those who worship idols.
O Lord my God, you have done many wonders for us.
Your plans for us are too numerous to list.
If I tried to recite all your wonderful deeds,
I would never come to the end of them…
I take joy in doing your will, my God,
For your instructions are written on my heart.

Whispers from *Your* Heart

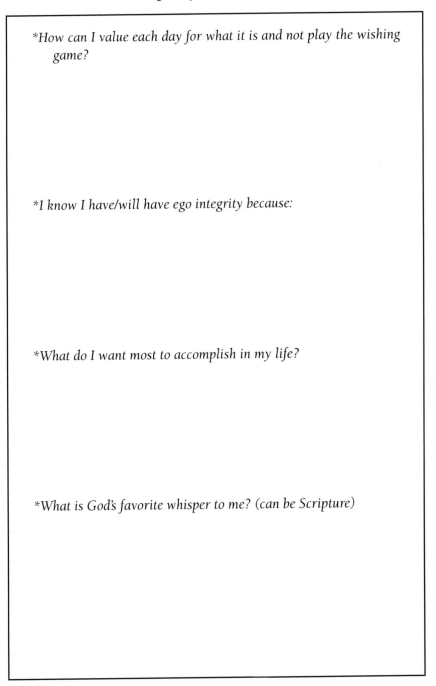

*How can I value each day for what it is and not play the wishing game?

*I know I have/will have ego integrity because:

*What do I want most to accomplish in my life?

*What is God's favorite whisper to me? (can be Scripture)

Notes

---

[1] Oswald Chambers, *My Utmost for His Highest* (Grand Rapids: Oswald Chambers Publications Association, Ltd., 1992), August 13.

[2] Sherwood Eliot Wirt, *Not Me God* (New York: Harper & Row 1966), 81. (From copyright page: "Grateful acknowledgment is made to Harcourt, Brace & World, Inc., New York, and to Geoffrey Bles Ltd., London, for permission to quote three verses of a poem from *Letters to Malcom: Chiefly on Prayer* by C. S. Lewis."

[3] Bill Hybels, *You're Too Busy Not to Pray* (Intervarsity Press 1998).

[4] Brother Lawrence and Frank Laubach, *Practicing His Presence* (Sargent, GA The Seed Sowers 1973), 91.

[5] *Psalter Hymnal*, (Grand Rapids: Publication Committee of the Christian Reformed Church, Inc. 1959), 518-519.

[6] Brother Lawrence and Frank Laubach, *Practicing His Presence* (Sargent, GA The Seed Sowers 1973), 15.

[7] Charles Stanley, *The Source of My Strength* (Nashville: Thomas Nelson Publishers 1994), 144.

[8] Ibid., 146-150.

[9] Larry Lea, *Could You Not Tarry One Hour?* (Lake Mary, FL: Creation House 1987), 35.

[10] Charles Stanley, *In Touch* (A Publication of In Touch Ministries).

[11] David Roper, *Elijah, A Man Like Us* (Grand Rapids: Discovery House 1997), 55.

[12] Oswald Chambers, *My Utmost for His Highest* (Grand Rapids: Oswald Chambers Publications Association, Ltd., 1992), August 4.

[13] David Roper, *Elijah, A Man of God* (Grand Rapids: Discovery House 1997), 52.

[14] Henry T. and Richard Blackaby, *Hearing God's Voice* (Nashville: Broadman & Holman 2002), 116.

[15] St. Frances deSales, *Be At Peace.*

[16] Brother Lawrence and Frank Laubach, *Practicing His Presence* (Sargent, GA: The Seed Sowers 1973), 52.

[17] Shirley Vogel, *Caring Ministries Brochure*, (Brewster Baptist Church 2000)

[18] Leighton Ford, *Transforming Leadership* (Downer's Grove, Illinois: InterVarsity Press 1991), 33.

[19] Ibid., 34.

[20] Eugene H. Peterson, *Run With the Horses,* (Downer's Grove, Illinois: InterVarsity Press 1983), 48.

[21] Oswald Chambers, *My Utmost for His Highest* (Grand Rapids: Oswald Chambers Publications Association, Ltd., 1992), May 13.

[22] David Roper, *Elijah, A Man Like Us,* (Grand Rapids: Discovery House Publisher 1997), 32.

[23] Brother Lawrence and Frank Laubach, *Practicing His Presence* (Sargent, GA The Seed Sowers 1973), 42.

[24] Ibid., 35.

[25] Charles R. Swindoll, *The Grace of Encouragement* desk calendar (Bloomington MN: Garborg's Heart and Home, Inc.), April 17.

[26] *The Celebration Hymnal*, (USA: Word/Integritiy 1997), 287.

[27] Richard J. Foster, *Prayer* (San Francisco: Harper 1992), 39.

[28] Ibid., 41.

[29] Dr. Bruce H. Wilkinson, *The Prayer of Jabez* (Sisters, OR: Multnomah Publishers 2000), 15.

[30] Ibid., 12.

[31] Ibid., 36.

[32] Rev. Vincent Fasano

[33] Henri Nouwen, *Here and Now* (New York: Crossroad 1994), 81.

[34] Oswald Chambers, *My Utmost for His Highest* (Grand Rapids: Oswald Chambers Publications Association, Ltd., 1992), April 26.

Notes

[35] Carol Kent, *When I Lay My Isaac Down*, (Colorado Springs: NavPress 2004),12-13.

[36] Ibid., June 1.

[37] Rev. Vincent Fasano

[38] Wayne Whitson Floyd and Dietrich Bonhoeffer *The Wisdom and Witness of Dietrich Bonhoeffer* (Minneapolis: Fortress Press 2000), 11.

[39] Anne Graham Lotz, *The Fragrance of Love*, Discipleship Journal (Colorado Springs: NavPress Mar/Apr 2004), 25.

[40] Anne Graham Lotz, *My Heart's Cry* (Nashville: W. Publishing Group, Division of Thomas Nelson, Inc.2002), 39, 41-42.

[41] Ibid., 150.

[42] Beth Moore, *Whispers of Hope* (Nashville: LifeWay Press 1998), 213.

[43] Oswald Chambers, *My Utmost for His Highest* (Grand Rapids: Oswald Chambers Publications Association, Ltd. 1992), November 23.

[44] Sherwood Eliot Wirt, *Not Me God* (New York: Harper & Row 1966), 81.

[45] Henry T. and Richard Blackaby, *Hearing God's Voice*, (Nashville: Broadman & Holman Publishers 2002), 193.

[46] Virelle Kidder, *Donkeys Still Talk* (NavPress 2004), 23-24.

[47] Ibid., 40-41.

[48] Henry T. and Richard Blackaby, *Hearing God's Voice*, (Nashville:Broadman & Holman Publishers 2002), 214.

[49] Virelle Kidder, *Donkeys Still Talk* (Colorado: NavPress 2004), 59.

[50] Oswald Chambers, *My Utmost for His Highest* (Grand Rapids: Oswald Chambers Publications Association, Ltd. 1992), August 3.

[51] Ibid., September 23.

[52] Ibid., February 20.

[53] Ibid., July 6.

[54] Augustus M. Toplady, *Rock of Ages*, Great Hymns of the Faith (Grand Rapids: Zondervan Publishing House 1970), 126.

[55] Larry Crabb, *Going Deeper With God*, Decision Volume 46, Number 10, October 2005 (Charlotte: Billy Graham Evangelistic Assoc.), 15.

[56] Sheri Rose Shepherd, *His Princess, Love Letters From Your King*, (Sisters OR: Multnomah Publishers 2004), 71.

[57] Dr. Bruce H. Wilkinson, *Secrets of the Vine* (Sisters OR: Multnomah Publishers, Inc. 2001), 72-73.

[58] Bob Sorge, *Secrets of the Secret Place* (Kansas City: Oasis House 2001), 125.

[59] Ibid., 212.

[60] Nouwen, Henri J. M., *With Open Hands* (New York: Ballantine 1972), 3.

[61] Ibid., 4-5.

[62] Erik Erickson, *Childhood and Society 2nd Edition*, (W. W. Norton and Co., 1963).

[63] Brother Lawrence and Frank Laubach, *Practicing His Presence*, (Sargent, GA: The Seed Sowers, 1973), 1-2.

[64] Oswald Chambers, *My Utmost for His Highest*, (Grand Rapids: Oswald Chambers Publications Association, Ltd 1992), September 2.

About the Author

Shirley Pieters Vogel was born in the tiny town of East Palmyra, New York and raised in the Christian Reformed Church where, at thirteen, Shirley accepted Jesus Christ as her Savior. Later, in the desperation of mid-life crises, Shirley went to her knees and there found God waiting to embrace and teach her how to love and trust Jesus more deeply and to rely on the reality of the Holy Spirit to empower her.

Listeners to Shirley's story often say, "Now I can go on..." That hope-filled confession makes Shirley passionate to continue encouraging women of all ages to trust God who not only cares, but is bigger than any situation in which they can ever find themselves.

Shirley's RN training and BS in Human and Community Services prepared her not only for her nursing positions, but also for work as a Hospice volunteer and twenty years of service to her church family at Brewster Baptist Church in Brewster, MA. Included are *Caring Ministries* and *wHispers*, an ecumenical women's ministry, both of which Shirley founded and directed.

Shirley and her husband, Stefan, live on Cape Cod and collectively are the parents of six loving children and grandparents to fourteen of the best!

Shirley and I first met thirteen years ago in 1995 when I was a candidate to be the next pastor at Brewster Baptist Church, and she the Chairperson of the Pastoral Search Committee. Shirley led that effort with the diligence, skill, and prayer that have marked all her efforts at the church ever since.

In my years as Senior Pastor of Brewster Baptist Church, Shirley has held several key leadership positions including serving as a Deacon and Chair of the Capital Campaign Fund Raising Team when the church undertook a significant expansion and raised over $2,400,000 without the help of a professional fundraising firm. As our church grew, Shirley founded and directed Caring Ministries with a host of helping ministries to meet the needs of all kinds of people. Most recently, Shirley felt led to reach out to women with a ministry that addressed their spiritual and relational needs for growth and support. In every ministry that she leads, Shirley always proceeds prayerfully, plans thoroughly, and does things with excellence. She has touched a lot of lives through the years. It has been a pleasure for me to serve with her at BBC and to see her own growth in faith and leadership as she has responded obediently to the Lord's leading in her life. She also makes the best chocolate, pecan, caramel brittle you've ever tasted!

—Rev. Dr. Douglas Scalise, Senior Pastor

Shirley would love to hear from you!

To write your comments, learn how to start a wHispers
ministry, or to book Shirley to speak at your event,
visit her website at www.shirleyvogel.com
email at whispers@ shirleyvogel.com
or call Shirley at 508.394.0646